ACBL Bridge Series

Commonly Used Conventions

by
Audrey Grant

ACBL BRIDGE SERIES

Commonly Used Conventions is the fourth in the ACBL Bridge Series of texts written by Audrey Grant, world famous bridge teacher and author. There are five texts in all.

Volume One —
   Bidding – The Club Series

Volume Two —
   Play of the Hand – The Diamond Series

Volume Three —
   Defense – The Heart Series

Volume Four —
   Commonly Used Conventions – The Spade Series

Volume Five —
   More Commonly Used Conventions – The Notrump Series

Trained teachers across North America offer bridge courses using these materials. Information on teachers in your area is available at the ACBL web site at www.acbl.org or by calling the ACBL Education Department in Memphis, Tennessee at 901–332–5586, extension 264.

Coordinated decks of E-Z Deal Cards which allow the reader to deal out the exercise deals at the end of each chapter are available for each bridge text. Social players can create a bridge party by dealing and playing the bridge hands and then looking in the text for information on the desired results.

The decks of cards can be ordered from the American Contract Bridge League online from the Product Catalog at www.acbl.org or by calling the ACBL Sales Department toll free at 1–800–264–2743 in the USA or at 1–800–264–8786 in Canada.

ISBN 0–943855–14–4

INTRODUCTION

The American Contract Bridge League's *Commonly Used Conventions* student text is the fourth in the ACBL Bridge Series of bridge books. The first book, *Bidding*, is followed by *Play of the Hand, Defense, Commonly Used Conventions,* and *More Commonly Used Conventions.* The books focus on introducing players to the game of bridge and helping them to advance.

This series of books is unusual in the field of bridge writing for several reasons. First, they were written by a professional educator, Audrey Grant, who also happens to be a bridge player. Accordingly these books encompass all of the sound principles that facilitate learning any subject and are built on the firm foundation of a basic understanding of the game of bridge.

Next, the technical approach to these books was determined by surveying a cross section of North American bridge teachers. This means that whether a student learns bridge from this book in Vancouver, British Columbia; St. Louis, Missouri; or Orlando, Florida, that student will be able to play bridge with virtually any other beginning bridge players in North America.

Third, the effectiveness of the teaching principles was field-tested in five cities prior to the publication of the first book in this series (*Bidding*), originally know as *The Club Series*, with more than 800 actual bridge students and at least 25 bridge teachers involved.

Finally, it is the first time in the more than 60-year history of ACBL that the sanctioning body for bridge in North America has produced its own basic bridge texts. The end result of the joint effort of Audrey Grant and ACBL is this series that enables the reader to learn bridge or to review and improve bridge techniques in a logical and progressive fashion. More importantly, the reader will have fun while learning the fundamental concepts of good bridge bidding, play and defense which will be beneficial for a lifetime.

The American Contract Bridge League

The American Contract Bridge League (ACBL) is dedicated to the playing, teaching, and promotion of contract bridge.

The membership of 170,000 includes a wide range of players — from the thousands who are just learning the joy of bridge to the most proficient players in North America.

ACBL offers a variety of services, including:

- **Tournament play.** Thousands of tournaments — North American Bridge Championships (three a year), as well as tournaments at the regional, sectional, local, and club levels — are sanctioned annually.

- **Two magazines.** *The Bridge Bulletin,* a monthly publication, offers articles on tournaments, card play, the Laws, personalities, special ACBL activities, and much more. A bi-monthly magazine, *Better Bridge,* is geared to the interests of new and advancing bridge players.

- **A ranking plan.** Each time a member does well in any ACBL event, whether at the club level or at a North American Bridge Championship, that member receives a masterpoint award. Players achieve rankings and prestige as a result of their cumulative masterpoint holdings.

- **A teaching program.** ACBL has trained more than 4,700 people through the Teacher Accreditation Program (TAP) to effectively teach beginning bridge lessons. You can find a teacher in your area at ACBL's web site at www.acbl.org.

- **A newcomer program.** ACBL offers special games and programs for players new to bridge and new to duplicate. The IN Programs at the three North America Bridge Championships are very popular.

- **Access to 3500 bridge clubs.** ACBL offers sanctioned bridge play at clubs across the United States, Canada, Mexico, Bermuda, on cruise ships, and even at a few foreign-based bridge clubs. You can locate a club in your area at ACBL's web site at www.acbl.org.

- **A charity program.** Each year the ACBL Charity Foundation selects a *"Charity of the Year,"* which is the main beneficiary of ACBL charity games and general donations by the membership. All ACBL clubs participate to raise money for the charity.

- **A cooperative advertising program.** ACBL assists teachers, clubs, units, and districts by subsidizing costs incurred for advertising programs designed to recruit students, and promote bridge lessons and games.

- **An education program.** The ACBL Educational Foundation is dedicated to bringing the enjoyment of bridge to people all ages and firmly believes this can be accomplished through bridge education. Grants are provided for special bridge projects.

- **A funded school lesson program.** ACBL and the ACBL Educational Foundation have joined together to provide materials and teachers for bridge lessons at all levels — elementary, secondary, and college.

- **A junior program for players age 25 and under.** ACBL offers a funded teaching program, student membership, special events, and a newsletter, *The Grapevine.*

- **Products.** ACBL offers a wide variety of bridge supplies, books, clothing, and other bridge products for new players and teachers through the ACBL Sales Department. Visit ACBL's Internet shop on the web at www.acbl.org.

- **Membership in the World Bridge Federation.** Each year ACBL sends premiere players to compete in the world championships. ACBL's Junior team participants in the World Junior Team Championship in odd-numbered years.

- **Membership benefits.** Credit card programs, member discounts on product purchases, special hotel rates at tournaments, airline discounts for NABCs, an 800 line for member services, discounted entry fees at most tournament play, recognition for levels of achievement, discounted Hertz car rental, and supplemental insurance products are offered.

ACBL has long been the center of North American bridge activity. 1997 was our 60th anniversary. We invite you to join us in the excitement of organized bridge play. You can enjoy the fun, friendship, and competition of bridge with an ACBL membership!

TABLE OF CONTENTS

Why play bridge?

You may be a little confused — why is Martina Navratilova writing the introduction to a bridge book?

The answer is that I believe it takes a strong mind, as well as a strong body, to live life to its fullest.

Bridge is more than just a card game. *It's a cerebral sport.* Bridge teaches logic, reasoning, quick thinking, patience, concentration and partnership skills.

Once at Wimbledon, when we got rained out, I spent my time playing bridge to keep me sharp and on my toes. An evening of bridge at home with family and friends is so much more fulfilling than sitting around watching TV.

The American Contract Bridge League has commissioned one of the world's most successful bridge teachers, Audrey Grant, to write this book. Audrey has taken what many people consider a complex game and made it easy and fun to learn.

Bridge has meant a lot to me in my travels. No matter where I go, I can always make new friends at the bridge table.

You know, tennis is a sport for a lifetime, and bridge is a game for a lifetime. It can be enjoyed by young and old, male and female, weak and strong. It crosses all barriers!

Take this book home with you today. Start learning a game and a sport — to last a lifetime!

MARTINA NAVRATILOVA
World Tennis Champion

CHAPTER 1
The Stayman Convention

THE STAYMAN CONVENTION

An opening notrump bid narrowly defines opener's strength and distribution. It's usual for the partnership to reach a good contract after this beginning. The accuracy can be further improved with the help of the conventional bids discussed in the next two chapters. Before getting into conventional responses, the partnership needs to agree on the range of strength shown by an opening notrump bid.

THE RANGES FOR OPENING NOTRUMP BIDS

An opening notrump bid shows a balanced hand within a defined range of strength. Most players agree that a notrump opening bid would show one of the following hand patterns: 4–3–3–3, 4–4–3–2, or 5–3–3–2. In North America, duplicate bridge players prefer a 15 to 17 point range for opening the bidding 1NT. Not everyone agrees on the best range to use. Traditionally players favored a 16 to 18 point range. Some modern partnerships use a mini-notrump range of 10 to 12 points. You and your partner need to agree on your range. Using a 15 to 17 point range, the opening bidder can describe any balanced hand of 12 or more points using an orderly progression of 2 to 3 point ranges.

Opening Balanced Hands – Based on 15 to 17 point 1NT	
12 to 14 points	Open one of a suit, intending to rebid notrump as cheaply as possible. This describes a hand too weak to open 1NT.
15 to 17 points	Open 1NT.
18 or 19 points	Open one of a suit, intending to jump rebid in notrump. This describes a hand too strong to open 1NT.
20 or 21 points	Open 2NT.
22 to 24 points	Open 2♣[1], intending to rebid 2NT.
25 to 27 points	Open 3NT (or open 2♣[1], intending to rebid 3NT)[2]

[1]The opening 2♣ bid is discussed further in Chapter 8.

[2]See the discussion of the *gambling 3NT* opening bid in the Appendix.

There are several reasons why this structure is popular among tournament and club players. Balanced hands with 12 (or fewer) points are more frequently opened in duplicate bridge. Hands with 15 to 17 points occur more often than those with 16 to 18 points. The auction after a 1NT opening bid is usually straightforward for the partnership, so it's an advantage to open 1NT more frequently.

The ranges of the 1NT and 2NT opening bids affect the meaning of the jump rebid to 2NT by opener. It's now used to show a balanced hand of 18 or 19 points and becomes an invitational, rather than forcing, rebid. Responder doesn't have to bid again holding a minimum response of 6 or 7 points.

Most tournament players use *weak two-bids* and open all strong hands with a *strong artificial* (conventional) 2♣. One consequence is that the partnership can define the range for a direct 2NT opening as 20 or 21. A 2NT rebid after a 2♣ opening shows 22 to 24. Since balanced hands of 20 or 21 points are more frequent than those with 22 to 24 points, this puts the 2NT opening to better use.

Duplicate players compete aggressively for partscores. Experience has shown that it's often possible to make a game contract of 3NT with as few as 25 points (or an occasional 24 points) in the combined hands, although it's still a good idea to have about 26 or more points for a contract of 4♥ or 4♠.

The notrump structure based on 15 to 17 points for 1NT is used for the remainder of the book. It's more in keeping with the current style used at clubs and tournaments.

Consider the following hands held by the opening bidder:

♠ K J 4   Open 1NT. There are 15 high-card points and an ex-
♥ A 10   tra point for the five-card diamond suit, bringing the
♦ K Q 9 7 3   total to 16.
♣ Q 8 2

♠ 10 7 5   Using the recommended notrump structure, open 2NT,
♥ A Q   showing a balanced hand of 20 or 21 points. Don't
♦ A K J 6   wait for *stoppers* (high cards) in all four suits before
♣ K Q J 4   opening 2NT. That approach has gone out of fashion.

♠ K J 3
♥ A 10 2
♦ K Q 8
♣ A J 9 4

Using a range of 15 to 17 points, this hand is too strong for a 1NT opening. Open 1♣, intending to rebid 2NT if partner responds at the one level. This shows a balanced hand of 18 or 19 points.

Opener's first decision can be influenced by the rebid. Consider these two hands.

♠ K J 8 4 3
♥ A Q 4
♦ K Q
♣ J 8 3

Open 1NT. Even if the partnership plays five-card majors, balanced hands that fall in the right range are best described with an opening notrump bid. If you open 1♠ with this hand and partner responds 1NT, 2♣, 2♦, or 2♥ you have an awkward choice of rebids. No rebid would accurately describe both the strength and distribution of the hand.

♠ A Q
♥ K 4
♦ K J 8 3
♣ Q 10 8 6 3

1NT usually shows a balanced distribution with no singletons or voids and at most one doubleton, but many players would open this hand 1NT. Although there are two doubletons, an opening bid of 1♣ leads to an awkward choice of rebid if partner responds 1♥ or 1♠. Players sometimes open 1NT with a six-card minor suit and 6–3–2–2 distribution — or when holding a singleton honor. There's nothing to prevent you from exercising your judgement occasionally, as long as partner expects you to have the usual balanced distribution.

The Effect of a 15 to 17 Notrump Range on Responses

If you and your partner are moving from a 16 to 18 point range to a 15 to 17 for an opening bid of 1NT, you don't need to adjust responder's guidelines for signing off, inviting, and bidding game. Use the following approach:

- With 0 to 7 points, responder wants to stop in partscore.
- With 8 or 9 points, responder wants to invite game.
- With 10 or more points, responder wants to insist on game.

You'll get to some game contracts with only 25 combined points, but you should make enough of them to more than compensate for those times you go down.

THE STAYMAN CONVENTION

If the partnership has eight or more combined cards in a major suit, it's usually best to play with that suit as trump. The power of the trump suit often produces more tricks. After an opening bid of 1NT, responder frequently wants to search for a major suit fit.

The *Stayman* convention uses a response of 2♣ after an opening bid of 1NT as an artificial bid asking opener to bid a four-card or longer major suit. With no four-card major suit, opener makes the conventional rebid of 2♦. Partner opens 1NT and you are responder; it's your call:

♠ K J 9 4   Responder has 11 high-card points and knows the
♥ K 9 8 5   partnership belongs in game. There are at least 26
♦ 8 3   points in the combined hands. The only question is
♣ A 7 4   whether the partnership belongs in 3NT, 4♥, or 4♠.
                  Responder starts by bidding 2♣, the *Stayman* con-
vention. If opener rebids 2♥, showing a four-card heart suit, responder has uncovered an eight-card fit and can raise to 4♥. If opener rebids 2♠, responder raises to 4♠. If opener rebids 2♦, showing no four-card or longer major suit, responder puts the partnership in 3NT, having checked for a major along the way.

Opener's Rebid

Once the partnership decides to use *Stayman*, opener's response to the 2♣ bid is dictated by the agreement. Consider West's rebid on the following hands after the auction begins:

WEST	NORTH	EAST	SOUTH
1NT	Pass	2♣	Pass
?			

♠ 10 8 7 4
♥ A Q 3
♦ A 7
♣ K Q J 2

Rebid 2♠. Responder's 2♣ bid asks if opener has a four-card major suit. It doesn't ask how good the suit is.

♠ Q 10 5
♥ A Q 7 6 3
♦ Q 7 5
♣ K Q

Rebid 2♥. This bid shows a four-card or longer suit. Opener rebids at the cheapest level.

♠ A Q 6
♥ J 4 2
♦ A 6
♣ K Q 8 7 3

Rebid 2♦. This bid has nothing to do with diamonds. It simply says you don't have a four-card major suit.

♠ A Q 6 3
♥ Q 10 4 2
♦ A 10 5
♣ K J

Rebid 2♥. Rebidding with both majors is similar to bidding four-card suits *up the line* when responding to an opening bid of 1♣ or 1♦. If it turns out that responder isn't interested in hearts, you can show the spade suit at your next opportunity.

Responder's Use of Stayman with a Game-Going Hand

With enough strength to put the partnership in game — 10 or more points — *Stayman* is used when responder has exactly four cards in a major suit.

WEST	NORTH	**EAST**	SOUTH
1NT	Pass	?	

♠ J 10 7 5
♥ A Q 7 3
♦ K J 8 4
♣ 7

Respond 2♣. You're interested in finding a major-suit fit. If opener rebids 2♥ or 2♠, raise to game. If opener rebids 2♦, denying a four-card major suit, jump to 3NT.

♠ 7 3
♥ K Q 10 5
♦ J 8 4
♣ A J 6 3

Respond 2♣. Responder doesn't need both majors to use *Stayman*. If opener rebids 2♥, raise to 4♥. If opener rebids 2♦ or 2♠, jump to 3NT.

Opener can override responder's decision to play in 3NT and put the contract in 4♠. Here's an example:

♠ K Q 10 5
♥ 7 3
♦ J 8 4
♣ A J 6 3

Respond 2♣. If opener rebids 2♠, raise to 4♠. If opener rebids 2♦ or 2♥, jump to 3NT, as in the previous example. The difference here is that after the rebid of 2♥ opener might also hold four spades, since opener bids four-card majors *up the line*. If that's the case, opener should now bid 4♠ following your jump to 3NT. Opener can draw the inference that you must be interested in spades if you aren't interested in hearts. This is a good test that both partners fully understand the mechanics of *Stayman*.

With a five-card or longer major suit, responder will have other options.

♠ K 3
♥ A 10 8 6 5
♦ K J 2
♣ 8 4 3

Respond 3♥. Using standard methods, with a five-card major responder jumps to 3♥. This is a forcing bid, asking opener to choose between 3NT and 4♥. With a doubleton heart, opener will rebid 3NT; with three or more hearts, opener will continue to 4♥. There is no need to use the *Stayman* convention. Even if the partnership is using the *Jacoby transfer* (see next chapter), the *Stayman* convention isn't used when responder has a game-going hand with a five-card major suit.

♠ K Q 9 7 6 5
♥ A 6 3
♦ 9 4
♣ 10 2

Respond 4♠. With a six-card major suit, there's no need for responder to use *Stayman*. Opener must hold at least two spades. Responder can take the partnership directly to 4♠.

In the following example, responder starts with the *Stayman* Convention to find out if opener has a four-card major. If opener rebids 2♦, responder continues by asking if opener has three-card support for spades.

♠ Q J 8 6 3
♥ A 10 7 5
♦ 4
♣ K 9 3

Respond 2♣. With a four-card major suit and a five-card or longer major suit, responder does start with 2♣, the *Stayman* convention. If opener shows either major, responder can jump to game in that major. If opener rebids 2♦, responder now jumps to 3♠, a forcing bid asking opener to choose between 3NT and 4♠. Responder finds out if opener has either a four-card heart suit or three or more spades — the best of all worlds.

Responder's Use of Stayman with an Invitational Hand

With enough strength to invite opener to game — 8 or 9 points — responder uses *Stayman* in two situations:

- To check for a major-suit fit, or

- To show an invitational hand with a five-card or longer major suit.

Use *Stayman* to check for a major-suit fit.

WEST	NORTH	**EAST**	SOUTH
1NT	Pass	?	

♠ Q 9 7 5
♥ A 10 6 3
♦ 5 3
♣ Q 8 2

Respond 2♣. If opener rebids 2♥, raise to 3♥. This is an invitational bid, showing 8 or 9 points. Opener can pass or continue to 4♥. If opener rebids 2♠, invite by raising to 3♠. If opener rebids 2♦, denying a four-card major suit, rebid 2NT, an invitational bid.

♠ 8 4
♥ A J 10 5
♦ 10 8 4
♣ K 9 6 3

Respond 2♣. Responder doesn't need both majors to use *Stayman*. If opener rebids 2♥, raise to 3♥. If opener rebids 2♦ or 2♠, bid 2NT. This is like raising to 2NT, but you have checked for a major suit fit along the way.

♠ A J 10 5   Respond 2♣. If opener rebids 2♠, raise to 3♠. If
♥ 8 4   opener rebids 2♦ or 2♥, bid 2NT. Opener could
♦ 10 8 4   have four spades after a rebid of 2♥, since opener
♣ K 9 6 3   bids four-card majors *up the line*. If that's the case,
                opener can now bid 3♠ with a minimum hand or
4♠ with a maximum hand, drawing the inference that you must be interested in spades if you aren't interested in hearts.

♠ K 10 6 3   Respond 2♣. With both a four-card major suit and a
♥ K 10 8 4 3   five-card or longer major suit, start with *Stayman*. If
♦ J 7   opener bids 2♥ or 2♠, invite by raising to the three
♣ 9 4   level. If opener rebids 2♦, denying a four-card major suit, bid 2♥. This is an invitational sequence,
showing a five-card or longer heart suit. Opener will pass with a minimum hand but bid again with a maximum-strength hand.

Stayman can also be used when responder has a hand of invitational strength and a five-card or longer major suit if other methods to invite are not available. Using standard methods, responder has to go through *Stayman* with any invitational-strength hand when there is interest in finding a major suit fit.

WEST	NORTH	**EAST**	SOUTH
1NT	Pass	?	

♠ K 6 3   Respond 2♣. An invitational hand with five hearts
♥ A 10 9 6 3   can be awkward using standard methods. Start with
♦ J 10 5   *Stayman*, and if opener rebids 2♥, raise to 3♥. If
♣ 9 2   opener rebids 2♦, bid 2♥, showing an invitational
                hand of 8 or 9 points with a five-card heart suit.
                The difficulty arises if opener rebids 2♠. It's a bit
much to bid 3♥ with this hand, since opener may have two hearts and a minimum-strength hand — now the partnership has nowhere to go. It's better to rebid 2NT, so opener can pass with a minimum. This sounds to partner as though you have an invitational hand with only four hearts. With a maximum hand, opener should technically bid 3♥ holding a three-

card heart suit, rather than accepting by bidding 3NT, to allow for this possibility — since opener has already denied four hearts — but few partnerships are this sophisticated. The use of the *Jacoby transfer* handles this type of hand much more effectively.

♠ K J 8 5 3 2   Respond 2♣. With this hand, responder is too strong
♥ 4 2   to sign off in 2♠, but not strong enough to commit
♦ 10 7   the partnership to game by bidding 4♠. Instead, re-
♣ Q 10 4   sponder starts with *Stayman*. If opener bids 2♠, raise
to 3♠. If opener rebids 2♦ or 2♥, bid 2♠, show-
ing an invitational hand with at least five spades. Partnerships using the *Jacoby transfer* would handle this hand differently.

Responder's Use of Stayman with a Weak Hand

In general, responder shouldn't use the *Stayman* convention with hands worth 0 to 7 points. It risks getting the partnership too high.

WEST	NORTH	**EAST**	SOUTH
1NT	Pass	?	

♠ J 8 4 3   Pass. Although responder could be lucky using *Stay-*
♥ Q 10 6 3   *man* with this hand if opener rebids 2♥ or 2♠. It's
♦ 5 3   best to pass and hope opener can take seven tricks in
♣ J 9 3   1NT. If opener rebids 2♦ over *Stayman*, responder
is badly placed. Passing would leave the partnership in a poor spot, but any rebid by responder would show at least invita-tional strength. If responder rebids 2NT, for example, opener might ac-cept by bidding 3NT. The partnership would be too high.

Here is an exception.

♠ J 8 4 3   Respond 2♣. An exception can be made when re-
♥ Q 10 6 3   sponder is short in clubs. Now responder can pass
♦ J 9 5 3   any rebid by opener. If opener rebids 2♥ or 2♠, the
♣ 3   partnership has found a fit and you can pass. If opener
rebids 2♦, pass and hope the partnership is at least in a playable spot.

Responder's Use of Stayman as a Minor-Suit Slam Try

Stayman can be put to uses other than searching for a major-suit fit. Many partnerships use the *Stayman* convention as the first step to show a five-card or longer minor suit with interest in a slam contract. Responder starts with 2♣; opener replies by bidding a four-card major or bidding 2♦ with no four-card major. Responder then bids 3♣ or 3♦ as a forcing bid, showing interest in slam and a five-card or longer suit.

The partnership must agree to use this particular variation of *Stayman*. There are other possible meanings that could be assigned to these bidding sequences. Consider the following examples:

WEST	NORTH	**EAST**	SOUTH
1NT	Pass	?	

♠ A 4
♥ J 8
♦ A Q 10 7 5 2
♣ K 9 4

Respond 2♣. With interest in slam and a strong diamond suit, start with *Stayman*. Opener will rebid 2♦, 2♥, or 2♠, treating the 2♣ response as an inquiry about major suits. Now rebid 3♦. This is a forcing bid, showing five or more diamonds. With a minimum-strength hand, opener can rebid 3NT to show no interest in a slam contract. With three-card or longer support for diamonds and some extra strength, opener can make any other bid to show encouragement. For example, opener could bid 3♥ to show high cards in hearts and interest in reaching a contract of 6♦. The partnership's slam-bidding methods would take over at this point.

♠ 10 4
♥ A J 6 5
♦ Q 4
♣ A K J 7 3

Respond 2♣. If opener rebids 2♥, showing a four-card or longer heart suit, use the partnership's slam-bidding methods to try to reach 6♥. If opener rebids 2♦ or 2♠, bid 3♣ as a forcing bid to find out if opener has any interest in moving toward a slam with clubs as trump. The partnership needs a firm understanding about this sequence, since some partnerships use this last sequence — a rebid of 3♣ after starting with 2♣ in response to 1NT — to show a weak hand with a long club suit. This is a common method for signing off in partscore with clubs as trump when the partnership uses *Stayman*.

Stopping in a Partscore In a Minor Suit

The partnership needs to agree on how to stop in a minor-suit partscore.

♠ 8 5 4
♥ 4
♦ J 3
♣ Q 9 7 6 5 4 2

The traditional way to play partscore with clubs as trump using *Stayman* is to respond 2♣ and then rebid 3♣ after opener's rebid. If the partnership is using this sequence as forcing, it needs another way of stopping in partscore in a minor suit. One method is to use an immediate jump to 3♣ or 3♦ as a weak signoff in response to 1NT. Using this approach, responder would bid an immediate 3♣ with this hand and opener would be expected to pass. Many partnerships use other methods to show weak hands with a long minor suit, and this is discussed in the next chapter.

Variations of the Stayman Convention

The above version of the *Stayman* convention is called *non-forcing Stayman*. The 2♣ response itself is a forcing bid, since it's conventional, but it isn't forcing to the game level. Responder's rebids at the two level or raises of opener's major to the three level are invitational — non-forcing — bids. For other variations of the *Stayman* convention, see the descriptions of *forcing Stayman*, *two-way (double-barreled) Stayman*, and *puppet Stayman* in the Appendix.

RESPONDING TO 2NT AND 3NT

After a 2NT Opening Bid

Stayman is usually used after an opening bid of 2NT.

WEST	NORTH	**EAST**	SOUTH
2NT	Pass	?	

♠ Q 10 8 5
♥ 8 2
♦ K 9 6 3
♣ J 8 6

Respond 3♣. This is the *Stayman* convention, asking opener to bid a four-card major. Since opener is showing 20 or 21 points, responder wants to be in game. If opener rebids 3♠, raise to 4♠. If opener rebids 3♦ or 3♥, bid 3NT. Holding both four hearts and four spades, opener will rebid 3♥. When you rebid 3NT, opener can bid 4♠, knowing you hold four spades to have used *Stayman*.

If the partnership uses a *strong conventional 2♣* opening bid (see Chapter 8), then *Stayman* is also used after the auction has started with a 2♣ opening bid, a 2♦ response, and a rebid of 2NT by opener — showing a balanced hand of 22 to 24 points.

After a 3NT Opening Bid

If the partnership uses an opening bid of 3NT to show a strong balanced hand of 25 to 27 points, *Stayman* can still be used, but having a firm agreement with partner beforehand is best. Some partnerships prefer to use a response of 4♣ as the *Gerber* convention.

Here is an example of using *Stayman* in response to an opening bid of 3NT:

WEST	NORTH	**EAST**	SOUTH
3NT	Pass	?	

♠ J 10 7 5 3
♥ Q 9 6 2
♦ 4
♣ 6 5 2

Respond 4♣. This is *Stayman*. If opener bids 4♥ or 4♠, you'll pass and the partnership should be in its best spot. If opener rebids 4♦, try 4♠, hoping partner has three of those. There's not much room over 3NT to explore all the possibilities. You have to make do with the tools you have available.

If the partnership uses the *strong conventional 2♣ opening* bid, *Stayman* can also be used after a 2♦ response and a rebid of 3NT by opener.

HANDLING INTERFERENCE

If your partnership decides to use a convention such as *Stayman*, you need to have agreements so you know what to do when the opponents interfere in the auction. For example, what do you do if an opponent overcalls 2♦ over your partner's 1NT opening bid and you want to ask if partner has a four-card major? Would 3♣ be *Stayman*? Without firm agreements, the partnership can run into difficulty in such situations.

Standard Methods

The standard agreement is to continue to use your conventional responses to 1NT if an opponent doubles, since no bidding room has been used. If an opponent overcalls, however, the partnership has to abandon most conventional responses because there is no longer enough bidding room. The standard agreements after partner opens 1NT and your right-hand opponent overcalls are the following:

- The bid of a suit at the two level is natural, showing five or more cards in the suit bid and is non-forcing. Opener is allowed to raise with a maximum, since responder could have passed with a very weak hand.

- The bid of a suit at the three level is natural. It shows five or more cards in the suit and is forcing.

- A bid of the opponent's suit — a *cuebid* — is forcing and acts as a substitute for the *Stayman* convention. Opener bids a four-card major, or rebids notrump with no major suit.

- 2NT is invitational. 3NT is to play.

- Double is for penalties.

You are East after the auction has gone:

WEST	NORTH	**EAST**	SOUTH
1NT	2♥	?	

♠ K J 10 8 3
♥ J 4
♦ 10 8 7 3
♣ Q 5

Bid 2♠. This is a natural, non-forcing response showing a five-card or longer suit. Opener will treat this as a mildly invitational bid, since you would have passed with a very weak hand.

♠ K 4 2
♥ 3
♦ 10 8 3
♣ A Q J 8 7 5

Bid 3♣. This is a natural bid, showing a five-card or longer club suit. It's a forcing bid, showing the strength the partnership needs to continue to game. Opener can bid 3NT with some strength in the opponent's suit. Otherwise, the partnership will probably be better off in a contract of 5♣, or even 6♣.

♠ 7 6
♥ K J 9 3
♦ A 8 6 2
♣ 10 9 5

Double. This is a penalty double of the opponent's overcall. Since partner has a balanced hand with 15 to 17 points, you can probably get a sufficient penalty to compensate for any contract your side might make.

♠ A J 8 3
♥ 4 3
♦ K Q 10 6
♣ 8 6 3

Bid 3♥. The *cuebid* of the opponent's suit replaces *Stayman*. Opener will bid 3♠ with a four-card or longer suit, and you can raise to game. With fewer than four spades, opener will rebid 3NT, which should be the best spot for your side.

♠ K 7 5
♥ J 3
♦ Q 10 9 7 5 2
♣ J 5

Bid 2NT. Using the methods described so far, there's no way to show an invitational-strength hand with a long diamond suit after the opponent's interference bid. A bid of 3♦ would be forcing, committing the partnership to the game level. 2NT is a reasonable compromise.

The situation is different if an opponent interferes following a conventional response. Bids carry the same meaning that they would with no interference. The opponent's bid may present other options. You are West and the auction starts this way:

WEST	NORTH	EAST	SOUTH
1NT	Pass	2♣	2♥
?			

♠ A Q 8 3
♥ J 5
♦ K 9 6 2
♣ A Q 5

Bid 2♠. South's overcall doesn't prevent you from showing your four-card major suit.

♠ A J 2
♥ Q 6
♦ A 10 6 3
♣ K Q 8 3

Pass. If South had passed, you would have responded 2♦ to show no four-card major suit. After the overcall, you're no longer obligated to bid. Pass and leave the next decision to partner.

♠ J 10
♥ K J 10 8
♦ A K 8 2
♣ A 9 5

Double. You were intending to respond 2♥ to partner's *Stayman* inquiry. It looks as though South has chosen the wrong time to wander into the auction. Your double suggests to partner that you would like to defend for penalty.

SUMMARY

There are a variety of bidding styles and conventions to handle an opening bid with a balanced hand. A popular blend of opening notrump bids and responses is the following:

Opening Balanced Hands —
Based on 15 to 17 point 1NT

12 to 14 points	Open one of a suit, intending to rebid notrump as cheaply as possible. This describes a hand too weak to open 1NT.
15 to 17 points	Open 1NT.
18 or 19 points	Open one of a suit, intending to jump rebid in notrump. This describes a hand too strong to open 1NT.
20 or 21 points	Open 2NT.
22 to 24 points	Open 2♣†, intending to rebid 2NT.
25 to 27 points	Open 3NT (or open 2♣†, intending to rebid 3NT).

†The opening 2♣ bid is discussed further in Chapter 8.

The Stayman Convention

After an opening bid of 1NT, a response of 2♣ can be used as the *Stayman* convention, asking opener to show a four-card or longer major suit. Opener responds as follows:

- 2♦ No four-card or longer major suit.
- 2♥ A four-card or longer heart suit.*
- 2♠ A four-card or longer spade suit.

* With both majors, opener rebids 2♥.

The *Stayman* convention can also be used after an opening bid of 2NT or 3NT.

After opener's rebid, responder rebids as follows:

Responder's Rebids after Using Stayman

- A rebid of 2 ♥ or 2 ♠ shows a five-card or longer suit and is invitational.

- A rebid of 2NT or a raise of opener's major to the three level is invitational.

- A jump to 3 ♥ or 3 ♠ is forcing, showing a five-card suit and asking opener to choose between 3NT and four of the major suit.

- A rebid of 3 ♣ or 3 ♦ shows a five-card or longer minor suit and slam interest.

- A jump to game is a sign-off bid[†].

Handling Interference over 1NT

- If the opening notrump bid is doubled, responder's bids retain their conventional meaning.

- If there is an overcall directly over the notrump bid, the standard approach is to treat all of responder's bids as natural, except a cuebid of the opponent's suit — which replaces *Stayman*.

[†]Except when responder bids 3NT after opener rebids 2 ♥ holding four hearts and four spades. Opener then bids 4 ♠.

NOTE: See the Appendix (pages 300–306) for a discussion of these supplemental conventions and/or treatments.

Gambling/Acol 3NT Opening

Forcing *Stayman*

Two-Way *Stayman*

Puppet *Stayman*

Negative Doubles after 1NT

Lebensohl

These exercises assume you are using the methods outlined in the summary.

Exercise One — Opening Notrump Bids

You are the dealer. What is your call on the following hands?

1) ♠ K 10 8
♥ A Q 9
♦ K J 7 3
♣ Q J 7

2) ♠ A J 10
♥ K 9 8 7 4
♦ Q 5
♣ A J 6

3) ♠ K Q 10
♥ J 4
♦ A K J 4
♣ A Q 10 5

4) ♠ J 10 6
♥ A 10 3
♦ A Q J 8 5
♣ K Q

5) ♠ Q 7 5
♥ K 9 4 3
♦ A 7
♣ K Q 6 2

6) ♠ K 3
♥ K 10 4
♦ A J
♣ K J 10 9 6 5

Exercise Two — Responding to Stayman

You open 1NT, and partner responds 2♣. What would you rebid with each of the following hands?

1) ♠ K J 6
♥ K Q 9
♦ J 8
♣ K Q J 7 3

2) ♠ K 10 8 6 3
♥ A 9 8
♦ K 10 5
♣ A J

3) ♠ A K J 7
♥ 10 8 6 4
♦ K 4
♣ K J 9

Exercise Three — Responding to 1NT

Partner opens 1NT. What would you respond with each of the following hands? What do you plan to do next?

1) ♠ Q 10 8 5
♥ A 8 6 3
♦ 8 3
♣ A J 6

2) ♠ 8 3
♥ Q J 8 3
♦ A 10 5
♣ J 8 6 5

3) ♠ Q 8 7 3
♥ 9 7 6 3
♦ J 7 5 4 3
♣ —

4) ♠ A 10 6 2
♥ K J 10 8 3
♦ Q 4 3
♣ 5

5) ♠ 6
♥ A 9 3
♦ A K J 8 6 3
♣ K 8 4

6) ♠ 9 3
♥ K Q
♦ 10 7 2
♣ A Q 8 7 5 2

Exercise One — Opening Notrump Bids

1) 1NT. Balanced hand, 16 HCPs.

2) 1NT. Balanced hand, 15 HCPs plus 1 for the five-card suit.

3) 2NT. Balanced hand, 20 HCPs.

4) 1♦. 17 HCPs plus 1 for the five-card suit; too strong for 1NT.

5) 1♣. 14 HCPs; too weak for 1NT.

6) 1NT (or 1♣). 15 HCPs plus 2 for the six-card suit; not quite balanced but no suitable rebid after 1♣ opening.

Exercise Two — Responding to Stayman

1) 2♦. No four-card or longer major suit.

2) 2♠. Shows four-card or longer major suit.

3) 2♥. Bid four-card suits 'up the line.

Exercise Three — Responding to 1NT

1) 2♣ *(Stayman)*. If opener rebids 2♥ or 2♠, raise to game; if opener rebids 2♦, bid 3NT.

2) 2♣ *(Stayman)*. If opener rebids 2♥, raise to 3♥; if opener rebids 2♦ or 2♠, bid 2NT.

3) 2♣ *(Stayman)*. Pass if opener rebids 2♦, 2♥, or 2♠.

4) 2♣ *(Stayman)*. If opener rebids 2♥ or 2♠, raise to game; if opener rebids 2♦, jump to 3♥ (forcing).

5) 2♣ *(Stayman)*. If opener rebids 2♦, 2♥, or 2♠, bid 3♦ (slam try in diamonds).

6) 3NT. No interest in a major suit but enough for game; 3NT should be easier than 5♣.

Exercise Four — Responder's Rebid

Partner opens 1NT, you respond 2♣, and opener rebids 2♥. What's your next bid with each of the following hands?

1) ♠ A 8 6 4
   ♥ K 10 8 3
   ♦ J 3
   ♣ 10 8 2

   _____

2) ♠ A J 9 5
   ♥ 7 3
   ♦ K Q 8 4
   ♣ J 6 2

   _____

3) ♠ K Q 9 7 3
   ♥ A Q 7 2
   ♦ 8 5
   ♣ 7 3

   _____

4) ♠ K Q 6 2
   ♥ 8 3
   ♦ A 7
   ♣ A Q J 8 5

   _____

5) ♠ J 9 7 6
   ♥ 10 8 6 2
   ♦ K 8 6 3
   ♣ 4

   _____

6) ♠ Q J 8 7 3
   ♥ K 4
   ♦ 9 8 2
   ♣ Q 7 6

   _____

Exercise Five — Opener's Second Rebid

As West, you open 1NT with the following hand:

♠ A Q 4 3
♥ K Q 6 2
♦ A Q 3
♣ 7 4

What's your next bid in the following auctions with North-South passing?

1)

West	East
1NT	2♣
2♥	3♦
?	

2)

West	East
1NT	2♣
2♥	2NT
?	

3)

West	East
1NT	2♣
2♥	2♠
?	

4)

West	East
1NT	2♣
2♥	3♣
?	

Exercise Four — Responder's Rebid

1) 3 ♥. With 8 HCPs plus 1 dummy point for the doubleton diamond, make an invitational raise.

2) 3NT. With 11 HCPs, there's enough for game and no major suit fit has been found so far.

3) 4 ♥. Having found a fit and with enough for game, there's no need to introduce a new suit.

4) 3 ♣. Having failed to find a spade fit, look for a possible slam in clubs (3 ♣ is forcing).

5) Pass. 2 ♥ should be a better contract than 1NT; there's not enough strength to invite game.

6) 2 ♠. This shows an invitational hand with five or more spades.

Exercise Five — Opener's Second Rebid

1) 4 ♥. With 17 HCPs, you have enough to accept partner's invitation.

2) 4 ♠. Partner must have spades to use *Stayman* and not raise hearts; partner is also showing an invitational-strength hand; accept the invitation and play in the eight-card fit.

3) 4 ♠. Partner is showing an invitational hand with five or more spades; accept with a maximum.

4) 3NT. Partner's 3 ♣ bid is forcing, showing a good club suit; 3NT shows no interest in clubs.

Exercise Six — Responding to 2NT

Partner opens the bidding 2NT (20 to 21). What do you respond with each of the following hands? What's your plan?

1) ♠ 9 5 4
   ♥ J 10
   ♦ J 8 7 6 3
   ♣ 10 4 3

2) ♠ K J 8 5
   ♥ 7 3
   ♦ Q J 6 4
   ♣ 9 7 2

3) ♠ J 7 3
   ♥ A Q 7 6 2
   ♦ 8 5
   ♣ 9 4 2

4) ♠ A 10 7 4 2
   ♥ Q 5 4 3
   ♦ J 7
   ♣ 5 4

5) ♠ Q 8
   ♥ 8 7 6
   ♦ Q 7 4
   ♣ K J 10 5 4

6) ♠ A J 8
   ♥ Q 10 3
   ♦ K Q 7 5
   ♣ 8 6 2

Exercise Seven — Handling Interference

Partner opens 1NT, and the opponent on your right overcalls 2♦. What do you bid with each of the following hands?

1) ♠ 10 2
   ♥ J 6 3
   ♦ 6 5 3
   ♣ Q 9 8 4 3

2) ♠ K Q 8 7 5
   ♥ 8 4
   ♦ Q 9 3 2
   ♣ 7 5

3) ♠ 3
   ♥ A Q J 6 5
   ♦ K 10 8 5
   ♣ J 8 2

4) ♠ Q 10 8 6 5 2
   ♥ A 10 3
   ♦ 7 6
   ♣ K 2

5) ♠ Q J 9 6
   ♥ A 10 8 5
   ♦ 6 3
   ♣ A 7 4

6) ♠ 8 7 3
   ♥ A 4
   ♦ K J 9 2
   ♣ 10 9 7 6

Exercise Six — Responding to 2NT

1) Pass. With only 2 HCPs plus 1 for the five-card suit, game is unlikely when opener has 20 to 21 points.

2) 3♣ *(Stayman)*. With 7 HCPs, there's enough combined strength for game; look for an eight-card spade fit; if opener rebids 3♦ or 3♥, put the partnership in 3NT.

3) 3♥. This response is forcing, asking opener to choose between 3NT and 4♥.

4) 3♣ *(Stayman)*. If opener rebids 3♥ or 3♠, you can raise to game in the major suit; if opener rebids 3♦, bid 3♠ to show the five-card spade suit and ask opener to choose between 3NT and 4♠.

5) 3NT. With no interest in a major, put the partnership in game in notrump; 3♣ would be *Stayman*.

6) 4NT. Enough to invite slam; with a minimum (20), opener can pass; with a maximum (21), opener can bid slam.

Exercise Seven — Handling Interference

1) Pass. Nothing to say.

2) 2♠. This shows a mildly invitational hand with a five-card suit; with less you would pass.

3) 3♥. A jump in a new suit is forcing.

4) 4♠. With 9 HCPs plus 2 for the six-card suit, there's enough for game.

5) 3♦. The cuebid takes the place of the *Stayman* convention.

6) Double. Looks like your opponent has walked into trouble.

Bid and Play — Deal 1

(E-Z Deal Cards: #1, Deal 1 — Dealer, North)

Suggested Bidding

WEST	NORTH	EAST	SOUTH
	1NT	Pass	2♣
Pass	2♥	Pass	3NT
Pass	4♠	Pass	Pass
Pass			

After North opens 1NT, South uses *Stayman* to look for a major-suit fit. With both four-card majors, North rebids 2♥, bidding up the line. South isn't interested in hearts and puts the partnership in 3NT, holding enough strength for a game. North draws the inference that South wouldn't use *Stayman* without interest in a major; since it isn't hearts, it must be spades. North puts the partnership in its eight-card fit.

Dlr: North   ♠ Q 10 7 3
Vul: None   ♥ A K 7 2
           ♦ K 9
           ♣ A 8 4

♠ 8 4   ♠ A 6 2
♥ Q 10 9 5   N   ♥ J 6 3
♦ 10 6 5 3 2   W E   ♦ 8 4
♣ K 6   S   ♣ Q J 10 9 5

          ♠ K J 9 5
          ♥ 8 4
          ♦ A Q J 7
          ♣ 7 3 2

Suggested Opening Lead

East is on lead. With the knowledge that South's 2♣ response was a conventional bid, East selects the ♣Q, top of a sequence.

Suggested Play

North can see one loser in spades, two in hearts, and two in clubs. The heart losers can be trumped in dummy or discarded on South's extra diamond winners after drawing trumps. North can afford to win the ♣A and lead spades, planning to drive out the ♠A and then draw the rest of the trumps. Following this line of play, North should lose at most one spade trick and two club tricks.

Playing duplicate bridge, North may want to try for an overtrick after the opening club lead by discarding a club loser on one of dummy's extra diamond winners before letting the defenders in with the ♠A. On the actual deal, East trumps the third round of diamonds as North discards a club. North still makes the contract, since there will be only one club loser left to go with the spade loser.

If North–South were to reach 3NT, rather than 4♠, East can lead clubs to defeat the contract. After the ♣A is driven out, North doesn't have enough tricks and will have to promote extra winners in spades. East–West get four club tricks, along with the ♠A.

Suggested Defense

Although East–West can't defeat a contract of 4♠, they must be careful not to let declarer make an overtrick. When East leads the ♣Q, West should play the ♣K on this trick to avoid blocking the suit. Otherwise, if declarer wins the first trick with the ♣A and drives out East's ♠A, the defenders can take only one club trick with West's ♣K. West has no club left to return, and declarer can discard a club loser on dummy's diamonds after drawing the remaining trumps.

Bid and Play — Deal 2

(E-Z Deal Cards: #1, Deal 2 — Dealer, East)

Suggested Bidding

WEST	NORTH	EAST	SOUTH
		2NT	Pass
3♣	Pass	3♦	Pass
3NT	Pass	Pass	Pass

With 20 high-card points, East opens the bidding 2NT if the partnership range for this bid is 20 or 21 points. After South passes, West uses the *Stayman* convention to look for an eight-card major-suit fit. With no four-card major, East makes the conventional rebid of 3♦. Holding 10 high-card points, West knows the partnership has enough combined strength for a game but not enough for a slam. Since there's no major suit fit, West signs off in 3NT.

```
Dlr: East        ♠ Q 10 9 5
Vul: N–S         ♥ 10 7 6 5
                 ♦ A Q 6
                 ♣ 8 4
♠ J 7 6 3            N        ♠ A K 2
♥ K 8 4 2        W     E      ♥ A Q 3
♦ 10 5              S         ♦ K 8 4
♣ A 6 3                       ♣ K J 10 5
                 ♠ 8 4
                 ♥ J 9
                 ♦ J 9 7 3 2
                 ♣ Q 9 7 2
```

Suggested Opening Lead

South is on lead and starts with the ♦ 3, fourth from longest and strongest. South should not be deterred by East's 3♦ bid, since that was a conventional response.

Suggested Play

East can count seven sure tricks — two spades, three hearts, and two clubs. East will also get a trick with the ♦ K once South has led the suit. The ninth trick could come from the spade suit, if the ♠ Q is doubleton. There might also be an extra trick from the heart suit if the missing hearts divide 3–3. The club suit offers a sure method for developing a ninth trick. Declarer can take a club finesse. If it wins, declarer has an extra trick and may make an overtrick. Even if the finesse loses, declarer has an extra trick because the ♣10 will be established as a winner once the ♣Q is driven out.

With all of these options, how should declarer play? Establishing an extra trick from the club suit is the surest way of making the contract. Declarer must be careful, however. The defenders have attacked diamonds. If declarer loses a trick to the ♣Q, the defenders may be able to take enough diamond tricks to defeat the contract. To prevent this, declarer should use the hold up play.

Suppose North wins the first trick with the ♦A and returns the ♦Q. Declarer should hold up with the ♦K, letting North win the trick. When North leads another diamond, declarer wins with the ♦K. Since declarer is planning to develop an extra trick in clubs, either a low spade or a low heart can be discarded from dummy. The advantage of holding up is that South now becomes the dangerous opponent while North becomes a non-dangerous opponent. If declarer loses a trick to South, South may be able to take enough diamond winners to defeat the contract. That makes South dangerous. If declarer loses a trick to North, North is unlikely to have any diamonds left to lead. If North does have a diamond left to lead, the defenders' diamonds must originally have been divided 4–4, so they can't take enough tricks to defeat the contract. That makes North non-dangerous.

Declarer now wants to tackle the club suit in a way that avoids losing a trick to the dangerous opponent. This can be done by playing the ♣K and then leading the ♣J, planning to finesse against the ♣Q in the South hand. On the actual hand, South holds the ♣Q and the finesse succeeds, giving declarer a ninth trick. If the finesse were to lose to the ♣Q in the North hand, declarer would still be safe. The ♣10 would be established as the ninth trick and North is the non-dangerous opponent — the defenders cannot take enough tricks to defeat the contract before declarer regains the lead.

The danger on this hand can be seen if declarer plays a club to dummy's ♣A and then plays a club to the ♣J, taking a finesse against the ♣Q in the North hand. When the finesse loses to the ♣Q in the South hand — the dangerous hand — South takes enough diamond tricks to defeat the contract.

Suggested Defense

South gets the defense off to a good start by leading the ♦3. Assuming North plays third hand high and wins the first trick with the ♦A, North should then return the ♦Q — high card from the short side — to avoid blocking the suit. Once East's ♦K is driven out, South's remaining diamonds are established as winners. If declarer lets South gain the lead with the ♣Q, the defenders can defeat the contract.

If the defense starts this way, but declarer holds up with the ♦K and avoids giving South a trick with the ♣Q (as discussed above), it would appear that the defenders have no chance to defeat the contract. There is a way, however, for the defenders to give declarer a much tougher challenge. Although it is usual to play third hand high when partner leads a low card against declarer's notrump contract, there are exceptions. Suppose North chooses to play the ♦Q rather than the ♦A on the first trick. Now it's difficult for declarer to hold up winning the ♦K. Declarer will be under the illusion that South holds the ♦A and will think that this is the only opportunity to win a trick with the ♦K. Assuming declarer does win the first trick with the ♦K, now both defenders become dangerous. If declarer loses a trick in another suit to either opponent, the defenders can take enough diamond tricks to defeat the contract. Declarer will have to guess which defender holds the ♣Q.

North won't lose a trick by playing the ♦Q rather than the ♦A on the first trick. If South holds the ♦K, the ♦Q will win the trick and North can play the ♦A and continue with the suit. If declarer wins with the ♦K, North will get the ♦A later and can continue leading the suit upon regaining the lead. The play of the ♦Q might cause some confusion for South, however. If declarer wins with the ♦K and then loses a trick to South's ♣Q, South is likely to think that declarer, not North, holds the ♦A. South may not lead the suit again. That's the trouble with plays like this. You might fool declarer, but you might also fool partner. Both defenders will really need to be on their toes to defeat this contract.

Bid and Play — Deal 3

(E-Z Deal Cards: #1, Deal 3 — Dealer, South)

Suggested Bidding

WEST	NORTH	EAST	SOUTH
			1NT
Pass	2♣	Pass	2♦
Pass	Pass	Pass	

South has 15 high-card points and a balanced hand. This is ideal for a 1NT opening bid if the partnership is using a range of 15 to 17 points. With only 5 high-card points, North does not have the usual strength required for the *Stayman* convention. With shortage in clubs, however, it is relatively safe to respond 2♣. North can pass any response by South. When South rebids 2♦, showing no four-card major, North passes and leaves the partnership in a partscore contract that is likely to be better than 1NT.

```
Dlr: South    ♠ J 9 4 3
Vul: E–W      ♥ K 9 6 2
              ♦ J 8 5 3 2
              ♣ —
♠ K 8                      ♠ Q 10 6 2
♥ 8 5 4         N          ♥ A 7 3
♦ A 10 9     W   E         ♦ 7 4
♣ Q J 9 6 2      S         ♣ A 10 7 5
              ♠ A 7 5
              ♥ Q J 10
              ♦ K Q 6
              ♣ K 8 4 3
```

Suggested Opening Lead

West would probably lead the ♣Q, top of a broken sequence.

Suggested Play

It's sometimes difficult to plan the play from declarer's perspective when the long trumps are in the dummy. It's often easier to view the hand as though it were being played by dummy. Dummy's hand has three spade losers, one heart loser, and one diamond loser (if the diamonds divide 3–2). That appears fine, since declarer can afford to lose five tricks.

Declarer should still be careful not to run out of trumps before all the work is done. If declarer trumps the first club lead in dummy and then starts to draw trumps, West may win the ♦A and lead another club. If declarer trumps this trick, declarer can't afford to draw the remaining trumps and then give up a heart trick. The defenders can take a club winner. Declarer may be able to make the contract by playing on hearts before drawing the last trump. When the hearts luckily divide 3–3, declarer can come to enough tricks. There's an easier way to keep control, however.

On the lead of the ♣Q, declarer should discard a spade loser from dummy. East will win this trick with the ♣A, but now declarer is in command. South's ♣K is a winner and can be used to discard another spade loser from dummy. The defenders can't force declarer to use dummy's trumps right away. On regaining the lead, South can drive out the ♦A, draw trumps, and then drive out the ♥A. South should finish with an overtrick, losing one spade — having discarded two spade losers on the clubs — one heart, one diamond, and one club.

The play of discarding a spade loser from dummy while losing the first trick to East's ♣A is referred to as a loser on a loser. This type of play arises in many situations and, by exchanging one loser for another, declarer can often gain a trick. In this hand, for example, declarer develops the ♣K into a winner while preserving dummy's trumps.

Suggested Defense

With the favorable lie of the cards for declarer — diamonds dividing 3–2 and hearts dividing 3–3 — the defenders will have a difficult time holding declarer to fewer than eight tricks. Holding declarer to eight tricks is a reasonable result, however, since South might take nine tricks.

If South declares 1NT, the defenders have a chance to defeat the contract. They can establish four club winners by giving South a trick with the ♣K. They must then restrict declarer to two heart and two diamond winners and the ♠A. They can do this, for example, if West holds up the ♦A for two rounds, and East holds up the ♥A for two rounds. Now South can never get to the dummy. The defenders eventually get a spade winner (maybe two) to go along with four club tricks and two aces.

Bid and Play — Deal 4

(E-Z Deal Cards: #1, Deal 4 — Dealer, West)

Suggested Bidding

WEST	NORTH	EAST	SOUTH
1NT	2♠	3♠	Pass
4♥	Pass	Pass	Pass

After West's 1NT opening bid, North can overcall 2♠ with the good six-card suit. When North has a good suit, it's unlikely that East–West will double the overcall for penalty. Even if 2♠ is doubled and defeated, the penalty is likely to be less than the value of East–West's potential contract.

```
Dlr: West      ♠ K Q J 7 5 2
Vul: Both      ♥ 7 3
               ♦ A Q 6
               ♣ 9 4
♠ A 8 4              ♠ 6 3
♥ A Q 8 5      N     ♥ K 10 6 4
♦ K 8 2     W   E    ♦ J 7 5 3
♣ K 10 5       S     ♣ A Q 8
               ♠ 10 9
               ♥ J 9 2
               ♦ 10 9 4
               ♣ J 7 6 3 2
```

With 10 high-card points, East has the strength to take the partnership to the game level and would like to investigate whether there is an eight-card heart fit. 2♣ is no longer available as the *Stayman* convention after the overcall. In this situation, a cuebid of the opponent's suit replaces *Stayman*. It is forcing and commits the partnership to game. Holding a four-card or longer major suit, opener shows it in response to the cuebid. Opener has the other major suit and shows it by bidding 4♥. Without a four-card heart suit, opener would rebid 3NT with some strength in spades or bid a four-card minor. East–West find their heart fit despite North's interference.

Suggested Opening Lead

North is on lead and starts with the ♠K, top of a sequence.

Suggested Play

West's 4♥ contract is a little precarious. West needs the defenders' hearts to divide 3–2 to avoid a heart loser. In addition, there are two spade losers and three diamond losers. One spade loser can be trumped in dummy, so declarer wants to restrict the diamond losers to two.

After winning the ♠A and drawing trumps, declarer tackles the diamond suit by leading toward one of the honors. Declarer might start by leading a low diamond from dummy toward the ♦K, hoping South holds the ♦A. When the ♦K loses to North's ♦A, declarer still has a chance. Later, declarer can lead a low diamond toward dummy's ♦J, hoping that North holds the ♦Q. The second finesse works.

On this layout, it doesn't matter whether declarer leads toward the ♦K or toward the ♦J first. As a matter of good technique, however, leading toward the ♦J first is better. The 2♠ overcall makes it more likely that North holds the ♦A. At the same time, it's unlikely North holds a lot of diamonds. Exchange North's ♦Q and ♦6 for two low clubs in the South hand to see why it might be a good idea to lead a low diamond from the West hand first. Also, if the ♦J does lose to South's ♦Q, declarer still has the option of "guessing" that North started with the doubleton ♦A. Try exchanging North's ♦Q for a low club in the South hand. Declarer might still make the contract. If North hesitates when a low diamond is led toward the ♦J, declarer could infer that North holds the ♦A. On the next round of diamonds, declarer might play a low diamond from both hands rather than leading a diamond toward the ♦K.

Suggested Defense

The defenders can't defeat 4♥ if declarer plays correctly. They may get a chance, however, if declarer slips slightly. Suppose declarer wins the ♠A, draws trumps, and then takes all the club winners before leading a diamond to the ♦K. North can win this with the ♦A, take a spade winner, and play another high spade, forcing declarer to trump in the dummy. With no club entries left, declarer will have to lead a diamond from dummy, away from the ♦J. South will win this trick and North will still have the ♦Q left to defeat the contract.

CHAPTER 2

The Jacoby Transfer

JACOBY TRANSFER

In this chapter, we will focus on the value of using transfer bids to overcome some of the disadvantages of the standard structure of responses to 1NT opening bids. For example, when responder makes a signoff bid of 2 ♦, 2 ♥, or 2 ♠, the contract is played by the weaker hand and the stronger hand goes down as dummy. This can make it easier for the opponents to defend. They can see the location of most of the high cards. Also, with responder as declarer, the opening lead comes through the strength in opener's hand, perhaps trapping one of the high cards. This can be a problem even when responder has enough values to sign off in a game contract such as 4 ♥ or 4 ♠. Another disadvantage comes when responder has to go through *Stayman* to show an invitational hand with a five-card or longer major suit. Opener can't tell whether responder is inviting with a five-card suit or a six-card or longer suit. Finally, the transfer provides a convenient way for responder to describe a two-suited hand after opener starts with 1NT.

JACOBY TRANSFER FOR THE MAJORS

To address these problems, Oswald Jacoby, one of the game's great players and theorists, developed the idea of transfer bids in response to a notrump opening. These conventional responses are called *Jacoby transfers*, in honor of their originator, and work like this:

- A response of 2 ♦ asks opener to bid 2 ♥.
- A response of 2 ♥ asks opener to bid 2 ♠.

Responder uses the transfer bid when holding a five-card or longer major suit. One advantage of this approach is that the weaker hand is usually the dummy and the stronger hand remains concealed as declarer. Consider the following deal:

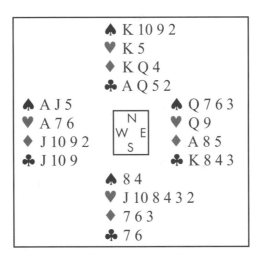

North opens 1NT. Playing standard methods, South responds 2♥, a signoff bid. That puts West on lead, and whether West leads the ♦ J or the ♣ J, the defenders are off to a good start. They have the advantage of leading through dummy's strength and will likely defeat the contract, especially since dummy's cards are exposed.

Playing the *Jacoby transfer*, South responds 2♦, asking North to bid 2♥. South passes, leaving North as declarer in the 2♥ contract. East is on lead making it much more difficult for the defense. East has to lead away from a high card into declarer's strength. It will also be more difficult later, since the defenders can't see declarer's (North's) high cards.

The basic idea of transferring is useful, but any change in your bidding methods has an impact on the structure of your system. The use of the *Jacoby transfer* has implications. You and your partner have to consider how using this convention will allow you to accomplish everything you want to do using standard methods, namely:

- sign off in partscore in a major suit.

- invite opener to game in a major suit.

- get to a game in a major suit.

Signing Off in Partscore in a Major Suit

After an opening 1NT bid, responder, with 0 to 7 points, has no interest in game. To sign off in a major suit, transfer to it and then pass. You are East and partner opens 1NT:

♠ 10 8 6 4 2   This isn't the kind of hand you want to play in a
♥ 9 3   notrump contract. You want to play partscore in a
♦ Q 8 6 4   likely fit in spades. Playing standard methods, re-
♣ 5 2   spond 2♠; opener would pass. Playing the *Jacoby*
                  transfer, respond 2♥, telling opener to bid 2♠.
                  When opener bids 2♠, pass. The contract is played
                  from opener's side. Your hand, the weaker hand, is
                  the dummy.

This is how the auction would go:

WEST	NORTH	EAST	SOUTH
1NT	Pass	2♥	Pass
2♠	Pass	Pass	Pass

Inviting Game in a Major Suit

Playing the *Jacoby transfer*, responder can invite game holding 8 or 9 points and a five-card or longer major suit by first transferring to the major suit. On the rebid, responder shows an invitational hand by:

• Bidding 2NT with a five-card major suit, or

• Raising to the three level with a six-card or longer major suit.

Here is an example of inviting game with a five-card major suit. You are East and partner opens 1NT.

♠ K 10 8 7 3   With 8 high-card points and five cards in a major
♥ Q 9 4   suit, start by responding 2♥ to show the spade suit.
♦ K 5   After opener obediently bids 2♠, rebid 2NT to show
♣ 8 4 2   an invitational-strength hand and precisely five
                  spades. Opener can now decide what to do.

The auction would start this way:

WEST	NORTH	EAST	SOUTH
1NT	Pass	2♥	Pass
2♠	Pass	2NT	Pass
?			

With a minimum hand, opener passes with a doubleton spade or signs off in 3♠ with three or more spades. With a maximum hand, opener bids 3NT with a doubleton spade or 4♠ with three or more spades.

Here's how responder would show an invitational hand with a six-card or longer major in response to 1NT when playing the *Jacoby transfer*.

♠ 9 6
♥ A J 10 4 3 2
♦ Q 7 2
♣ 8 3

With a six-card heart suit, start by bidding 2♦, a *Jacoby transfer bid*. When opener dutifully bids 2♥, raise to 3♥, inviting opener to continue to game. This shows a six-card or longer suit. With a five-card heart suit, you would rebid 2NT to invite game.

The auction would start this way:

WEST	NORTH	EAST	SOUTH
1NT	Pass	2♦	Pass
2♥	Pass	3♥	Pass
?			

With a minimum hand, opener passes. With a maximum hand, opener accepts the invitation by bidding 4♥.

Bidding Game in a Major Suit

With 10 or more points, responder knows there is enough combined strength for game. The only decision is the denomination of the contract.

- With a five-card major suit, responder transfers opener to the suit and then jumps to 3NT, asking opener to choose between game in notrump and game in the major suit. This replaces the jump to 3♥ or 3♠ using standard methods.

- With a six-card or longer major suit, responder transfers opener to the suit and then raises to the game level.

Let's look at some examples. You are East.

WEST	NORTH	**EAST**	SOUTH
1NT	Pass	?	

♠ K Q 8 7 6 4
♥ 8 5 2
♦ A 7
♣ 6 3

Respond 2♥. With a six-card major suit, start by making a transfer bid of 2♥. When opener rebids 2♠, jump to 4♠. Using standard methods, responder would jump immediately to 4♠ with this hand.

♠ 8 4 2
♥ K J 10 8 3
♦ A 9 5
♣ Q 3

Respond 2♦. Holding a five-card major suit, start by transferring to hearts. Over opener's 2♥ rebid, jump to 3NT. Opener can pass with a doubleton heart, or bid 4♥ with three or more hearts.

Responder only transfers to a major with a five-card or longer suit.

♠ K Q 7 4
♥ 9 2
♦ A 8 6 4
♣ J 7 5

Respond 2♣. With a four-card major suit, start by bidding *Stayman*. If opener rebids 2♠, raise to 4♠. If opener rebids 2♦ or 2♥, jump to 3NT. Note that if opener started with both four hearts and four spades and rebid 2♥, opener can now bid 4♠ over the 3NT bid. Since you used *Stayman*, opener knows you have one of the major suits.

♠ K Q 6
♥ J 10 5
♦ A Q 8 3
♣ 6 4 2

Jump to 3NT. With no interest in a major suit game, jump directly to 3NT. You make the same response whether or not you play transfer bids.

Opener's Rebid after the Transfer

When responder transfers opener to a major suit, opener is expected to accept the transfer by bidding the requested suit at the cheapest level.

WEST	NORTH	EAST	SOUTH
1NT	Pass	2 ♦	Pass
?			

♠ A Q 8 4
♥ 10 3
♦ K Q 9 6
♣ A Q 7

Rebid 2 ♥. Simply accept partner's transfer. Partner may have a weak hand with a long heart suit and be trying to sign off with hearts as trump. You've no reason to override partner's decision. Of course, partner may continue with another bid, such as 2NT, showing an invitational-strength hand with a five-card heart suit. Now you could show your maximum strength and dislike for hearts by rebidding 3NT.

♠ K 8 4
♥ J 9 8 3
♦ A K J
♣ K 8 3

Rebid 2 ♥. Partner's 2 ♦ response is a transfer to hearts and you have four-card support. With a minimum-strength hand for the 1NT bid, however, you've no reason to expect that the partnership belongs any higher than the partscore level. Partner may have no points and a five-card heart suit. Accept the transfer and wait to hear what partner does next. If partner passes and you play in 2 ♥, your length in hearts will be an added bonus. If partner were now to jump to 3NT, showing a game-going hand with a five-card heart suit, you would bid 4 ♥ with the knowledge that your side has a nine-card major-suit fit.

There's one exception. With four-card support for responder's major and a maximum-strength hand, opener can jump to the three level in responder's suit. This is referred to as *super acceptance*.

♠ A 8
♥ Q J 8 5
♦ K 10 3
♣ A K 10 5

Jump to 3 ♥. When partner responds 2 ♦, you could simply accept the transfer by rebidding 2 ♥. But with four-card support and a maximum-strength hand for the 1NT opening bid, jump to 3 ♥ to show a *super acceptance* of the transfer. This isn't a forcing bid.

With nothing but a long heart suit, responder can pass — responder could be trying to play in a quiet partscore of 2 ♥ and you may have taken the partnership too high. Nonetheless, if responder has a little something, you want to send the message that you're willing to play at the game level in hearts. If partner has a strong hand and was intending to go to the game level anyway, you want to suggest that slam is a possibility.

THE SUBSEQUENT AUCTION

After the initial transfer and opener's acceptance of the transfer, the auction can proceed in several ways.

- Responder can pass to play partscore in the major suit.

- Responder can invite game by bidding 2NT or raising the major suit.

- Responder can jump to game in notrump or in the major suit.

- Responder can bid a new suit.

Most partnerships have the agreement that a new suit by responder below the game level is natural and forces the partnership to keep bidding to at least the game level. Here are examples:

West	WEST EAST	East
♠ J 9	1NT 2♥	♠ Q 10 8 6 3
♥ A 10 6	2♠ 2NT	♥ K 9 2
♦ A K 8 5	Pass	♦ 7 4
♣ K 6 5 3		♣ Q 9 4

After the opening 1NT bid, East transfers to show the spade suit and then bids 2NT to show an invitational-strength hand with a five-card spade suit. With a minimum-strength hand for the 1NT bid and no fit in spades, West rejects the invitation and the partnership stops in a partscore contract in notrump.

West	WEST	EAST	East
♠ K 5	1NT	2♥	♠ Q 10 8 7 3
♥ K 9 6 2	2♠	3♥	♥ A Q J 7 3
♦ A 8 4	4♥	Pass	♦ 3
♣ K Q 10 2			♣ 9 3

With both five-card major suits and enough strength to put the partnership in a game-level contract, East starts by transferring to the higher-ranking of the two five-card suits. After West accepts the transfer, East shows the other major suit. This is a forcing bid, offering West a choice of major suits. West prefers hearts as the trump suit. By inference, East is showing at least five-cards in both majors in this bidding sequence. With a four-card major and a five-card major, East would start with the *Stayman* convention.

West	WEST	EAST	East
♠ A K J 9	1NT	2♦	♠ 5
♥ A 8	2♥	3♣	♥ K Q 7 6 3
♦ K 9 8 6	3NT	Pass	♦ Q 10 3
♣ 10 6 5			♣ A Q J 4

With a five-card heart suit and a mild interest in reaching a slam contract, East starts by transferring West to hearts. East then shows the club suit. West doesn't care for either of East's suits and expresses this opinion by rebidding 3NT. East has nothing further to say and respects West's decision.

West	WEST	EAST	East
♠ A J	1NT	2♦	♠ 5
♥ A 10 5 2	3♥	4♣	♥ K Q 7 6 3
♦ A K J 5	4♦	4NT	♦ Q 10 3
♣ 10 6 5	5♠	6♥	♣ A Q J 4

East has the identical hand to the previous example and starts by transferring to hearts. With a maximum-strength hand and four-card support, West *super accepts* by jumping to 3♥. This encourages East to look for slam by showing a control in clubs. When West shows values in diamonds, East uses the *Blackwood* convention to check for aces, and then bids the good slam.

SIGNING OFF IN A MINOR SUIT

Since a response of 2♣ is *Stayman* and a response of 2♦ is a transfer to hearts, responder needs another way to sign off in a minor suit. Here is one method that is commonly used.

2♠ as a Minor-Suit Sign-off

A popular extension to the *Jacoby transfer* can be used to stop in partscore in a minor suit. Here is an example:

• A response of 2♠ asks opener to bid 3♣. Responder can then pass to play partscore in clubs or bid 3♦ as a sign-off in diamonds.

This reveals one small disadvantage to using transfers. Using standard methods, you could sign off in 2♦. Since this is now a transfer to hearts, you'll have to play in 3♦, rather than 2♦, when you have a weak hand with a long diamond suit. For example, suppose this is your hand as East:

♠ 8
♥ 9 4 2
♦ K 8 6 5 4 2
♣ J 7 3

Playing *2♠ as a minor-suit sign-off*, the auction would go like this:

WEST	NORTH	EAST	SOUTH
1NT	Pass	2♠	Pass
3♣	Pass	3♦	Pass
Pass	Pass		

You make a transfer bid to clubs, and opener bids 3♣ as requested. You now show your diamond suit and opener passes your signoff bid.

Here are other examples of signing off when responder has a minor suit.

WEST	NORTH	**EAST**	SOUTH
1NT	Pass	?	

♠ 9 2
♥ 10 5
♦ Q 3
♣ J 9 8 6 4 3 2

Respond 2♠. With a seven-card minor suit and no interest in playing in a game contract, start with 2♠. This asks opener to bid 3♣. You will pass and the partnership will rest in partscore with opener as declarer.

♠ 8 7 4
♥ 9
♦ Q J 9 7 5 4
♣ 6 3 2

Respond 2♠. This requests opener to bid 3♣. You'll correct to 3♦, and opener is expected to pass. You will be declarer in 3♦. This is a weakness in this method, since responder is still declarer and, playing standard methods, responder would be able to sign off in 2♦.

♠ 9 4
♥ 10 7
♦ Q 9 8 6 5
♣ J 6 4 3

Pass. Although you could start with the 2♠ response to get the partnership to 3♦, with this type of hand it's best to pass. Partner may have difficulty taking seven tricks in 1NT, but there's no guarantee that trying to take nine tricks in a diamond partscore will be any better.

Other Responses to 1NT

If the partnership adopts both *Stayman* and *Jacoby transfers*, then it's common to assign special messages to some other bids in response to 1NT.

3♣ and 3♦

Responder has a way to show a weak hand with a long minor suit, by bidding 2♠ to transfer opener to 3♣ and then passing or bidding 3♦. Responder also has a way to show a strong hand with a long minor suit, by bidding 2♣ and then bidding the minor suit after opener's response (see Chapter 1). Missing is a response that shows an invitational-strength hand with a minor suit. For this purpose, a jump response of 3♣ or 3♦

can be used to show a hand of invitational strength with a six-card or longer minor suit For example:

WEST	NORTH	**EAST**	SOUTH
1NT	Pass	?	

♠ 10 8 3
♥ Q 7
♦ A J 9 7 4 2
♣ 9 3

Jump to 3 ♦ . With a six-card minor suit, jump to the three level in your minor suit, inviting opener to bid game with a maximum hand. If opener passes, turning down the invitation, you'll play in a partscore contract with diamonds as trump.

3♥ and 3♠

Responder has a way to handle signoff, invitational, and game-going hands with a major suit, through the use of the *Jacoby transfer*. This frees up jump responses to the three level in a major suit for other purposes. A common use of these bids is that a jump response of 3♥ or 3♠ shows a hand of at least slam-invitational strength with a six-card or longer major suit. For example:

WEST	NORTH	**EAST**	SOUTH
1NT	Pass	?	

♠ 5 4
♥ A K J 10 7 2
♦ K J 6
♣ Q 4

Jump to 3♥ . With a good six-card major suit and a hand worth 16 points — 14 high-card points plus 2 points for the six-card suit — you're too strong to sign off in a game contract. Jump to the three level in your major suit. Opener will know that you are interested in going beyond the game level, since you would respond 2♦ — transferring to hearts — and then jump to game if you weren't interested in going any further. With a poor fit for hearts and a minimum hand, opener can rebid 3NT. You can then give up on the slam bonus. With good support for hearts but a minimum-strength hand, opener can simply raise to 4♥ . With good support for hearts and a maximum-strength hand, opener can make a stronger move toward slam. (Slam bidding methods are discussed in the fifth book in the ACBL Bridge Series, *More Commonly Used Conventions.)*

Responses of 4♣ or Higher

Most partnerships agree to use a 4♣ response to 1NT as the *Gerber* convention asking for aces and a 4NT response to 1NT as a *quantitative* — invitational — raise, inviting opener to continue to slam.

Some partnerships assign special meanings to immediate jump responses of 4♦, 4♥, and 4♠ (see, for example, the description of the *Texas transfer* in the Appendix), but many partnerships prefer not to add any further conventions at this point. With no agreement to the contrary, jumps to 4♥ and 4♠ by responder are natural signoff bids, as in standard methods. With a six-card major suit and a game-going hand, responder has a choice between jumping to game directly (and becoming declarer) or transferring and then bidding game (making opener the declarer).

WHEN THE OPPONENTS INTERFERE

If your partnership uses transfer bids, you need to have agreements about what to do when the opponents interfere in the auction. What do you do if an opponent overcalls 2♦ over your partner's 1NT opening bid and you want to show a heart suit? Does a 2♥ bid now show hearts, or is it a transfer to spades? Without firm agreements, the partnership quickly runs into difficulty.

The standard agreement is to continue to use transfer responses to 1NT if an opponent doubles, since no bidding room has been used. If an opponent overcalls, however, the partnership has to abandon transfer bids because there is no longer sufficient bidding room. Here are examples of hands you might hold as South after the auction has gone:

WEST	NORTH	EAST	**SOUTH**
	1NT	2♦	?

♠ J 4
♥ K J 10 8 3
♦ 10 8 7 3
♣ Q 5

Bid 2♥. This is natural and non-forcing, showing a five-card or longer suit. It isn't a transfer to spades. Opener will treat this as mildly invitational, since you would have passed with a very weak hand.

♠ A K J 4 2
♥ 10 7 5
♦ 8 3
♣ A 8 5

Bid 3 ♠. This is a natural bid, showing a five-card or longer spade suit. It's forcing, showing enough strength for the partnership to continue to game. Opener can bid 3NT with a doubleton spade or raise to 4 ♠ with three-card or longer support.

The situation is different if an opponent interferes following a conventional response. Bids carry the same meaning that they would if there were no interference. However, the opponent's bid may present other options. For example, suppose you are North and the auction starts:

WEST	NORTH	EAST	SOUTH
	1NT	Pass	2 ♦
Double	?		

♠ A Q 8
♥ Q J 5
♦ 8 6 2
♣ A K 9 5

Bid 2 ♥. Accept the transfer bid with three-card support for partner's suit.

♠ A Q 2
♥ 6 4
♦ A 10 6
♣ K Q 8 6 3

Pass. If West had passed, you would accept the transfer and bid 2 ♥. West's double gives you the option of passing. With only two hearts, you've no particular reason to bid at this point. Your side can still stop in 2 ♥, but partner may choose to bid something else with the knowledge that you don't have heart support.

♠ A K 4
♥ 10 3
♦ A J 10 8 3
♣ A 9 5

Redouble. This suggests to partner that your side's best contract could be 2 ♦ redoubled. If you can take eight tricks, you'll get a game bonus. Of course, partner could have another opinion and could bid again.

RESPONDING TO 2NT AND 3NT

After a 2NT Opening Bid

If the partnership uses *Jacoby transfers* over 1NT opening bids, it uses similar methods after an opening bid of 2NT:

- 3♦ is a transfer to 3♥.

- 3♥ is a transfer to 3♠.

Here are examples of responder's actions after an opening bid of 2NT (20 or 21 points).

WEST	NORTH	EAST	**SOUTH**
	2NT	Pass	?

♠ 9 7 6 5 3 2
♥ J 6
♦ 7 3
♣ 8 4 2

Respond 3♥. This is a transfer to 3♠. After opener accepts the transfer, pass. The partnership will be in a partscore in the major suit, played from opener's side of the table. This is one of the advantages of using transfer bids. Playing standard methods, a response of 3♠ would be forcing, and the partnership couldn't stop below the game level.

♠ 8 2
♥ K J 7 5 3
♦ K 9 4
♣ 7 6 2

Respond 3♦, transferring opener to 3♥. After opener bids 3♥, follow with 3NT. This sequence shows a hand with enough strength to raise to game and a five-card heart suit. Opener can pass with two hearts and convert to 4♥ with three or more hearts.

♠ Q 10 7 5 2
♥ 8 3
♦ Q 9 2
♣ 7 6 5

Awkward. There's not enough bidding room available to show an invitational-strength hand with a five-card major suit. You have several options. To play in partscore, pass 2NT or transfer opener to 3♠ and then pass. To play in game, transfer to 3♠ and then bid 3NT, asking opener to choose between 3NT and 4♠. You'll have to use your judgment — there's still room for that even with all the conventions available to the partnership.

♠ 2
♥ K 9 8 7 5 3
♦ 7 2
♣ Q 8 4 2

Respond 3♦. This transfers opener to 3♥, and you can then raise to 4♥. This allows the contract to be played at the game level from partner's side. You could jump to 4♥ and play the hand from your side of the table. Some partnerships prefer to distinguish between the two sequences — transferring and then raising to game versus bidding game directly — using one sequence as a signoff in game, while the other sequence is mildly invitational to slam. Such distinctions are for experienced partnerships and are more commonly used when the partnership uses both *Jacoby* and *Texas transfer bids*.

If the partnership uses a *strong artificial 2♣ opening* (see Chapter 8), then the above methods are also used after the auction has started with a 2♣ opening bid, a 2♦ response, and a rebid of 2NT by opener — showing a balanced hand of 22 to 24 points.

After a 3NT Opening Bid

The partnership can also use the *Jacoby transfer bid* after an opening bid of 3NT showing a strong balanced hand of 25 to 27 points or, if the partnership uses the *strong artificial 2♣ opening* bid, after an opening 2♣ bid, a 2♦ response, and a rebid of 3NT by opener.

- 4♦ is a transfer to 4♥.   • 4♥ is a transfer to 4♠.

Here are examples of responder's actions after an opening bid of 3NT:

WEST	NORTH	EAST	**SOUTH**
	3NT	Pass	?

♠ 3
♥ J 9 8 7 6 3
♦ 10 5 4 2
♣ 8 3

Respond 4♦. This is a transfer to 4♥. There's no guarantee the contract will make, but it's likely to be better than 3NT.

♠ 7 6 5 4 3 2
♥ 6 5
♦ 7 4 2
♣ 6 4

Respond 4♥. This is a transfer to 4♠. You'll have to hope that partner remembers this is a transfer bid. Otherwise, playing 4♥ from your side of the table will prove to be an interesting contract!

SUMMARY

If the partnership uses both *Stayman* and the *Jacoby transfer bid* as discussed in this chapter, responder's bids send the following messages:

Responses to 1NT

- 2♣ is the *Stayman* convention.
- 2♦ (*Jacoby transfer bid*) asks opener to bid 2♥.
- 2♥ (*Jacoby transfer bid*) asks opener to bid 2♠.
- 2♠ (*Jacoby transfer bid*) asks opener to bid 3♣.
- 2NT is invitational to 3NT (8 or 9 points).
- 3♣ and 3♦ are invitational to 3NT (8 or 9 points with a six-card suit).
- 3♥ and 3♠ are invitational to slam, showing a six-card or longer suit.
- 3NT, 4♥, and 4♠ are sign-off bids.

After the transfer bid, opener rebids as follows:

Opener's Rebid

In response to a transfer bid of 2♦ or 2♥:

- Opener simply bids the requested suit at the two level.
- Opener can *super accept* by jumping to the three level in the requested suit holding a maximum-strength hand and four-card support for responder's suit.

In response to a transfer bid of 2♠:

- Opener bids 3♣. Responder may then pass to play a partscore in clubs. If responder bids 3♦, opener passes to play a partscore in diamonds.

Responder's Rebid after a Jacoby Transfer Bid

- Responder passes, with minimum values, to play a partscore in the major suit.
- A rebid of 2NT is invitational, showing five cards in the major suit.
- A raise to 3 ♥ or 3 ♠ is invitational, showing a six-card or longer suit.
- A raise to 4 ♥ or 4 ♠ is a sign-off bid.
- A jump to 3NT shows five cards in the major suit and asks opener to choose between 3NT and four of the major suit.
- The bid of a new suit is natural and forcing.

Handling Interference

If the opening notrump bid is doubled:

- Responder's bids retain their conventional meanings.

If there is an overcall directly over the notrump bid:

- The *Jacoby transfer* no longer applies. All responder's bids are natural — except a cuebid of the opponent's suit, which replaces *Stayman*.

If there is interference after the transfer bid:

- Opener can pass with a minimum and a doubleton in the requested suit. Otherwise, opener can bid if there is room available.

Jacoby transfer bids can also be used after opening bids of 2NT or 3NT.

NOTE: See the Appendix (pages 306–310) for a discussion of these supplemental conventions and/or treatments.

Four-Suit Transfer Bids

Minor-Suit Stayman

Texas Transfers

Smolen Transfers

Singleton-Showing Responses (Splinter)

These exercises assume you are using the methods outlined in the summary.

Exercise One — Using *Jacoby Transfer* Bids

Partner opens 1NT. What do you respond with each of the following hands? What do you plan to do next?

1) ♠ 4
   ♥ J 10 8 7 5 3
   ♦ Q 8 3 2
   ♣ 9 8   _2D PASS_

2) ♠ K J 9 6 5 4
   ♥ 8 3
   ♦ K 6
   ♣ 7 4 2   _2H 3S_

3) ♠ A K
   ♥ 10 9 7 6 5 2
   ♦ K 7 6
   ♣ 5 4   _2D 4H_

4) ♠ Q J 6 4 2
   ♥ Q 8 3
   ♦ 8 4 2
   ♣ K 6   _2H 2NT_

5) ♠ K Q 6
   ♥ A 10 8 5 2
   ♦ 10 3
   ♣ Q 4 3   _2D 3NT_

6) ♠ K Q J 8 2
   ♥ —
   ♦ A Q 9 7 4
   ♣ 10 8 3   _2H 3D_

Exercise Two — Opener's Response to a *Jacoby Transfer*

You are North and open 1NT with the following hand:

♠ K 6
♥ K Q 8 2
♦ A J 9 3
♣ K J 4

What is your rebid in each of the following auctions?

1)
WEST	**NORTH**	EAST	SOUTH
	1NT	Pass	2♥
Pass	? _2S_		

2)
WEST	**NORTH**	EAST	SOUTH
	1NT	Pass	2♦
Pass	? _3H_		

3)
WEST	**NORTH**	EAST	SOUTH
	1NT	Pass	2♥
Pass	2♠	Pass	3NT
Pass	? _P_		

4)
WEST	**NORTH**	EAST	SOUTH
	1NT	Pass	2♥
Pass	2♠	Pass	2NT
Pass	? _3NT_		

Exercise One — Using *Jacoby Transfer* Bids

1) 2♦ (transfer). Pass partner's 2♥ bid.

2) 2♥ (transfer). Raise to 3♠, invitational.

3) 2♦ (transfer). Raise to 4♥.

4) 2♥ (transfer). Bid 2NT, invitational.

5) 2♦ (transfer). Jump to 3NT.

6) 2♥ (transfer). Bid 3♦ (forcing) to show the second suit.

Exercise Two — Opener's Response to a *Jacoby Transfer*

1) 2♠. Accept the transfer.

2) 3♥. With a maximum and four-card support, super accept the transfer.

3) Pass. Partner is showing a game-going hand with a five-card spade suit, asking you to choose between 3NT and 4♠.

4) 3NT. Partner has shown an invitational hand with five spades; accept in notrump with a maximum but no spade fit.

Exercise Three — Responding with Minor Suits

Partner opens 1NT. What do you respond with each of the following hands? What do you plan to do next?

1) ♠ 9 4 3
   ♥ 8
   ♦ 8 6 3
   ♣ Q 10 8 7 6 4 *2S PASS 3C*

2) ♠ 6
   ♥ Q 9 5
   ♦ J 9 8 6 5 4 2
   ♣ J 5 *2S-3D*

3) ♠ 3 2
   ♥ 8 5 4
   ♦ J 7 6
   ♣ K 10 8 6 4 *PASS*

4) ♠ 9 4 2
   ♥ K 8
   ♦ K J 10 8 6 3
   ♣ 8 4 *3D*

5) ♠ 7 4 2
   ♥ K Q
   ♦ A Q J 9 7 3
   ♣ 10 8 *3 NT*

6) ♠ A 4
   ♥ 6 4
   ♦ K Q 7
   ♣ K Q J 10 8 3 *2C - 3C*

Exercise Four — The Subsequent Auction

As North, you open 1NT with the following hand:

♠ A Q 6 3
♥ K Q J 5
♦ Q 6 5
♣ J 4

What is your next bid in each of the following auctions?

1)
WEST	NORTH	EAST	SOUTH
	1NT	Pass	2♠
Pass	? *3C*		

2)
WEST	NORTH	EAST	SOUTH
	1NT	Pass	2♠
Pass	3♣	Pass	3♦
Pass	? *P*		

3)
WEST	NORTH	EAST	SOUTH
1NT	Pass	3♣	
Pass	? *P*		

4)
WEST	NORTH	EAST	SOUTH
	1NT	Pass	2♣
Pass	2♥	Pass	3NT
Pass	? *4S*		

5)
WEST	NORTH	EAST	SOUTH
	1NT	Pass	2♣
Pass	2♥	Pass	3♣
Pass	? *3NT*		

Exercise Three — Responding with Minor Suits

1) 2♠ (extended transfer). Pass partner's 3♣ bid.

2) 2♠ (extended transfer). Bid 3♦ as a signoff bid in diamonds.

3) Pass. Since you can't sign off at the two level in clubs, the choice is between playing partscore in 1NT or transferring to 3♣; it should be easier to take seven tricks in 1NT than nine tricks in 3♣.

4) 3♦ (invitational). With 7 HCPs plus 2 points for the six-card suit, make an invitational bid of 3♦; partner can pass to play a partscore in diamonds, or accept and play game in notrump (or diamonds).

5) 3NT. With enough strength for game but not enough for slam, bid game in notrump; it should be easier to take nine tricks than 11.

6) 2♣ *(Stayman)*. Rebid 3♣ (forcing) after hearing partner's response to show slam interest.

Exercise Four —The Subsequent Auction

1) 3♣. Accept the transfer.

2) Pass. Partner is showing a weak hand with a long diamond suit.

3) Pass. Partner is showing an invitational hand with a long club suit; with a minimum-strength hand, decline the invitation and settle for partscore in clubs.

4) 4♠. Partner has a game-going hand with a four-card spade suit; play game in the major-suit fit.

5) 3NT. Partner is showing a hand with a club suit and slam interest; with no fit and a minimum-strength hand, show no interest in slam by rebidding 3NT.

Exercise Five — Handling Interference

Partner opens 1NT, and the opponent on your right overcalls 2♥. What call do you make with each of these hands?

1)   ♠ 8 4 2
    ♥ J 7
    ♦ Q 8 6 4 3
    ♣ 10 5 3
    _P_

2)   ♠ K J 7 6 5
    ♥ 8 2
    ♦ Q 9 6 4
    ♣ J 8
    _2S_

3)   ♠ A Q J 8 3
    ♥ 5
    ♦ 10 8 5
    ♣ K J 9 6
    _3S_

4)   ♠ Q J 8 7 4 2
    ♥ 10 3
    ♦ A K 6
    ♣ 9 5
    _4H_

5)   ♠ A J 7 4
    ♥ 9 2
    ♦ A Q 6 5
    ♣ 7 4 2
    _3H_

6)   ♠ 9 7 3
    ♥ J 4
    ♦ Q 8 2
    ♣ K Q 7 6 3
    _2NT_

Exercise Six — Responding to 2NT

Partner opens the bidding 2NT (20 or 21). What do you respond with each of these hands? What's your plan?

1)   ♠ 7 5
    ♥ 10 8 6 4 3 2
    ♦ 7 5 3
    ♣ 4 2
    _3D - P_

2)   ♠ Q J 8 6 5
    ♥ K 7 3
    ♦ 9 2
    ♣ 10 7 3
    _3H - 3NT_

3)   ♠ J 10 4
    ♥ Q 10 7 6 5 2
    ♦ K 3
    ♣ 8 6
    _3D · 4H_

4)   ♠ K 10 7 5 2
    ♥ Q 8 6 3
    ♦ 9 5
    ♣ J 7
    _3C_

5)   ♠ J 8 3
    ♥ 6
    ♦ Q 9 7 6 4
    ♣ K 8 5 4
    _3NT_

6)   ♠ K J 8
    ♥ Q 10 4
    ♦ K 7 6 5
    ♣ A J 2
    _6NT_

Exercise Five — Handling Interference

1) Pass. With a weak hand it's best to defend 2♥ and hope to defeat the contract.

2) 2♠, natural and invitational, showing a five-card or longer suit. *Jacoby transfers* no longer apply after an overcall; with a weak hand, you would have passed.

3) 3♠, forcing, asking opener to choose between 3NT and 4♠. *Jacoby transfers* no longer apply after an overcall.

4) 4♠. You want to be in game in spades and can no longer use a *Jacoby transfer.*

5) 3♥. A cuebid of the opponent's suit replaces *Stayman* when there is interference.

6) 2NT. Make an invitational raise, as you would have done without the interference.

Exercise Six — Responding to 2NT

1) 3♦ (transfer). Pass. Partner will play the partscore contract of 3♥.

2) 3♥ (transfer). Bid 3NT, giving opener the choice of 3NT or 4♠.

3) 3♦ (transfer). Raise to game, 4♥; opener will play the contract.

4) 3♣ *(Stayman).* If opener shows a four-card major, raise to game; if opener bids 3♦, you then bid 3♠, showing the five-card suit and asking opener to choose between 3NT and 4♠. If you were to transfer to 3♠ right away, you would not have room to search for a fit in hearts.

5) 3NT. Settle for game in notrump, even with an unbalanced hand; there's no way to explore for a minor-suit fit using standard methods.

6) 6NT. The partnership has at least 34 combined points, enough for slam; with no interest in a major-suit fit, take the partnership directly to the best spot.

Bid and Play — Deal 1

(E–Z Deal Cards: #2, Deal 1 — Dealer, North)

Suggested Bidding

WEST	NORTH	EAST	SOUTH
	1NT	Pass	2♦
Pass	2♥	Pass	Pass
Pass			

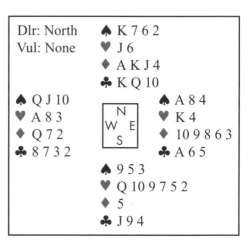

Dlr: North
Vul: None

♠ K 7 6 2
♥ J 6
♦ A K J 4
♣ K Q 10

♠ Q J 10   ♠ A 8 4
♥ A 8 3   ♥ K 4
♦ Q 7 2   ♦ 10 9 8 6 3
♣ 8 7 3 2   ♣ A 6 5

♠ 9 5 3
♥ Q 10 9 7 5 2
♦ 5
♣ J 9 4

After North opens 1NT and East passes, South knows the partnership belongs in a partscore in hearts. Using the *Jacoby transfer bid,* South responds 2♦, asking opener to bid hearts. North accepts by rebidding 2♥. South now passes to leave the partnership in its best partscore contract.

Suggested Opening Lead

East is on lead. East will likely select the ♦ 10, top of a sequence.

Suggested Play

One consequence of playing transfer bids is that the contract is played from the short side — the hand with fewer trumps. In such situations, it's sometimes easier for declarer to count the losers from dummy's perspective. Looked at in this manner, there are three spade losers in the South hand, two heart losers, and one club loser.

North could hope that West has the ♠A and plan to eliminate a loser by leading toward the ♠K. After a diamond lead from East, however, there's a much easier solution. Whether or not West plays the ♦Q, declarer will get three diamond tricks. Before drawing trumps, declarer can discard two of South's spade losers on the extra diamond winners. Then it's safe to lead hearts. Declarer should finish with an overtrick, losing one spade, two hearts, and one club.

Notice that the 2 ♥ contract might be less successful if played from South's side of the table. West might lead the ♠Q, trapping North's ♠K. The defenders could get three spade tricks, two heart tricks, and the ♣A to defeat the contract. The transfer bid makes quite a difference to the outcome.

Suggested Defense

East–West will have difficulty defeating a 2 ♥ contract played from the North hand. The only winning defense is for East to find a heart lead! West can get a trick with the ♥A and then lead the ♠Q to trap North's ♠K. Defending this way, the defenders could get three spade tricks, two heart tricks, and one club trick. From East's point of view, a heart lead is very unattractive, especially when North is known to hold most of the high cards. Without seeing all four hands, East will almost certainly make the standard lead of a diamond.

This hand illustrates one of the advantages of the *Jacoby transfer bid*. The opening leader has to choose a lead that plays into the strong hand. This frequently costs the defense one or more tricks.

South does well to remove partner from the 1NT contract. After a diamond lead against 1NT, careful defense will restrict North to three diamond tricks and two club tricks. That's down two in a notrump contract.

Bid and Play — Deal 2

(E–Z Deal Cards: #2, Deal 2 — Dealer, East)

Suggested Bidding

WEST	NORTH	EAST	SOUTH
		Pass	1NT
Pass	2♥	Pass	2♠
Pass	4♠	Pass	Pass
Pass			

After South opens 1NT, North uses the *Jacoby transfer bid* of 2♥ to request that partner bid spades. After South accepts the transfer, North has enough strength to put the partnership in a game contract. Knowing there is at least an eight-card spade fit, North raises to 4♠. The advantage of the transfer bid is that South is now the declarer and West will have to make the opening lead.

```
Dlr: East      ♠ A K J 9 6 3
Vul: N–S       ♥ 8 4 2
               ♦ J 9
               ♣ 7 5
♠ 8 4                        ♠ 10 2
♥ A 9 3          N           ♥ Q J 10 7 5
♦ K 5 2        W   E         ♦ 8 7 4
♣ Q J 10 6 2     S           ♣ K 8 4
               ♠ Q 7 5
               ♥ K 6
               ♦ A Q 10 6 3
               ♣ A 9 3
```

Suggested Opening Lead

Because of the use of the transfer bid, West is on lead and would make the standard opening lead of the ♣Q, top of a sequence.

Suggested Play

South has two potential heart losers, a potential diamond loser, and two club losers. South's plan should be to draw trumps and then take the diamond finesse. If East has the ♦K, South will avoid a diamond loser. Even if West has the ♦K, South can discard all of dummy's hearts on the established diamond winners and avoid losing two heart tricks — West can't lead hearts without giving declarer a trick with the ♥K. South has to lose only one club trick because the second club loser can be trumped in the dummy.

The only danger for declarer is if East can gain the lead. East could then lead a heart, trapping South's ♥K if West holds the ♥A. If declarer wins the first trick with the ♣A and the diamond finesse loses later, West can lead a club to East's ♣K and East can lead a heart. To avoid this possibility, declarer should let West win the first trick with the ♣Q. Now there's no danger that East can ever get the lead and trap South's ♥K. Of course, duplicate bridge players may be reluctant to give up a club trick to ensure the contract. If the diamond finesse is successful, they can discard all of dummy's clubs and make an overtrick. Even if the diamond finesse is unsuccessful, they would still be okay if East holds the ♥A or the defense is less than accurate.

Suggested Defense

Although East–West can't legitimately defeat a contract of 4♠ played by South, they may get an opportunity. When West leads the ♣Q, East should play the ♣8 as an encouraging signal. If declarer wins the first trick with the ♣A, draws trumps, and then takes the diamond finesse, West can win the ♦K and lead a club to East's ♣K. East can finish off a fine defense by leading the ♥Q to trap declarer's ♥K.

If North–South aren't using transfer bids, East–West will have an excellent chance to defeat the contract. East would be on lead and could lead the ♥Q, giving the defenders the first two tricks. If they now switch to clubs, they can take a club trick after declarer loses the finesse to West's ♦K.

Bid and Play — Deal 3

(E–Z Deal Cards: #2, Deal 3 — Dealer, South)

Suggested Bidding

WEST	NORTH	EAST	SOUTH
			Pass
1NT	Pass	2♦	Pass
2♥	Pass	2NT	Pass
4♥	Pass	Pass	Pass

With an invitational-strength hand and a five-card major suit, East transfers West to 2♥ and then bids 2NT. With a maximum-strength hand for the 1NT opening bid, West has enough to accept the invitation. With the knowledge that East has five hearts, West puts the partnership in game in the eight-card fit.

```
Dlr: South      ♠ J 10 3
Vul: E–W        ♥ A 6
                ♦ J 10 9 6 3
                ♣ Q 5 2
   ♠ A K 8 5           ♠ 7 4 2
   ♥ Q 10 5       N    ♥ K J 7 4 3
   ♦ A 7 4     W   E   ♦ 8 5
   ♣ K J 4         S    ♣ A 7 6
                ♠ Q 9 6
                ♥ 9 8 2
                ♦ K Q 2
                ♣ 10 9 8 3
```

Suggested Opening Lead

North is on lead and starts with the ♦ J, top of a sequence.

Suggested Play

West has two spade losers, a heart loser, two diamond losers, and a club loser. With only three spades and two diamonds in the dummy, West can probably restrict each of these suits to one loser. Since there's nothing that can be done about the heart loser, West will have to try to avoid losing a club trick. One choice is to take the club finesse — hoping South holds the ♣Q — but there's another option. If the missing spades are divided 3–3, one of dummy's clubs can be discarded on the established spade winner. West should organize the play to take advantage of both possibilities.

After winning the ♦A, West should lead trumps to drive out the ♥A. On regaining the lead, West should plan to draw trumps and then play spades. When the spades divide 3–3, West no longer needs the club finesse.

Suggested Defense

The defenders will establish a diamond trick with the opening lead and they have a second sure trick with the ♥A. They will eventually get a spade trick, but that will be all unless declarer chooses to take the club finesse rather than establish the spade suit.

If East–West reach 3NT, rather than 4♥, the defenders have an opportunity to defeat the contract. North will start with the ♦J and South must be careful to play a high diamond on this trick to avoid blocking the suit. If South plays the two high diamonds early, North–South can get four diamond tricks to go along with the ♥A.

Bid and Play — Deal 4
(E–Z Deal Cards: #2, Deal 4 — Dealer, West)

Suggested Bidding

WEST	NORTH	EAST	SOUTH
1NT	Pass	2♠	Pass
3♣	Pass	3♦	Pass
Pass	Pass		

After West's opening 1NT bid, East would like to play in a partscore in diamonds. Since a 2♦ response would be a transfer to hearts, East starts by responding 2♠ which asks West to bid 3♣. East now bids 3♦, a signoff bid, and West passes.

If the partnership uses four-suit transfers, East would respond 2NT as a transfer to diamonds. Without a good fit for diamonds, West would simply accept the transfer by bidding 3♦, and the contract would be played by West instead of East.

```
Dlr: West      ♠ K 8 4 2
Vul: Both      ♥ 10 9 5 3
               ♦ A 5
               ♣ Q J 10
♠ A Q J 10          N        ♠ 3
♥ A 8 6         W       E    ♥ 7 4 2
♦ J 9               S        ♦ Q 10 8 7 6 3
♣ A 8 5 3                    ♣ 9 6 4
               ♠ 9 7 6 5
               ♥ K Q J
               ♦ K 4 2
               ♣ K 7 2
```

Suggested Opening Lead

South is on lead and can start with the ♥K, top of a sequence.

Suggested Play

After the opening lead, East has two immediate heart losers to go along with the two top trump losers. East also has two club losers. The best chance to make the contract is to use dummy's spades. After winning the ♥A, East should lead the ♠A and then the ♠Q. If North covers the ♠Q with the ♠K, East ruffs and can start to draw trumps, having established two spade winners in dummy on which to discard clubs. If the defenders switch to clubs before the high diamonds have been driven out, East will have to play the spade winners before leading any more trumps and attempt to discard two losers.

If North doesn't play the ♠K when the ♠Q is led from dummy, East should discard a heart loser. Even if it turned out that South held the ♠K, East would still have eliminated a loser and established the remaining spade honors in dummy as winners. This type of play is called 'discarding a loser on a loser' — if you lose the trick, you've eliminated a loser anyway, so nothing is lost.

Suggested Defense

The lead of the ♥K establishes two winners for the defense. If declarer doesn't discard either of the losers before leading trumps, the defenders can take their heart winners and switch to clubs. Now it will be too late for declarer to establish any spade winners before the defenders can regain the lead and take their club winners to defeat the contract.

If West is left to play in 1NT, the defenders can defeat that contract. Declarer can develop three spade tricks to go along with the ♥A and ♣A, but that should be all. Even if declarer can establish an extra trick in the club suit, that's still one trick short.

CHAPTER 3

Major-Suit Openings and Responses — Part I

MAJOR-SUIT OPENINGS AND RESPONSES — PART I

Opening bids of 1♥ and 1♠ cover a wide spectrum of hands. The opening bidder could have a balanced hand that falls outside the range of a 1NT bid, or an unbalanced hand. Opener could have a minimum-strength hand of about 13 or 14 points, or a hand just below the requirements for a *strong two-bid*. The partnership can have agreements and make use of conventions to help responder get a clearer picture of opener's hand.

OPENING BIDS OF 1♥ AND 1♠

Before using any conventions, it's important for the partnership to agree on its basic style for opening bids of 1♥ and 1♠. In most areas of North America, it's popular to use a *five-card major* system. An opening bid of 1♥ or 1♠ shows at least a five-card suit. You are the dealer on the following hands.

♠ A K 7 3
♥ 9 7 6 5 2
♦ A Q 8
♣ 2

Open 1♥. The longest suit is opened, not the strongest. Playing five-card majors, there's no requirement that the opening bid show a good suit — only five cards or more.

♠ A K J 6 2
♥ 2
♦ A Q 10 7 5 2
♣ 3

Open 1♦. Although this hand has a five-card spade suit, it should be opened 1♦. With a choice of suits to bid, it is usually better to open the longer suit first. There may be exceptions, however.

♠ Q 10 6 5 2
♥ A K Q 7 3
♦ 5
♣ A 8

Open 1♠. With two five-card or six card suits, open the higher-ranking.

♠ A 9 7 5
♥ K Q 10 8
♦ K 3
♣ J 8 4

Open 1♣. Playing five-card majors, this hand is opened 1♣. Without a five-card major, open the longer minor — with four cards in both minors, the usual guideline is to open 1♦, and with three cards in each minor, most partnerships open 1♣.

Strength Requirements

The common guideline is that 13 points are required to open the bidding; this is a guideline, not a rule. There are different methods for valuing hands. Players generally agree that the value of a hand is a combination of both high-card strength and distributional strength. Not everyone, however, will agree on what constitutes an opening bid. Consider the following hands:

♠ K J 8 7 5 2
♥ 6 4
♦ A K 5
♣ 9 3

Open 1♠. There are 11 high-card points. Some partnerships add two points for length, bringing the total to 13. Others add one point for each doubleton, again bringing the total to 13. Some use the *Rule of 20* — open the bidding if the sum of your high-card points plus the number of cards in your two longest suits is 20 or more — 11 points + 6 cards + 3 cards = 20. All roads lead to the same place.

♠ K J 4
♥ Q 10 8 7 3
♦ 5
♣ K Q 9 3

This hand would be borderline. Those counting length points reach 12 — 11 high-card points plus 1 for the five-card suit. Those counting points for short suits add 2 points for the singleton, getting to 13 total points. Using the *Rule of 20,* add 9 — the number of cards in the two longest suits — and you get a total of 20. Opening the bidding 1♥ with this hand is neither right nor wrong. It's a matter of judgment. Partners should agree on their general style.

♠ A Q J 8 7 5
♥ K Q J
♦ A Q
♣ 10 5

Open 1♠. You and your partner should have the same feeling about the upper range for an opening bid at the one level. Most partnerships would feel that this hand is worth an opening bid of 1♠, but there are those that open this with a *strong two-bid*. It comes down to a matter of style.

In third or fourth position, there are additional criteria that affect the strength required for opening the bidding. This is discussed in the next chapter.

RAISING PARTNER'S MAJOR-SUIT OPENING

When the partnership has found an eight-card or longer major-suit fit, the challenge is to determine whether to stop in partscore, bid to the game level, or bid a slam. It's important to have a sound understanding of the raise structure since raises of major suits occur frequently. Conventional agreements can help the partnership reach the appropriate level.

The Single Raise

Playing five-card major-suit openings, a single raise to the two level is usually played as three-card or longer support and 6 to 9 or 6 to 10 points. When you raise partner's suit, *dummy points*[1] are used in place of length points. For example, suppose you are East:

WEST	NORTH	**EAST**	SOUTH
1♥	Pass	?	

♠ 7 4
♥ Q 9 3
♦ K J 7 6 4
♣ 10 8 3

Raise to 2♥. This hand is worth 7 points — 6 high-card points plus 1 dummy point for the doubleton spade. The raise lets partner know you have found a fit and it's now up to partner to make the next move. You would make the same bid if North overcalled 1♠ or 2♣.

♠ J 10 7 3
♥ 10 7 5 2
♦ 6
♣ Q 8 4 2

Raise to 2♥. There are 3 high-card points and 3 dummy points for the singleton. There's no need to mention the spade suit since you have at least a nine-card fit in hearts. If North overcalled, you could make a preemptive jump raise to 3♥. This is discussed in Chapter 6.

[1] Dummy points — or short suit points — are usually used instead of length points to value a hand when you are planning to raise partner's suit. The following approach is most common: void — 5 points; singleton — 3 points; doubleton —1 point.

♠ Q 9 3
♥ K Q 7
♦ Q J 7 5
♣ 9 6 3

Raise to 2♥. Some partnerships limit the raise to the two level to 6 to 9 points but an upper range of 10 points is equally popular. Exercise your judgment. With this balanced hand, a raise to the two level is enough. If partner can't bid again, it's unlikely you will miss game.

♠ K J 9 6 3
♥ J 7 3
♦ 8 2
♣ K 7 5

Respond 1♠ or raise to 2♥. With three-card support, you can raise directly to 2♥ but many players would respond 1♠. Although you have an eight-card heart fit, you might have a nine-card spade fit. The 1♠ response might be more descriptive if you can show the heart support next — if partner rebids 1NT, for example. If East were to overcall 2♣ or 2♦, you would have no choice but to raise hearts directly.

Limit Raises

When you are raising partner's suit and skip one level of bidding, you are making a *jump raise* or a *double raise*. You are East:

WEST	NORTH	EAST	SOUTH
1♥	Pass	3♥	

The strength shown by the jump raise depends on the bidding style adopted by the partnership. Although it traditionally showed heart support and 13 or more points (a *forcing raise)*, the modern trend is toward a more natural style where a raise to the two level shows support with 6 to 9 points and a jump raise to the three level shows the next range of 10 to 12 points. Since this means that the jump raise is an invitational bid, limited to a maximum of 12 points, this style is called *limit raises*.

A limit raise is usually made with four-card or longer support. With three-card support and 10 to 12 points, responder bids a new suit, planning to show support and strength on the next round of bidding.

Partner opens 1♥. The player on your right passes. It's your call.

♠ A 7
♥ Q J 6 3
♦ K 9 7 2
♣ 6 4 3

Respond 3 ♥. Playing *limit raises*, the jump raise to the three level shows 10 to 12 points and at least four-card support. Partner can pass with a minimum opening bid or accept the invitation with a little extra — a good 14 or 15 points or more.

♠ Q 9 7 5 2
♥ 9 8 6 4
♦ A J
♣ K 5

Respond 3 ♥. There's no need to look for another fit once you have four-card support for partner's major suit. Agree on hearts right away to avoid any confusion. The quality of your hearts isn't important. If you don't have high cards in hearts, you'll have them elsewhere to compensate.

♠ A J 7 3
♥ Q 9 8
♦ J 2
♣ K 9 7 2

Respond 1 ♠. Avoid making a limit raise with three-card support for partner's major. Start by bidding a new suit. You'll show support and strength on the next round. If partner rebids 2 ♥, for example, you will raise to 3 ♥, inviting partner to game.

You may see the point range required for a limit raise stated as 9 to 11 points, 10 to 12 points, or 11 or 12 points, depending on the books you read or the players you talk with. The variation in the ranges comes about mainly from the interpretation of *points*. Some players are talking about high-card points, others about high-card points plus dummy points. There is agreement that a limit raise shows a hand too strong for a single raise to the two level but not strong enough for a forcing raise to game. Partner opens the bidding 1 ♠ and you hold the following hand:

♠ Q J 8 4
♥ A 8 7
♦ Q 9 6 3 2
♣ 8

You have 9 high-card points but, counting 3 dummy points for the singleton club, you have a total of 12 points. When playing limit raises, respond 3 ♠, inviting opener to game.

Forcing Raises

Partner opens the bidding 1 ♥ and you have the following hand:

♠ 8 2
♥ K Q 6 5
♦ A J 8 4
♣ Q 9 3

This hand has 12 high-card points plus 1 dummy point for the doubleton spade since you're planning to support partner's major suit. Partner has promised 13 or more points with the opening 1 ♥ bid, and you have enough to drive the partnership to the game level.

The traditional approach was to use a jump raise of opener's major as a *forcing raise*, showing a hand with enough strength and support to play in a game contract. Unless the opponents intervened, opener couldn't pass until the partnership reached at least 4 ♥. The modern style is to use a jump to the three level as a *limit raise*, an invitational bid which opener could pass. Using that approach, responder can't afford to bid 3 ♥ with this hand since a game contract might be missed.

There are two ways for responder to handle this type of hand. One is to use a conventional forcing raise, which will be discussed later in this chapter. The alternative is to start with a new suit, 2 ♦ on the above hand, planning to show support and strength on the next round. If opener were to rebid 2NT, for example, responder would now jump to 4 ♥, guaranteeing that the partnership reaches game in the trump fit.

Why not go directly to game with the above hand by responding 4 ♥? There is the possibility that opener might hold a strong hand and be interested in exploring the prospect of a slam contract once opener knows you have 13 or more points. By bidding 4 ♥, you leave no room for the partnership to investigate the possibility of slam without going beyond the game level. It is better to reserve the immediate jump to game for other purposes.

Preemptive Raises

Most players use the direct jump to game to show a weak hand, about the strength for a raise to the two level, but one that has at least five-card support for partner's suit. You might jump to 4♥ over partner's opening 1♥ bid with the following hand:

♠ 8
♥ K 9 6 5 3
♦ K 10 8 4
♣ 10 9 3

With 6 high-card points plus 3 dummy points for the singleton spade, you have enough strength to raise to the two level. The purpose of jumping to the four level is two-fold. First, your length in the trump suit, combined with the singleton spade, is likely to give partner a reasonable chance to make ten tricks despite the shortage of high cards. Second, the jump to 4♥ is a form of *preemptive bid*, taking bidding room away from the opponents if they want to compete. Since you have only one spade, the opponents could have an eight-card or longer spade fit. Since you and your partner have a lot of hearts, you could expect that one of the opponents will have a singleton or void in hearts. The opponents may be able to make a 4♠ contract. Your preemptive jump to 4♥ will make it difficult for them to exchange information and find their best contract.

JACOBY 2NT

Suppose partner opens 1♠, and you have the following hand:

♠ K 10 8 4
♥ A J 7
♦ A Q J 6
♣ 8 3

If you play *limit raises*, you can't afford to bid 3♠ since partner might pass. With 15 high-card points plus 1 point for the doubleton club, you want to reach at least the game level, even if partner has a minimum for the opening bid. In keeping with the raise to 2♠ showing 6 to 9 points and the raise to 3♠ showing 10 to 12 points, the most natural progression would seem to be to raise to 4♠ with 13 or more points. This would give up the use of 4♠ as a preemptive raise and would not leave room to explore the possibility of a slam contract without getting past the game level.

Oswald Jacoby developed the idea of using the 2NT response to show a forcing raise. This conventional response, known as *Jacoby 2NT*, has become popular with club and tournament players:

- A response of 2NT to an opening bid of 1♥ or 1♠ shows a game-forcing raise of the major suit and asks for a further description of opener's hand.

This convention gives up the natural meaning of a 2NT response — a balanced hand with a desire to play in notrump. You are compensated by having more room left to explore for slam when you have a fit and at least enough combined strength for a game contract. Here are a few points to keep in mind:

- Responder needs 13 or more dummy points to use *Jacoby 2NT*. This response forces the partnership to keep bidding to at least the game level in the major suit.

- Most partnerships prefer that responder have at least four-card support for the major suit to use *Jacoby 2NT*, similar to the requirement for a limit raise. With enough strength for a game-level contract but only three-card support, responder can start by bidding a new suit and then take opener to game in the major suit. A few partnerships, however, prefer a style of using *Jacoby 2NT* with good three-card support or more.

- Since responder requires enough strength to force to the game level after an opening bid of 1♥ or 1♠, most partnerships do not use the *Jacoby 2NT* convention when responder passed originally. Occasionally, responder will have a hand that was not strong enough to open the bidding but revalues to 13 or more dummy points once partner opens 1♥ or 1♠. Even so, responder needs to proceed cautiously since partner may have fewer than 13 points when opening in third or fourth position. Most partnerships would treat a jump response of 2NT by a passed hand as a natural bid. (*Drury* is another popular method of handling good hands with a fit for partner's major suit once you have passed originally. See Chapter 4.)

- *Jacoby 2NT* is only used in response to major-suit opening bids — 1♥ or 1♠. When partner opens the bidding 1♣ or 1♦, you are usually looking for a major-suit fit, or to play in notrump, before agreeing to play with the minor suit as trump.

You are East after the bidding has started:

WEST	NORTH	**EAST**	SOUTH
1♥	Pass	?	

♠ 9 2
♥ A J 7 5
♦ K Q J 6
♣ K 8 2

Respond 2NT. With four-card support for opener's major and a hand worth 15 dummy points — 14 high-card points plus 1 for the doubleton spade — respond 2NT. This lets partner know that hearts is the agreed trump suit and the partnership is headed for at least the game level. The partnership is now in a position to explore the possibility of a slam contract.

♠ K 3
♥ A K J 7 3
♦ A Q 2
♣ 9 6 2

Respond 2NT. *Jacoby 2NT* is an unlimited forcing raise. There may be slam on this hand and the best start is to agree with partner on the trump suit. You'll have a better idea of slam prospects once you hear partner's rebid.

♠ 3
♥ K J 3
♦ K 10 4 2
♣ A Q 8 7 2

Respond 2♣. This hand is certainly strong enough for you to want to make sure the partnership gets to the game level or higher. You also know that there is an eight-card heart fit. However, *Jacoby 2NT* is usually used only when responder has four-card or longer support. Respond 2♣. This is a forcing response. After opener's rebid, you can show your support for hearts. This way, partner will know you like hearts, but you don't have four of them.

Opener's Rebid after Jacoby 2NT

Once the partnership agrees to use *Jacoby 2NT* to show a forcing raise in response to 1 ♥ or 1 ♠, it must also decide on the meaning of opener's rebids. The standard agreement is the following.

The first consideration is for the opener to show shape regardless of the strength of the hand — either shortness in a side suit or length in a side suit.

- The bid of a new suit at the three level shows *shortness* in that suit, a singleton or a void. This information will be useful to responder in evaluating the prospect of a slam contract. Responder will know that the opponents can't take the first two tricks in the suit, even if they have both the ace and king, since opener will be able to trump at least the second round. If responder holds the ace in opener's short suit, the partnership will have no losers in the suit.

- A jump to the four level in a new suit shows at least five cards in that suit. Most partnerships prefer that this rebid is made holding a good five-card suit, K–J–10–x–x or better. Otherwise, opener simply bids the short suit at the three level.

With no distributional features to describe, opener makes a bid that describes the strength of the hand:

- With minimum strength (12 to 14), jump to game. It's the most discouraging bid opener can make in terms of interest in a slam contract.

- With medium strength (15 to 17), rebid 3NT.

- With maximum strength (18 or more), rebid the agreed trump suit at the three level.

You hold the following hands as West after the auction has started:

WEST	NORTH	EAST	SOUTH
1 ♥	Pass	2NT	Pass
?			

♠ A 9 5
♥ K J 7 6 5
♦ 8
♣ K Q 10 3

Rebid 3 ♦. Although this hand has only 13 high-card points, it also has a short suit — which could prove useful if partner is interested in a slam. 3 ♦ is the conventional bid to show a singleton diamond.

♠ 8 3
♥ A K J 4 2
♦ A Q 10 6 3
♣ 4

Jump to 4 ♦. This shows a good five-card side suit. If partner can look after the losers in the other two suits, the prospects for a slam contract are good.

♠ 9 3
♥ A Q 8 4 2
♦ K J 7 5
♣ Q 6

Jump to 4 ♥. With a minimum-strength hand — 12 high-card points plus 1 point for the five-card heart suit — and no singleton or void, jump directly to game in the agreed suit. This will discourage responder from looking for slam without considerable extra strength.

♠ K J
♥ K 10 8 4 2
♦ A J 10 7
♣ K 9

Rebid 3NT. With 15 high-card points plus 1 point for the five-card suit, this hand is too strong for a jump to 4 ♥. 3NT shows a medium-strength hand with no singleton or void.

♠ A 6
♥ A Q J 8 7 2
♦ K 8
♣ K 9 4

Rebid 3 ♥. With 17 high-card points plus 2 points for the six-card suit, this hand is much too strong to make a sign off bid of 4 ♥. Instead, rebid 3 ♥ to show a maximum strength hand without a singleton or void.

♠ 4
♥ A Q J 8 3
♦ K 6
♣ Q 10 8 5 2

Rebid 3 ♠. Although this hand has a side five-card suit, it isn't a particularly good one. You would need some help from responder to avoid losing two or three tricks in the club suit. Instead of showing your second suit, bid 3 ♠ to show the singleton. This is forward-going without overstating the value of your side suit.

♠ A 10 5
♥ K 10 9 7 4 2
♦ K Q 4 3
♣ —

Rebid 3 ♣. The bid of a new suit at the three level shows either a singleton or a void. If responder is interested in a slam, you may get an opportunity later in the auction to clarify that you have a void in clubs, rather than a singleton.

THE SUBSEQUENT AUCTION

After hearing opener's rebid, responder is usually in a position to decide whether to consider a slam contract. Here are sample auctions:

West	WEST	EAST	East
♠ Q 9	1♥	2NT	♠ 10 8 4
♥ K J 8 7 5	4♥	Pass	♥ A 9 6 2
♦ K 8			♦ A Q 7 3
♣ A 10 7 5			♣ K 6

After the *Jacoby 2NT* response, opener jumps to game to show a minimum hand with no singleton or void. East has nothing extra and is happy to settle for a game contract.

West	WEST	EAST	East
♠ A Q J 9 3	1♠	2NT	♠ K 10 8 4
♥ Q 6 4 2	3♦	4♠	♥ A J 3
♦ 5	Pass		♦ K Q 7 4
♣ A 5 2			♣ J 7

After the artificial forcing raise, opener rebids 3 ♦ to show shortness in that suit. This tells responder that the ♦ K and ♦ Q are *wasted* values — opposite partner's singleton there will still be a diamond loser. Responder decides to settle for a game contract, and opener has no reason to disagree.

West	WEST	EAST	East
♠ A J 10 7 4 2	1♠	2NT	♠ K Q 9 3
♥ A 9 6	3♣	4NT	♥ 2
♦ Q 8 3	5♥	6♠	♦ A K J
♣ 8	Pass		♣ 10 7 6 5 4

When opener shows a singleton club following the forcing raise, responder is encouraged to try for slam. East uses the *Blackwood* convention to ask for aces and bids the slam when opener shows two. The partnership reaches the excellent slam contract holding only 24 high-card points between the two hands. This auction demonstrates the value of identifying opener's shortness when considering a slam contract. If opener's clubs and diamonds were exchanged, even 5 ♠ would be in danger of being defeated.

West	WEST	EAST	East
♠ K 7	1♥	2NT	♠ A 6 3
♥ K 10 8 4 3	4♣	4NT	♥ A 9 7 6 2
♦ 5	5♦	5NT	♦ A 10 3
♣ A Q 9 7 3	6♥	7♥	♣ K 8
	Pass		

East starts with a forcing raise, and opener's rebid shows a good five-card club suit. This encourages responder to use the *Blackwood* convention to check for aces and kings. Responder finds that opener holds an ace and two kings and bids the excellent grand slam. The combined partnership hands contain only 27 high-card points, but the grand slam will be made if the three missing hearts are divided 2-1.

Using Jacoby 2NT over Interference

If there is an overcall or takeout double directly over the 1 ♥ or 1 ♠ opening bid, the standard agreement is that *Jacoby 2NT* is 'off' — it no longer applies. The major advantage of *Jacoby 2NT*, as a start to investigating slam possibilities, becomes less important once the opponents start competing for the contract. Slam is still possible, but less likely.

Although an overcall typically doesn't prevent responder from bidding 2NT — if the overcall is at the one or two level — the 2NT response in such situations is more useful as a natural, invitational bid. With a game-forcing hand and support for opener's major, responder can *cuebid* the opponent's suit.

It might appear that there is no reason to give up *Jacoby 2NT* after a takeout double, since the double takes up no bidding room. However, it isn't as common for responder to hold enough strength for a game-forcing raise when there is a takeout double. There are other methods to handle strong hands with support for opener's suit after a takeout double, and 2NT can be put to a more effective use (see *Truscott 2NT*). Some partnerships continue to use *Jacoby 2NT* after a double, but it isn't the recommended practice.

Here are examples after interference. You're East, and the auction starts off:

WEST	NORTH	**EAST**	SOUTH
1♠	2♦	?	

♠ K J
♥ K 8 3
♦ Q 10 4 2
♣ Q 6 4 2

Bid 2NT. After the overcall, this is a natural response, showing about 10 to 12 points, a balanced hand, and some strength in the opponent's suit. It's invitational, and opener can pass with a minimum-strength hand. With something extra, opener can bid again and the partnership will reach a game contract. This type of hand is the reason *Jacoby 2NT* doesn't apply after an overcall. Responder would find it awkward after the 2♦ overcall if 2NT were not available as a natural bid.

♠ K Q 7 5
♥ A J 3
♦ J 4
♣ Q J 6 2

Bid 3♦. The cuebid of the opponent's suit is available after an overcall to take the place of *Jacoby 2NT*. It's a forcing bid and shows a fit with opener's suit. It doesn't say anything about your holding in the opponent's suit, it merely shows a raise of partner's suit. With the values for a forcing raise, responder will make sure the partnership reaches at least the game level.

♠ A J 8 6 5 2
♥ 5 2
♦ 7
♣ 9 7 5 3

Bid 4♠. This is a preemptive raise, as if there were no overcall. With a weak hand but five-card or longer support, you want to get to the game level as quickly as possible. If partner can't make the 4♠ contract, the opponents can most likely make a contract of their own — that's the idea behind preemptive raises. Partner won't expect you to have much in the way of high cards; with a stronger hand you would have cuebid.

Sometimes, an opponent interferes after responder has made the conventional 2NT response. If the 2NT response is doubled, no room has been taken up so opener can make the conventional rebid. If there is an overcall at the three level. This is a useful set of agreements to follow.

- Pass shows shortness — a singleton or void — in the overcaller's suit.

- The bid of a new suit shows shortness in that suit.

- Double shows a minimum-strength balanced hand (5–3–3–2 shape).

- A bid of game in the agreed major suit tends to show a minimum-strength unbalanced hand with no singleton (5–4–2–2 shape, for example).

- 3NT shows a medium- or maximum-strength hand with no shortness.

Here are some examples where you hold the West hand after the auction has proceeded:

WEST	NORTH	EAST	SOUTH
1 ♥	Pass	2NT	3 ♦
?			

♠ A 9 4
♥ K Q 8 7 3
♦ 5
♣ K 10 6 2

Pass. Without the interference, you would have responded 3 ♦ to show shortness in diamonds. Now you can do the same thing by passing. With a lot of wasted strength in diamonds, partner will have the option of doubling the opponents for penalty rather than bidding higher in hearts. Otherwise, you'll reach your normal contract.

♠ 5
♥ A J 10 8 4 3
♦ J 7 5
♣ A Q 10

Bid 3 ♠. The overcall doesn't prevent you from showing your shortness in the spade suit. If partner is the one who is short in diamonds, your side may be headed toward slam. This is the same response you would have made without the interference.

♠ A J 8
♥ K J 8 4 3
♦ Q 7
♣ Q 8 4

Double. This shows a minimum-strength balanced hand. Partner has the option of passing to defend for penalty. Otherwise, partner can bid 3NT or 4♥ to play, or make some other bid with interest in reaching a slam contract.

♠ K Q
♥ A Q J 8 5
♦ 9 2
♣ 10 7 6 3

Bid 4♥. With a minimum-strength hand and no shortness in any suit, jump right to game. This is the same response you would make if South had not interfered.

♠ K 8
♥ A Q J 4 3
♦ K 10 6
♣ A 9 5

Bid 3NT. This shows extra values with no short suit. Partner can take it from there.

There are variations of the above responses, so make sure your partnership is in agreement.

NOTE: See the Appendix (pages 310–315) for a discussion of these supplemental conventions and/or treatments.

Splinter Bids

Extended Splinter Bids

Swiss

Bergen Major-Suit Raises

Weak Jump Raises

3NT as a Balanced Forcing Raise

SUMMARY

When responding to an opening bid of 1 ♥ or 1 ♠, most partner-ships use a style of limit raises where a single raise shows about 6 to 9 points and a jump raise shows about 10 to 12 points. A direct raise to the game level (e.g., 1 ♥–4 ♥) is usually played as a weak raise, showing five-card or longer support but less than the strength for a limit raise.

To accommodate forcing raises of opener's major, the *Jacoby 2NT* convention can be used. Responder bids 2NT with four-card or longer support and a game-going hand of 13 or more points. Opener rebids as follows:

Opener's Rebid after Jacoby 2NT

The first consideration is for opener to show shape regardless of the strength of the hand — either shortness in a side suit or length in a side suit:

- The bid of a new suit at the three level shows *shortness* in that suit, a singleton or a void. This information will be useful to responder in evaluating the prospect of a slam contract. Responder will know that the opponents can't take the first two tricks in the suit, even if they have both the ace and king, since opener will be able to trump the second round. If responder holds the ace in opener's short suit, the partnership will have no losers in the suit.

- A jump to the four level in a new suit shows at least five cards in that suit. Most partnerships prefer that this rebid is made when holding a good five-card suit, K–J–10–x–x or better. Otherwise, opener simply bids the short suit at the three level.

With no extreme distribution to describe, opener makes a bid that describes the strength of the hand:

- With minimum strength (12 to 14), jump to game. It's the most discouraging bid opener can make in terms of interest in a slam contract.

- With medium strength (15 to 17), rebid 3NT.

- With maximum strength (18 or more), rebid the agreed trump suit at the three level.

After opener has described the hand, responder can decide whether to pursue slam possibilities or settle for game in the major suit.

Using Jacoby 2NT after Interference

Interference before the *Jacoby 2NT* response:

- If the opponents overcall directly over the opening bid, the *Jacoby 2NT* convention no longer applies and a bid of 2NT by responder will be natural and invitational.

- If the opponents make a takeout double, the *Jacoby 2NT* convention is also off, but 2NT is used to show at least a limit raise in opener's suit (*Truscott 2NT*).

Interference after the Jacoby 2NT Response:

- If the opponents interfere with a double after the *Jacoby 2NT* response, opener can make the conventional rebid.

- If the opponents overcall at the three level or higher, the partnership needs to agree on the meaning of opener's rebids.

The following exercises assume you are using the methods outlined in the summary.

Exercise One — Major-Suit Openings

You are the dealer. What is your opening call with each of the following hands?

1) ♠ A 8
    ♥ K 9 7 6 5
    ♦ K Q 10 7 3
    ♣ 5
    _1 H_

2) ♠ A J 10 7
    ♥ Q 9 6 4
    ♦ Q 8 2
    ♣ A 3
    _1 D_

3) ♠ A Q 7 4 2
    ♥ 3
    ♦ A
    ♣ Q J 8 6 5 3
    _1 C_

4) ♠ K 9 4
    ♥ Q 10 8 5 3
    ♦ A Q 6 2
    ♣ 7
    _1 H (P)_

5) ♠ K Q 10 8 7 4
    ♥ A K 9
    ♦ K Q 5
    ♣ J
    _1 S_

6) ♠ J 10 8 6 3
    ♥ A 10
    ♦ K Q 8 5 3
    ♣ 7
    _1 S (P)_

Exercise Two — Major-Suit Raises

Partner opens the bidding 1 ♥ and the next player passes. What do you respond with the following hands?

1) ♠ J 9 7 5 3
    ♥ 5
    ♦ Q 8 6 5
    ♣ 9 6 2
    _P_

2) ♠ A 6
    ♥ 10 8 4
    ♦ J 10 7 5
    ♣ K 8 6 2
    _2 H_

3) ♠ J 8
    ♥ K 9 7 5
    ♦ Q 7 3
    ♣ A J 7 6
    _3 H_

4) ♠ 5
    ♥ K J 8 7 4
    ♦ 10 8 7 6 3
    ♣ 9 4
    _4 H / 2 H_

5) ♠ A 7 3
    ♥ Q 10 7 3
    ♦ 2
    ♣ Q 9 7 5 2
    _3 H_

6) ♠ K 9 2
    ♥ K 8 3
    ♦ 9 5
    ♣ K Q 10 6 3
    _2 C_

Exercise One — Major-Suit Openings

1) 1♥. With two five-card suits, open the higher-ranking.

2) 1♦. With no five-card or longer major suit, open the longer minor.

3) 1♣. Open the longer suit, even with a five-card major.

4) 1♥ (or Pass). With a borderline hand, opener can apply the *Rule of 20*. 11 high-card points + 5 hearts + 4 diamonds = 20.

5) 1♠. 18 high-card points plus 2 length points for the six-card suit is not enough for a strong two-bid. Open at the one level and show the extra strength on the next round.

6) 1♠ (or Pass). 10 high-card points + 5 spades + 5 diamonds = 20. That makes this hand an opening bid if the *Rule of 20* is applied.

Exercise Two — Major-Suit Raises

1) Pass. 3 high-card points plus 1 length point is not enough to respond. Don't try to improve the contract, you may get the partnership into deeper water.

2) 2♥. Raise with three-card support. The hand is worth 8 high-card points plus 1 for the doubleton spade. The quality of the heart suit is unimportant.

3) 3♥. With 11 high-card points plus 1 for the doubleton spade, make a limit raise to 3♥.

4) 4♥/2♥. The strength of the hand falls in the range of a raise to 2♥ but a preemptive raise to 4♥ is likely to be more effective. Partner may make the contract or the opponents may be kept from their best spot.

5) 3♥. Counting dummy points, this hand is worth a limit raise — 8 high-card points plus 3 points for the singleton diamond.

6) 2♣. Although this hand has the strength for a limit raise, avoid making a jump raise with three-card support when you have an alternative. Show the club suit and then raise hearts at the next opportunity.

Exercise Three — Jacoby 2NT

Partner opens the bidding 1♠, and the next player passes. What do you respond on the following hands?

1) ♠ Q 10 4
   ♥ K 9 7 6 3
   ♦ 7 4
   ♣ J 8 5 _2 S_
   ___

2) ♠ Q J 7 4
   ♥ A 5
   ♦ K 9 7 6
   ♣ 8 7 3 _3 S_

3) ♠ K Q 10 8
   ♥ Q 7
   ♦ K 9 8
   ♣ A 10 9 7 _2 N T_

4) ♠ J 10 9 7 5
   ♥ —
   ♦ Q J 7 6 4 2
   ♣ 10 7 _4 S_

5) ♠ A 7 3
   ♥ 3
   ♦ A 9 2
   ♣ K Q 10 8 6 4 _2 C_

6) ♠ A K 7 6
   ♥ K Q
   ♦ A J 10 8
   ♣ 10 7 5 _2 N T_

Exercise Four — Rebids by Opener after Jacoby 2NT

As West, what do you rebid on each of the following hands after the auction starts:

WEST	NORTH	**EAST**	SOUTH
1♥	Pass	2NT	Pass
?			

1) ♠ K 9
   ♥ A 10 7 5 3
   ♦ A 7 4
   ♣ J 6 3 _4 H_

2) ♠ 5
   ♥ J 10 8 6 3
   ♦ A K 8 6
   ♣ K J 2 _3 S_

3) ♠ Q 6
   ♥ K Q 7 6 2
   ♦ K Q 6 2
   ♣ A 8 _3 N T_

4) ♠ 9
   ♥ A J 10 8 3
   ♦ A Q J 7 2
   ♣ Q 7 _4 D_

5) ♠ A J 2
   ♥ A 10 9 7 6 3
   ♦ —
   ♣ Q J 7 6 _3 D_

6) ♠ A K 8
   ♥ K Q 9 7 5 3
   ♦ A 9
   ♣ J 7 _3 H_

Exercise Three — Jacoby 2NT

1) 2♠. Make a standard raise to the two level with three-card support and 6 high-card points.

2) 3♠. This calls for a limit raise, showing four-card support and 10 to 12 points.

3) 2NT *(Jacoby)*. With four-card support and enough strength to commit the partnership to game, use the *Jacoby 2NT* convention to get a further description of opener's hand.

4) 4♠. With a weak but distributional hand, make a preemptive raise to the four level; partner won't expect much since you would use *Jacoby 2NT* with a strong hand.

5) 2♣. Although you have enough strength to take the partnership to game in spades, avoid *Jacoby 2NT* with three-card support when you have a suitable alternative.

6) 2NT *(Jacoby)*. The 2NT response is unlimited. After partner's rebid, you will be in a better position to decide whether to venture toward a slam contract.

Exercise Four — Rebids by Opener after Jacoby 2NT

1) 4♥. With a minimum hand and no singleton or void, jump directly to game in the agreed suit.

2) 3♠. The rebid of a new suit at the three level is artificial and shows a singleton or void.

3) 3NT. Rebid 3NT to show a medium-strength hand with no single-ton or void.

4) 4♦. A jump in a new suit to the four level shows a good five-card side suit.

5) 3♦. A new suit at the three level shows a singleton or a void.

6) 3♥. A rebid of the agreed suit at the three level shows a maximum strength hand.

Exercise Five — Responder's Rebid after Jacoby 2NT

You hold the following hand as East:

> ♠ K Q 7 6
> ♥ A 8
> ♦ 9 4 3
> ♣ K J 6 2

What is your next bid in each of the following auctions?

1)

WEST	NORTH	EAST	SOUTH
1♠	Pass	2NT	Pass
4♠	Pass	? _P_	

2)

WEST	NORTH	EAST	SOUTH
1♠	Pass	2NT	Pass
3♣	Pass	? _4S_	

3)

WEST	NORTH	EAST	SOUTH
1♠	Pass	2NT	Pass
3♦	Pass	? _3H/4NT_	

4)

WEST	NORTH	EAST	SOUTH
1♠	Pass	2NT	Pass
4♣	Pass	? _4H_	

5)

WEST	NORTH	EAST	SOUTH
1♠	Pass	2NT	Pass
3NT	Pass	? _4S_	

Exercise Five — Responder's Rebid after Jacoby 2NT

1) Pass. Partner has shown a minimum-strength opening bid with no singleton or void.

2) 4♠. Partner has a singleton or void in clubs, which won't be very useful opposite your strength in the club suit. Give up on slam and settle for a game contract.

3) 3♥ or 4NT. Partner has a singleton or void in diamonds, which means that your high cards will all be useful. Make a try for slam, either by cuebidding 3♥ or using the *Blackwood* convention.

4) 4♥. Partner is showing a good five-card club suit on the side; the hands fit well together and you should make a move toward slam by cuebidding the ♥A.

5) 4♠. Partner has a medium-strength hand (17 to 18) points with no short suit; your hand is worth about 14 points, so slam is unlikely. Settle for a game contract.

Exercise Six — Handling Overcalls when Using Jacoby 2NT

As East, what do you bid on each of the following hands after the auction starts:

WEST	NORTH	EAST	SOUTH
1♠	2♥	?	

1) ♠ K Q 9 7
   ♥ A 4
   ♦ K Q 6 2
   ♣ 10 7 3 _3 H_

2) ♠ A J
   ♥ K 10 3 2
   ♦ 8 7 2
   ♣ Q J 7 3 _2NT_

3) ♠ A 10 9 7 6
   ♥ 3
   ♦ Q 9 7 6 2
   ♣ 8 4 _4 S_

Exercise Seven — Interference after Jacoby 2NT

You hold the following hand as West:

♠ K Q 10 6 4
♥ 8
♦ K 9 4 3
♣ A 6 2

What is your next bid in each of the following auctions?

1)
WEST	NORTH	EAST	SOUTH
1♠	Pass	2NT	Double
? _3 K_			

2)
WEST	NORTH	EAST	SOUTH
1♠	Pass	2NT	3♣
? _3H_			

3)
WEST	NORTH	EAST	SOUTH
1♠	Pass	2NT	3♥
? _P_			

Exercise Six — Handling Overcalls when Using Jacoby 2NT

1) 3♥. The cuebid of the opponent's suit replaces *Jacoby 2NT* when the opponents interfere. You'll make sure the partnership reaches at least a game contract in spades.

2) 2NT. A response of 2NT is natural and non-forcing after an overcall. It shows about 10 to 12 points.

3) 4♠. Make a preemptive raise to the four level. Partner won't expect too much since you could have cuebid the opponent's suit with a strong hand.

Exercise Seven — Interference after Jacoby 2NT

1) 3♥. Show the singleton heart. The opponent's double hasn't taken away any bidding room.

2) 3♥. You can still show the singleton after the opponent's overcall.

3) Pass. Passing shows shortness in the opponent's suit (if you have this agreement with partner).

Bid and Play — Deal 1

(E–Z Deal Cards: #3, Deal 1 — Dealer, North)

Suggested Bidding

WEST	NORTH	EAST	SOUTH
	1 ♥	Pass	2NT
Pass	4 ♥	Pass	Pass
Pass			

With four-card support for partner's major suit and 14 points — 13 high-card points plus 1 dummy point for the doubleton club — South should use the *Jacoby 2NT* convention after North opens the bidding 1 ♥. North has a minimum-strength hand and no singleton or void. To show this, North jumps to 4 ♥, which ends the auction since South has nothing further to add.

Dlr: North   ♠ K 7
Vul: None   ♥ A Q 7 6 3
              ♦ 10 9 5
              ♣ K 8 3

♠ Q 8 3 2   ♠ J 10 9 4
♥ J 10 8   ♥ K
♦ A 8 7   ♦ J 4 2
♣ Q 10 4   ♣ J 9 7 5 2

              ♠ A 6 5
              ♥ 9 5 4 2
              ♦ K Q 6 3
              ♣ A 6

Suggested Opening Lead

East is on lead and should select the ♠ J, top of a sequence.

Suggested Play

North can trump the club loser in dummy but still has two potential losers in the diamond suit. With no losers in the spade suit, North can make the contract for certain by losing no more than one trick in the trump suit. The best play to accomplish this is to draw a round of trump with the ♥ A, and if the ♥ K doesn't appear, cross to dummy to lead a heart toward the ♥ Q. This is successful on the actual layout, since East's ♥ K falls under the ♥ A. North still has to lose a trick to West's ♥ J, but the contract is safe even if two diamond tricks are lost. Playing the suit in this manner would also restrict the heart losers to one if the missing trumps are divided 2–2, or if they divide 3–1 and West holds the ♥ K. Only if the missing trump divide 4–0 or East has three trumps including the ♥K, would declarer lose more than one trick — and there is nothing that can be done anyway, if that is the situation. Playing the ♥A first is called a *safety play.*

North might be tempted, however, to draw trumps by taking an immediate finesse of the ♥Q. This would avoid losing any heart tricks if the suit divides 2–2 and West holds the ♥K. On this hand, that approach results in two heart losers and North will now have to restrict the diamond losers to one to make the contract.

Suggested Defense

If declarer takes an immediate heart finesse, the defenders have a chance of defeating the contract. The defenders will get two heart tricks and will need to take two diamond tricks. After finding the bad news in the heart suit, North will probably lead a low diamond to dummy's ♦Q or ♦K, hoping that East holds the ♦A. If West wins this trick with the ♦A, declarer will likely fall back on the last real chance, leading the ♦10 and finessing against East's ♦J. On the actual deal, this finesse is successful and declarer makes the contract.

West can give declarer a much tougher problem, however, by not taking the ♦A on the first round. North can't have a singleton diamond since the 4♥ response to Jacoby 2NT showed no singleton or void. West can probably derive this information if the partnership uses count signals in this situation — East's ♦2 on the first round would show an odd number of diamonds. Nothing is lost by ducking the first round of the suit. If West does this without a change in tempo, declarer has a challenge. When declarer crosses to the North hand to lead the ♦10 and East plays the ♦4, declarer will have to guess which opponent really has the ♦A. If North thinks East holds the ♦A, North will play the remaining high honor from dummy and West wins this trick with the ♦A. Now East's ♦J becomes the setting trick.

It takes some minor miscalculations from North and excellent defense by East–West to defeat the contract, but it could happen.

Bid and Play — Deal 2
(E–Z Deal Cards: #3, Deal 2 — Dealer, East)

Suggested Bidding

WEST	NORTH	EAST	SOUTH
		1♠	Pass
2NT	Pass	3♦	Pass
4♠	Pass	Pass	Pass

After East's opening bid of 1♠, West uses the *Jacoby 2NT* as a game-forcing raise. East's 3♦ rebid shows a singleton diamond. This tells West that the ♦K Q J are probably wasted high cards for the purposes of slam, since East–West will still have to lose a trick in that suit. West, therefore, gives up on trying for slam and jumps to game. East has nothing further to contribute.

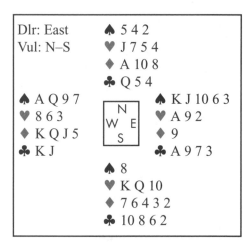

Dlr: East
Vul: N–S

```
              ♠ 5 4 2
              ♥ J 7 5 4
              ♦ A 10 8
              ♣ Q 5 4
♠ A Q 9 7              ♠ K J 10 6 3
♥ 8 6 3        N       ♥ A 9 2
♦ K Q J 5    W   E     ♦ 9
♣ K J          S       ♣ A 9 7 3
              ♠ 8
              ♥ K Q 10
              ♦ 7 6 4 3 2
              ♣ 10 8 6 2
```

Suggested Opening Lead

South is on lead and should lead the ♥K, top of a broken sequence.

Suggested Play

The East hand has two heart losers, one diamond loser, and two club losers. Declarer should plan to draw trumps and then eliminate the two club losers by trumping them, or by promoting diamond winners in the dummy on which to discard two clubs. Since three rounds of trumps must be played to draw all the opponents' spades, declarer should promote diamond winners in dummy before ruffing a club in the dummy. If declarer ruffs a club after playing three rounds of trump, it will be too late to establish the diamonds — the defenders can take two heart tricks and a club trick after winning the ♦A.

At duplicate bridge, East might consider finessing the ♣J immediately, hoping South holds the ♣Q. If successful, this would result in an overtrick, since declarer could then play the ♣K, come back to the East hand with a trump, and play the ♣A, discarding a heart from dummy. Now, when the ♦A is driven out, the defenders can take only one heart winner. On the actual lie of the cards, however, finessing the club is spectacularly unsuccessful, since the finesse loses and the defenders are in a position to take two heart tricks and the ♦A to defeat the contract.

As can be seen, East–West don't want to be any higher than 4♠ with these two hands.

Suggested Defense

After leading the ♥K, there isn't much the defenders can do if declarer plays safely for the contract. When North wins a trick with the ♦A, they can take two heart tricks to stop declarer from making an overtrick. Only if declarer takes a club finesse do the defenders have a chance, since they can take two heart tricks and the ♦A after North wins a trick with the ♣Q.

The most important thing for the defense is to get off to the best lead, the ♥K. If anything else is led, declarer can drive out the ♦A and discard both heart losers on dummy's extra diamond winners. Declarer can then make 12 tricks by ruffing the two club losers in the dummy. South should start with the ♥K, since this will at least develop the ♥Q into a trick and may result in more tricks if North holds either the ♥A or the ♥J. Holding the ♥J, North should play the ♥7 — an encouraging card — since South must also hold the ♥Q.

Bid and Play — Deal 3

      (E–Z Deal Cards: #3, Deal 3 — Dealer, South)

Suggested Bidding

WEST	NORTH	EAST	SOUTH
			1 ♠
Pass	2NT	Pass	3 ♣
Pass	3 ♦	Pass	3 ♥
Pass	4NT	Pass	5 ♥
Pass	6 ♠	Pass	Pass
Pass			

    After North makes a forcing raise of spades (by using the *Jacoby 2NT* response), South shows a singleton club. This encourages North to look for slam, since the partnership won't have any losers in the club suit. North's 3 ♦ bid is a cuebid showing the ♦ A. South shows the ♥ A in a similar manner. That's enough encouragement for North to use the *Blackwood* convention and bid a slam after finding that South holds two aces.

```
Dlr: South      ♠ K Q 7 5
Vul: E–W        ♥ Q 4
                ♦ A J 7
                ♣ A J 6 5
♠ 4                        ♠ 3 2
♥ J 10 9 8 6      N        ♥ K 7 3 2
♦ Q 4 3        W     E     ♦ 8 6 2
♣ K 7 4 2         S        ♣ Q 10 9 8
                ♠ A J 10 9 8 6
                ♥ A 5
                ♦ K 10 9 5
                ♣ 3
```

Suggested Opening Lead

    West is on lead and should start with the ♥ J, top of a sequence.

Suggested Play

    South has a heart loser and a diamond loser. With the ♥ J lead, there is a remote chance that West has led the top of an interior sequence such as ♥ K J 10 9 8, declarer can play the ♥ Q, hoping to win the trick. Unfortunately, East produces the ♥ K, and declarer has to win with the ♥ A — leaving a loser in the heart suit.

It would appear that South must now guess which defender has the ♦ Q. If it's West, declarer can take the ♦ K and finesse the ♦ J; if it's East, declarer can take the ♦ A and lead the ♦ J to trap the ♦ Q. If declarer guesses wrong, the defenders will win a trick with the ♦ Q and take a heart trick. If declarer guesses right, the contract will probably be made with an overtrick, since dummy's heart may be discarded on the fourth round of diamonds.

By careful play, however, declarer can let the opponents do the work and avoid guessing which defender has the ♦ Q. To bring this about requires some foresight. After winning the first trick with the ♥ A, declarer should immediately lead a club to dummy's ♣ A and trump a club. This is an unusual play, since it's not usually a good idea for declarer to spend time trumping dummy's losers. However, the reason for this will become apparent later. Next, declarer plays a trump to dummy's ♠ Q — drawing one round of trumps — and leads another club and trumps it. Now declarer plays a trump to dummy's ♠ K — drawing the opponents' remaining trump — and leads dummy's last club and trumps it. Finally, declarer gives up the heart trick to the opponents. The reason for all of this preparation becomes a little clearer when you look at the cards remaining in the North and South hands after declarer gives up the heart trick:

NORTH

♠ 7 5

♥ —

♦ A J 7

♣ —

SOUTH

♠ A

♥ —

♦ K 10 9 5

♣ —

The hearts and clubs have been eliminated from the North–South hands, and all the spades have been eliminated from the defenders' hands. It doesn't matter which defender is on lead. Whatever card is led, South can take the rest of the tricks. If the defender that wins the heart trick leads a heart or a club, South can discard — sluff — the ♦ 7 from dummy and trump — ruff — the trick with the ♠ A. After taking the ♦ A and ♦ K, declarer has the rest of the tricks. If, instead, either defender leads a diamond, declarer plays a low diamond and waits to see if the ♦ Q appears. Whether it appears or not, declarer takes three diamond tricks and makes the contract.

This type of play is often called an endplay, since the defenders are usually thrown into the lead at the end of play so that whatever they lead will help declarer. When there is a trump suit involved, the defenders are put in the position of leading a suit they don't want to lead — the diamonds in the above hand

— or giving declarer a sluff and a ruff — which allows declarer to discard a loser from one hand while trumping in the other. To prepare for an endplay, declarer often has to eliminate, or strip, one or more suits — all the North–South clubs and the East–West spades in the above hand — and then throw in one of the defenders — with the heart suit in the above hand. So this type of play is also referred to as a *strip and endplay* — a phrase popularized by Ely Culbertson.

Suggested Defense

While the defenders can't defeat the contract if declarer finds the correct play — or guesses well — they should give it their best effort. West must lead a heart to give declarer a problem. If West doesn't lead a heart, it won't matter if declarer misguesses the location of the ♦Q, since one of dummy's hearts can be discarded on the fourth round of diamonds, and declarer won't have to lose a heart trick.

If the defenders do establish their heart trick right away and declarer doesn't find the endplay, then the defenders must be careful not to give declarer any help in guessing the location of the ♦Q. Both defenders should hold on to all of their diamonds as long as possible. If, for example, East were to discard one or two diamonds, declarer could draw the inference that West holds the ♦Q. In fact, it would be a tricky play for West to discard a diamond — perhaps lulling declarer into thinking that East holds the ♦Q.

Bid and Play — Deal 4

(E–Z Deal Cards: #3, Deal 4 — Dealer, West)

Suggested Bidding

WEST	NORTH	EAST	SOUTH
1 ♥	Double	2NT	Pass
3 ♥	Pass	Pass	Pass

After West's opening bid, North has a perfect hand for a takeout double. With 10 high-card points, East could redouble, but that will give North-South an opportunity to find their best spot. Instead, with good support for West's suit and the values for a limit raise, East jumps to 2NT. After the takeout double, this isn't the *Jacoby 2NT* convention. It conventionally shows a hand that would have made a limit raise of 3 ♥ if there were no double. An immediate jump to 3 ♥ after the takeout double would be weak and preemptive.

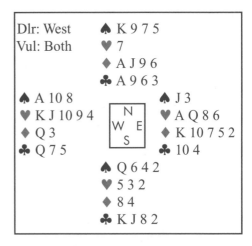

Dlr: West
Vul: Both

♠ K 9 7 5
♥ 7
♦ A J 9 6
♣ A 9 6 3

♠ A 10 8
♥ K J 10 9 4
♦ Q 3
♣ Q 7 5

♠ J 3
♥ A Q 8 6
♦ K 10 7 5 2
♣ 10 4

♠ Q 6 4 2
♥ 5 3 2
♦ 8 4
♣ K J 8 2

The 2NT response takes the auction a little too high for South to come in. With a minimum-strength hand, West rebids 3 ♥, putting the partnership in partscore in the agreed trump suit and rejecting East's invitational raise. North has nothing extra to show, and neither does East. South might consider a balancing bid of 3 ♠, but it's quite risky, especially since North–South are vulnerable.

Suggested Opening Lead

North doesn't have a good lead and will probably decide on the ♠ 5, fourth highest, hoping partner has either the ♠ A or ♠ Q. Another reasonable choice would be the lead of the singleton trump, hoping that it won't give up a trick and may prevent declarer from ruffing too many losers in the dummy.

Suggested Play

In a contract of 3 ♥, West has two spade losers, a diamond loser, and three club losers. If North leads a spade, one of West's spade losers disappears. West plays second hand low from dummy and captures South's ♠Q with the ♠A. West can later drive out North's ♠K with the ♠J, promoting the ♠10 into a winner. West can draw trumps in three rounds, and eventually trump a club loser in the dummy.

If North leads the ♦A, that establishes both the ♦Q and ♦K as winners. After drawing trumps, West can plan to discard a spade loser on the ♦K and ruff the third club loser in dummy. Even if North starts by leading a club or a trump, West should have little difficulty restricting the losers to four tricks: one spade, one diamond, and two clubs. West can plan to ruff both a spade loser and a club loser in the dummy, or West can go about establishing dummy's diamond suit as extra winners. If the defenders don't lead spades early enough, West might make an overtrick by finessing the ♦10 after driving out the ♦A, and then trumping a diamond to establish the suit.

The play is interesting if North–South buy the contract with spades as trump. They have to lose at least two spade tricks, one heart trick, and one diamond trick but could make nine tricks by avoiding the loss of a club trick. That's difficult to do, since West holds the ♣Q and most declarers would try the finesse of the ♣J, hoping East holds the ♣Q. If declarer is sure that West holds the ♣Q — West did open the bidding — there is a play that works. The ♣J can be led from the South hand, and it will win the trick unless West covers with the ♣Q. When West does cover with the ♣Q, the ♣A is won in the North hand and another club is led to trap East's ♣10. This is called a *backward finesse*. It's unlikely that most declarers would find this play, so a contract of 3 ♠ by North-South will probably be defeated one trick.

Suggested Defense

There is little that can be done to stop East-West from taking nine tricks in a heart contract. The defenders have to be careful, however, not to let East–West take ten tricks. If they take the ♣A and ♣K too quickly, they will establish declarer's ♣Q as a winner on which one of dummy's spades can be discarded. Declarer will avoid the loss of a spade trick. Also, if declarer goes about establishing the diamond suit, the defenders have to establish their spade winner before declarer can discard both spade losers on dummy's diamonds.

CHAPTER 4

Major-Suit Openings and Responses — Part II

MAJOR-SUIT OPENINGS AND RESPONSES — PART II

The previous chapter discussed major-suit opening bids and how responder shows support. This chapter covers additional topics related to major-suit opening bids and responses.

Third and Fourth Position Openings

It's common to be flexible when you are in third or fourth position and no one has opened the bidding. Your partner has passed originally, so you can occasionally open the bidding with fewer than 13 points or with a four-card major.

The critical difference between first and second positions and third and fourth positions is that a *new suit response by a passed hand is not forcing*. If responder hasn't had a chance to bid, then a new suit response is virtually unlimited in strength and opener cannot pass, even with a minimum hand. Responder could easily have 13 or more points and a game would be missed. If responder passed originally, then responder's hand is limited to at most 11 or 12 points. Unless opener has more than 13 points, there's little likelihood of game.

This gives you leeway to open *light* — with fewer than 13 points — in third or fourth position. There isn't much danger that the partnership will get too high, because you won't have to keep bidding once you've found a reasonable spot. You are generally looking to make a partscore when partner is a *passed hand* and you have fewer than 13 points. If either partner holds 11 or 12 points and doesn't open the bidding, the partnership could be missing a good partscore with a combined total of 22 to 24 points.

Opening Light in Third Position

Apart from the possibility of making a partscore contract, there are tactical reasons for opening light in third position. Even if you can't win the contract, your bidding may cause the opponents to misjudge and bid too much or too little. If your side defends, your opening bid could get the partnership off to the best lead. Here are some examples. You are East after the auction has started:

WEST	NORTH	**EAST**	SOUTH
Pass	Pass	?	

♠ K J 10 7 5
♥ J 3
♦ A 9 7
♣ Q 5 3

Open 1 ♠. If partner has 10 or 11 points, your side can expect to make a partscore. If partner raises spades or bids 1NT, you're happy to pass. If partner responds in a new suit, you can pass and hope to get a plus score. A new suit by a *passed hand* is not forcing. If partner doesn't have a good hand, your bid could keep the opponents out of their best contract or get partner off to the winning lead.

♠ Q J 5
♥ A K Q 10
♦ 8 3 2
♣ 9 7 2

Open 1 ♥, not 1 ♣. Although you usually need a five-card suit to open 1 ♥ or 1 ♠, you can use your judgment. If you open this hand in third position, it makes sense to treat the hearts as a five-card suit. You plan to pass whatever partner bids. If the opponents buy the contract, you'd like partner to lead a heart rather than a club.

♠ K 8 2
♥ Q J 7 5 3
♦ K 10 5
♣ J 8

This hand doesn't qualify for an opening bid, but many players would risk opening 1 ♥ in third position. If your partnership style is to occasionally open a hand with as few as 9 or 10 points, you might want to use the *Drury* convention.

♠ A J
♥ A K 10 8 7 3
♦ K Q 8 6
♣ 4

Open 1 ♥. It's important for both partners to remember that an opening bid of 1 ♥ or 1 ♠ in third position usually shows a full opening bid, and the partnership will continue bidding as usual.

Opening Light in Fourth Position

You can use the same tactics in fourth position as in third position —
occasionally opening light or with a four-card major suit — but there is
one caution. You have the option of passing and moving on to the next
deal. Avoid opening the bidding with a substandard hand only to let the
opponents win the auction or push your side too high. The key is the
spade suit. If you open the bidding and the opponents compete in spades,
they can outbid you at each level — you'll have to let them buy the
contract or go one level higher to make your suit trump.

For this reason, some players use the guideline of the *Rule of 15*. Add
the high-card points to the number of spades in the hand. If the total is 15
or more, open the bidding; otherwise, pass. Here are examples after the
auction has gone:

WEST	NORTH	EAST	**SOUTH**
Pass	Pass	Pass	?

♠ 10 2
♥ K J 7 5 3
♦ K Q 8 5
♣ Q 8

Pass. With 11 high-card points, pass and get on with
the next deal. If you open 1 ♥, the opponents could
come to life with an overcall or takeout double. You
could lose points, rather than getting a plus score.
The *Rule of 15* suggests passing — your 11 high-
card points plus two spades come to a total of 13.

♠ A J 10 7 5
♥ K 8 2
♦ 10 5
♣ K 9 3

Open 1 ♠. Most players would take a chance and open
1 ♠, hoping for a small plus score. You plan to pass
partner's response, since partner also has fewer than 13
points. Even if partner responds with a natural 2 ♦, pass
and hope to take eight tricks. Partner needs about 10 or
11 points to bid a new suit at the two level. This hand qualifies under the
Rule of 15 — 11 points plus five spades totals 16, more than enough.

♠ 2
♥ Q 3
♦ K Q J 9 5
♣ K J 8 4 2

Pass. Without either major suit, it could be best to pass
with a borderline hand. Even though you would open
the bidding in any other position, if you open 1 ♦ you
might be giving the opponents a chance to compete

in a major suit. If it turns out that partner has some length in the major suits, your hands won't fit well together. The *Rule of 15* leads to the same conclusion.

THE *DRURY* CONVENTION

It's a common tactic to occasionally open the bidding with a weaker hand in third or fourth position. When responder has 10 to 12 points and a fit with opener's suit, this can present a challenge. A new suit response is no longer forcing — so it can't be used as a *temporizing* bid before showing support — and a jump response may get the partnership too high if opener doesn't have full values. To resolve this situation, some partnerships use a convention developed by Douglas Drury, a well-known American bridge teacher and player. He used to play with Eric Murray — a Canadian barrister who often opened the bidding with fewer than 13 points in third and fourth positions.

Standard *Drury*

Here is the standard way of using the *Drury* convention:

- When partner opens the bidding 1♥ or 1♠ in third or fourth position, a response of 2♣ is artificial (conventional) and asks about the strength of the opening bid.

- With a *light* opening bid of fewer than 13 points, opener rebids 2♦, a conventional bid.

- With a normal opening bid of 13 or more points, opener rebids something other than 2♦.

West						East
♠ A 7 4	WEST	NORTH	EAST	SOUTH		♠ 10 6 2
♥ 10 8 6 3	Pass	Pass	1♥	Pass		♥ K J 9 5 2
♦ K Q J	2♣	Pass	2♦	Pass		♦ 8 3
♣ J 8 2	2♥	Pass	Pass	Pass		♣ A Q 5

After two passes, East opens in third position with only 10 high-card points plus 1 for the five-card suit. Since West has passed already, East is hoping to reach a partscore contract or keep North–South from finding their best contract. With 11 high-card points and four-card support for East's major, West's standard response would be a limit raise to 3 ♥, inviting partner to game. Using *Drury*, West starts with 2 ♣, asking about the strength of East's opening bid. East's 2 ♦ response denies the values for a full opening bid, so West settles for partscore in the major suit. After East's light opening bid with only 21 high-card points between the two hands, the partnership stops safely in a contract of 2 ♥.

A disadvantage of using *Drury* is that the partnership gives up the natural 2 ♣ response to a major-suit opening bid in third or fourth position, but there is adequate compensation. Here are additional points:

- Responder should have at least three-card support for opener's suit and 10 or more support points to use *Drury*. Otherwise, responder should make a natural response (other than 2 ♣).

- If responder doesn't use *Drury*, the inference is that responder doesn't have both a fit with opener's suit and a hand worth 10 or more points.

- If there is a takeout double or overcall after the third- or fourth-position opening bid, most partnerships agree that 2 ♣ is still *Drury* if that bid is available. In the above example, if South doubled or overcalled 1 ♠, West's 2 ♣ response would still be *Drury*.

- If the overcall is 2 ♣, then double is the *Drury* convention. In the above example, if South overcalled 2 ♣ after East's 1 ♥ opening bid, West would double to ask about the strength of East's opening.

- If responder wants to bid clubs — holding about 11 or 12 points and a five-card or longer club suit — most partnerships play that a jump response to 3 ♣ shows this hand. This is an invitational response and opener can pass, return to the major suit with a minimum hand, or accept the invitation with better than a minimum.

Here are more *Drury* auctions:

West		East
♠ A 7 4		♠ 10 6
♥ 10 8 6 3		♥ A K J 9 5 2
♦ K Q J		♦ 8 3
♣ J 8 2		♣ A Q 5

WEST	NORTH	EAST	SOUTH
Pass	Pass	1 ♥	Pass
2 ♣	Pass	2 ♥	Pass
3 ♥	Pass	4 ♥	Pass
Pass	Pass		

East has a full opening bid and shows it by rebidding hearts when West uses the *Drury* convention. The partnership then reaches its game contract. After hearing the 2 ♣ response, East could simplify the auction by jumping directly to 4 ♥. Since West promises at least three-card support and 10 or more points by using *Drury*, East knows the partnership belongs in game but has no interest in slam since partner passed originally.

West		East
♠ A 7		♠ 10 6 2
♥ 6 3		♥ K J 9 5 2
♦ K J 10 7 4 2		♦ 8 3
♣ J 8 2		♣ A Q 5

WEST	NORTH	EAST	SOUTH
Pass	Pass	1 ♥	Pass
2 ♦	Pass	Pass	Pass

After opening light in third position, East feels free to pass West's 2 ♦ response. East hopes the partnership can make a partscore, and any further bid is likely to get the partnership too high. Since West passed originally, the 2 ♦ response is not forcing — the partnership can't have enough combined strength for a game contract. East also knows that the partnership doesn't belong in a heart contract. With three-card support for hearts and enough strength to bid a new suit at the two level, West would have used the *Drury* convention.

West		East
♠ A 7 4		♠ 10 6 2
♥ A 8 3		♥ K J 9 5 2
♦ K 9 7 5 2		♦ 8 3
♣ 8 2		♣ A Q 5

WEST	NORTH	EAST	SOUTH
Pass	Pass	1 ♥	2 ♣
Double	Pass	2 ♦	Pass
2 ♥	Pass	Pass	Pass

After South's overcall of 2♣, a double by West acts as *Drury*. East bids 2♦ showing a weak opening bid, and West is content to play in partscore. Without *Drury*, West would be badly placed after the 2♣ overcall. A response of 2♦ might be passed, leaving the partnership in the wrong suit. A bid of 2♥ would be an underbid and the partnership might miss a game if East held a sound opening bid. An immediate bid of 3♥ might get the partnership overboard if East has opened light.

West					East
♠ A 8 3	WEST	NORTH	EAST	SOUTH	♠ K J
♥ 7 3	Pass	Pass	1♥	Pass	♥ A Q 9 5 2
♦ J 4	3♣	Pass	3NT	Pass	♦ A 10 7 2
♣ K Q 10 8 5 2	Pass	Pass			♣ J 6

After East's opening bid in third position, West can't respond 2♣ since that would be *Drury*. Instead, West jumps to 3♣ to show an invitational-strength hand of 11 or 12 points with a good club suit. With more than a minimum opening bid, East accepts the invitation by bidding game. East knows the partnership does not belong in hearts, since West would have used *Drury* with three-card or longer support for hearts.

Reverse Drury

Many partnerships prefer to reverse the manner in which opener shows a light opening bid when the partnership uses *Drury*. After the 2♣ response, opener rebids the major suit with a substandard opening bid. Any other rebid shows a full opening bid. This is called *reverse Drury*. It is the recommended style since the partnership arrives more quickly in the best partscore when opener's bid is light, leaving less opportunity for the opponents to enter the auction.

West					East
♠ K 6 2	WEST	NORTH	EAST	SOUTH	♠ A Q 8 7 4
♥ A 8 6 3				Pass	♥ Q 7 2
♦ K J 7 2	Pass	Pass	1♠	Pass	♦ 9 4 3
♣ 8 3	2♣	Pass	2♠	Pass	♣ K 4
	Pass	Pass			

With 11 high-card points, West doesn't have enough to open the bidding in second position. The auction comes around to East in fourth position. East has 11 high-card points plus 1 for the five-card suit. This is below the standard partnership requirements of 13 points for an opening bid and East must decide whether to pass the hand out or try for a partscore contract. East, applying the *Rule of 15*, makes a light opening bid. With support for spades, 11 high-card points, and a doubleton club, West's standard approach would be to initiate an invitational sequence, getting the partnership to at least the three level. Since partner opened in fourth position, West first uses *Drury* to ask whether East has a full opening bid. Using the *reverse Drury* style of responses, East's 2 ♠ rebid denies a full opening bid. West then settles for partscore at the two level and the partnership avoids getting too high.

West	WEST	NORTH	EAST	SOUTH	East
♠ K 6 2				Pass	♠ A Q 8 7 4
♥ A 8 6 3	Pass	Pass	1 ♠	Pass	♥ K 2
♦ K J 7 2	2 ♣	Pass	2 ♦	Pass	♦ Q 9 4 3
♣ 8 3	3 ♦	Pass	4 ♠	Pass	♣ K 4
	Pass	Pass			

East shows a full opening bid by doing something other than rebidding the original suit. Having already implied support for spades by using *Drury*, West now shows support for East's second suit. This information is enough to persuade East that game should be a reasonable proposition.

RESPONSES TO 1 ♥ OR 1 ♠ THAT DO NOT PROMISE SUPPORT

With support for partner's major suit, responder's priority is to let opener know that there is a fit. We have previously discussed the various ways this can be handled. Now we'll consider situations where responder does not have support for opener's suit. If responder isn't raising opener's major suit, there are a number of options.

1NT Response

Using standard methods, a response of 1NT is used as an invitational bid showing 6 to 9 or 10 points. It doesn't promise a balanced hand, and opener can pass the response with a minimum balanced hand. A forcing 1NT response is part of the *Two-Over-One system* and is described in the fifth book in the ACBL Bridge Series, *More Commonly Used Conventions*. Here are examples of responding as South:

WEST	NORTH	EAST	**SOUTH**
	1♥	Pass	?

♠ Q J 5
♥ 6 3
♦ A J 7 3
♣ J 9 6 5

Respond 1NT. This is a perfect hand for this response. Responder can't support opener's major, doesn't have a suit that can be bid at the one level, and isn't strong enough to bid a new suit at the two level. If opener has a minimum-strength balanced hand, 1NT should be the best contract.

♠ J 7 6
♥ 5
♦ Q 8 6 4
♣ J 8 6 5 3

Pass. 1♥ might not be a great contract — although it could be a good spot — but at this point you could get the partnership into more trouble by bidding. If you respond 1NT, opener could jump to 3♥ or raise to 3NT, expecting you to have some values. There's nothing to prevent you from occasionally deviating from your agreed range of 6 to 9 or 10 points — you're allowed to exercise your judgment — but partner could start to distrust your responses, which isn't good for the partnership.

♠ 10 3
♥ 9
♦ K J 8 6 5 3
♣ Q 9 6 4

Respond 1NT. This doesn't promise a balanced hand. It says you have 6 to 9 or 10 points, can't support partner's major, can't bid a new suit at the one level, and don't have the strength required to bid a new suit at the two level. If opener passes your response, 1NT may not be the best contract but it's all you can do. If there's more bidding, you might get a chance to show the diamond suit, having already denied more than 10 points.

♠ J 10 8 3
♥ K 4
♦ 9 8 6 4
♣ A 7 3

Respond 1♠. Although responder can't support opener's suit and has a balanced hand, the priority still is to look for a major-suit fit. Opener could have four spades, as well as five hearts, and a response of 1NT would likely result in the partnership missing its major-suit fit. Some partnerships prefer to bypass a weak four-card spade suit in this situation, but it isn't standard practice.

2NT Response

A response of 2NT can be used as a natural bid, describing a balanced hand with the strength agreed upon by the partnership — either 11 or 12 points (invitational) or 13 to 15 (forcing). This is discussed in the next chapter on responses to minor-suit opening bids. 2NT as a natural response is more commonly used only after minor-suit opening bids. As discussed earlier, many partnerships prefer to assign a conventional meaning to the response of 2NT after a major-suit opening bid, such as *Jacoby 2NT*.

3NT Response

A response of 3NT is commonly used to show a hand similar to an opening 1NT bid — a balanced hand of 15 to 17 points — but with only two cards in partner's major suit. For example, after an opening bid of 1♠, responder would jump to 3NT with this hand:

♠ J 8
♥ A Q 10
♦ K J 8 5
♣ K Q 6 2

This response isn't forcing. Opener now has a good picture of responder's hand and can judge whether to bid any further.

A New Suit Response at the One Level

A new-suit response is forcing, unless responder has already passed — limiting responder's hand to fewer than 13 points. There's no upper limit to responder's strength, although with certain hand types responder might choose to make a *jump shift*.

At the one level, a new suit shows at least four cards in the suit and a hand worth 6 or more points. After responding at the one level, responder doesn't have to bid again unless opener makes a forcing rebid (a *reverse* or a *jump shift*).

WEST	NORTH	**EAST**	SOUTH
1♦	Pass	?	

♠ A Q J 8 5
♥ K J 9 3
♦ 6 2
♣ A 5

Respond 1♠. The 1♠ response shows 6 or more points and is forcing. You want to leave the maximum amount of room to find the best fit, you can decide on the appropriate level.

♠ Q J 7 4
♥ 10 8 4 2
♦ 9 5
♣ K 6 2

Respond 1♥. This is about the minimum you can hold for a one-level response. Respond *up-the-line* with a choice of four-card suits. You don't plan to take a second bid with this hand unless opener makes a forcing rebid.

♠ K 9 4 3
♥ 10 2
♦ Q 8
♣ Q 10 8 7 5

Respond 1♠. You don't have enough to bid a new suit at the two level. You can show the spade suit at the one level, however, without promising more than 6 points.

A New Suit Response at the Two Level

The bid of a new suit at the two level shows a hand worth 11 or more points — some partnerships agree on as few as 10 points, while other styles might require 13 or more (see *Two-Over-One* in *More Commonly Used Conventions*). The bid of a new suit at the two level usually shows a four-card or longer suit, although some awkward hand types could require a response on a three-card suit. There's one important exception: a response of 2♥ to an opening bid of 1♠ should only be made with a five-card or longer suit. After responding at the two level, responder must make at least one more bid unless the partnership has already reached the game level.

WEST	NORTH	**EAST**	SOUTH
1 ♠	Pass	?	

♠ 8 4
♥ K 8
♦ A Q 10 8 4 3
♣ K 9 4

Respond 2 ♦. The best contract for the partnership is not yet apparent, so responder starts by bidding a new suit. Opener must bid again. After hearing opener's rebid, responder will have a better idea of where the partnership is headed.

♠ J 3
♥ K J 10 7 3
♦ J 8 7
♣ A 8 5

Respond 2 ♥. This is about the least you should have for a response of 2 ♥. You have 10 high-card points plus 1 point for the five-card suit. After partner's rebid, you have to make another bid, which could prove awkward. If partner rebids 2 ♠, for example, you could rebid 3 ♠, but if partner rebids 2NT, you're almost cornered into raising to 3NT which could get the partnership too high. Some partnerships don't require responder to make a second bid after bidding a new suit at the two level if opener simply rebids the original suit or rebids 2NT. That agreement isn't standard practice. Some players prefer to respond 1NT with a borderline hand — it's a matter of judgment.

♠ 8 6
♥ K J 4
♦ A Q J 8
♣ K 10 6 3

Respond 2 ♣. If the partnership isn't using *Jacoby 2NT*, you can respond with a natural, forcing 2NT, or you have to bid a new suit. When responding with four-card suits, bid them *up the line*.

Jump Shift by Responder

A jump response in a new suit — a *jump shift* — shows a strong hand with interest in reaching a slam contract. It generally shows a hand of 17 or more points. Responder isn't compelled to jump shift with a strong hand. A jump shift is usually reserved for one of the following hand types:

- A strong one-suiter.
- A hand with good support for opener's suit but unsuitable for an immediate forcing raise.
- A strong, semi-balanced hand.

Consider each of the following hands for South after the auction has started:

WEST	NORTH	EAST	SOUTH
	1♥	Pass	?

♠ A K Q J 8 7 5
♥ 8
♦ A K 9
♣ 9 3

Respond 2♠. With 17 high-card points and a strong one-suiter, this is a perfect hand for a jump shift. You want to settle on spades as the trump suit by rebidding them at your next opportunity. Then you can investigate slam possibilities.

♠ 3 2
♥ K Q 3
♦ A K J 8 7
♣ A 9 6

Respond 3♦. You plan to support hearts at your next turn, showing the fit and your interest in a possible slam contract..

♠ A Q 7
♥ 9 6
♦ A Q 10
♣ K Q J 10 5

Respond 3♣. A direct jump to 3NT would show 16 or 17 points. You're too strong for that. Instead, start with a jump shift, intending to rebid 3NT at your next opportunity to show a very strong balanced hand.

♠ K Q 8 7 5
♥ A 3
♦ A K Q 7 4
♣ J

Respond 1♠. Although you have a very strong hand — and a slam contract is almost a certainty — this isn't the time to jump shift. First you need to explore for a suitable trump suit. Spades, hearts, and diamonds are all possibilities, and the partnership might also belong in notrump. A jump to 2♠ would take away the room you need to investigate all of the possibilities. Start with 1♠, a forcing response. After you hear partner's rebid, you'll have more information and can make your next move.

2NT AFTER A TAKEOUT DOUBLE (TRUSCOTT/JORDAN/DORMER)

When opener's 1 ♥ or 1 ♠ bid is doubled for takeout, responder could ignore the double and respond as if there had been no interference. Many partnerships, however, modify the meaning of some of responder's bids after a takeout double.

Preemptive Raises

When an opponent makes a takeout double of the opening bid of 1 ♥ or 1 ♠, the *redouble* or *Jordan 2NT* can be used to show a hand of 10 or more points. The mechanics of the redouble are discussed in more detail in *More Commonly Used Conventions*. One consequence is that responses at the two level or higher no longer have to promise 10 or more points — since you can start with a redouble or respond 2NT holding that much strength. This allows the partnership to use a jump raise to the three level in opener's suit to show a hand with good trump support but with little or limited defensive values. This type of raise is called a *preemptive raise,* rather than a limit (or forcing) raise. For example, consider the following hand after the auction starts:

WEST	NORTH	**EAST**	SOUTH
1 ♥	Double	?	

♠ 7 5
♥ K J 8 5
♦ J 9 7 6 5
♣ 9 3

Jump to 3 ♥. With four-card support for partner's suit, you could raise to 2 ♥, but that is unlikely to be effective in keeping the opponents out of the auction. South doesn't need much strength to compete to 2 ♠ or three of a minor suit in response to North's double. Most players today would jump to 3 ♥, a *preemptive raise*. That makes it more difficult for the opponents to compete. South may not have enough to bid 3 ♠ or four of a minor suit, and the opponents may never get any further into the auction. If South stretches to bid, the opponents may get too high. Partner will not expect much strength outside the heart suit, since you could redouble with a hand of 10 or more points. So your side is unlikely to get too high. Since the partnership has at least nine hearts in the combined hands, it will be difficult for North–South to double and collect a large penalty, even if your side can't take nine tricks.

With 10 or more points, use the redouble or better still *Jacoby 2NT*. There's a disadvantage to starting with a redouble when you have 10 or more points *and* four-card or longer support for partner's major suit. By the time it's your turn to rebid, the opponents' bidding might make it difficult for you to describe the hand to partner. For example, suppose you have the following hand as East and the auction starts like this:

WEST	NORTH	**EAST**	SOUTH
1 ♥	Double	Redouble	2 ♠
Pass	4 ♠	?	

♠ Q 4　　　　　What can you do now? You don't have enough strength
♥ K J 7 3　　　to bid 5 ♥, and your hand isn't ideally suited to a
♦ K 8 7 3　　　penalty double of 4 ♠. You can pass and leave the
♣ J 3 2　　　　decision to partner, but partner doesn't have the
　　　　　　　　information that you have such fine support for hearts.

Jordan (Truscott) 2NT

To prevent this occurrence — while still leaving preemptive jump raises available — many players use a response of 2NT to describe a hand with 10 or more points and four-card or longer support for partner's suit. If the opponents now intervene, partner will be in a much better position to decide what to do. This conventional treatment was introduced in North America by Alan Truscott, a top player and bridge columnist for *The New York Times*. It's sometimes referred to as *Truscott 2NT*, although it's perhaps best known as *Jordan 2NT* (or even *Dormer 2NT*).

The 2NT response is available for this use after a takeout double, since with a natural 2NT response showing a strong balanced hand, responder can redouble. Even partnerships that play *Jacoby 2NT* prefer to use this convention, which covers limit as well as forcing raises after a takeout double. The main purpose of *Jacoby 2NT* is to look at slam possibilities — which become extremely remote once an opponent has enough strength for a takeout double.

WEST	NORTH	**EAST**	SOUTH
1♠	Double	?	

♠ Q J 7 3
♥ J 4
♦ A Q 8 2
♣ 10 8 5

Respond 2NT. This shows four-card or longer support for opener's suit and the values for at least a limit raise. Opener will be well positioned to decide what to do should the opponents compete.

♠ A J 7 3
♥ Q 4
♦ J 7 3
♣ K Q 5 2

Respond 2NT. This is no longer the *Jacoby 2NT* convention after the takeout double. It does, however, serve a similar purpose on this hand. The 2NT bid shows a limit raise *or better*. Even if partner rebids 3♠, you plan to continue to game. That will give partner the appropriate message. The partnership will be well placed if the opponents compete further. There's no real need for *Jacoby 2NT* with this hand. The likelihood of slam is very low once North has announced enough values for a takeout double.

♠ J 10 7 5
♥ 4 2
♦ Q 8 6 3 2
♣ 5 4

Respond 3♠. Since 2NT would show the strength for a limit raise or better, responder can use the jump to the three level as a *preemptive (weak) raise*. This bid may make it difficult for North–South to judge how high to compete. Partner won't be expecting much outside strength from your hand since you didn't redouble or use the *Jordan 2NT* bid.

Although a 2NT response shows a limit raise *or better*, opener should initially treat it as a limit raise:

- With a minimum-strength hand that would not continue to game opposite a limit raise, opener rebids the major at the three level. If responder actually holds a game-forcing raise, responder can still bid higher; otherwise, responder can pass and the partnership will rest in partscore at the three level.

- With a hand strong enough to accept the invitation of a limit raise, opener can bid game or bid a new suit with bigger things in mind.
- If the opponents intervene, opener can pass with a minimum-strength hand or double the opponents' contract for penalty with good defensive prospects. With more than a minimum hand, opener should take some action: doubling the opponent's contract for penalty, bidding higher in the agreed trump suit, or bidding a new suit.

Here are examples as West after the auction has started:

WEST	NORTH	EAST	SOUTH
1♥	Double	2NT	Pass
?			

♠ J 7
♥ K J 8 7 6
♦ A 10 5
♣ Q J 9

Rebid 3♥. You have a bare minimum opening bid, so you don't want to be at the game level opposite a limit — invitational — raise. Put the partnership in partscore. With a hand containing 13 or more points, partner can raise to game. If South had bid 3♠ instead of passing, you would pass to show a minimum hand.

♠ K 7
♥ A Q 10 8 3
♦ A Q 6 3
♣ 7 4

Rebid 4♥. Opposite a limit raise, the partnership should have enough combined strength for a game contract. If South were to bid 3♠, instead of passing, you would still bid 4♥. But if South were to bid 4♠, you should double. The partnership should have enough combined strength to defeat that contract, and there's no reason to believe your side can take 11 tricks with hearts as trumps if partner has only a limit raise.

♠ 7
♥ A K 10 9 6
♦ 10 3
♣ A K Q 6 5

Rebid 3♣. There's a possibility of making slam if partner has the right cards, so let partner know where your values are. Even if South jumped to 4♠, rather than passing, you should probably bid 5♣. Prospects for making 5♥ or 6♥ are probably better than those for extracting a large penalty by doubling 4♠ — although your decision could work out poorly. You can't pass and leave the decision to partner. Partner may not bid again with only the strength for a limit raise.

NOTE: See the Appendix (pages 315–316) for a discussion of these supplemental conventions and/or treatments.

Weak Jump Shifts

Soloway Jump Shifts

Preemptive Re-Raises

SUMMARY

Occasionally opening *light* — with fewer than 13 points — is common practice in third or fourth position. The objectives of this tactic are to reach a partscore contract and to make the auction more difficult for the opponents. An important consideration in using this tactic is that *a new suit response by a passed hand is not forcing*; opener can pass the response holding fewer than 13 points.

In fourth position, the *Rule of 15* can be used to decide whether to open the bidding or to pass. The number of spades is added to the high-card points. If the total is 15 or more, the hand is opened; otherwise, the hand is passed.

Partnerships that frequently open light in third or fourth position can use the *Drury* convention to avoid getting too high.

Drury

- When partner opens the bidding 1 ♥ or 1 ♠ in third or fourth position, a response of 2 ♣ is artificial (conventional) and asks about the strength of the opening bid.

- The 2 ♣ response shows three-card or longer support for opener's major and 10 or more points in support of opener's suit.

- A response other than 2 ♣ shows a hand unsuitable for *Drury* (less than three-card support and/or fewer than 10 points). A jump to 3 ♣ shows an invitational-strength hand with five or more clubs.

- *Drury* can be used after a takeout double or a 1 ♠ overcall. After a 2 ♣ overcall, double takes the place of *Drury*.

There are two common styles of response to *Drury*:

Standard Drury

- A rebid of 2 ♦ by opener shows a *light* opening bid; any other rebid shows a full opening bid.

Reverse Drury

- A rebid of the major suit by opener shows a *light* opening bid; any other rebid shows a full opening bid.

Responding to 1♥ or 1♠ without Support

- 1NT — 6 to 9 or 10 points, not necessarily a balanced hand.
- 2NT — Not applicable if using *Jacoby 2NT*.
- 3NT — 15 to 17 points, balanced, usually two cards in opener's major.
- A new suit at the one level shows a four-card or longer suit and 6 or more points. (It is forcing unless responder is a *passed hand.*)
- A new suit at the two level promises 10 or more points. A response of 2 ♥ shows a five-card or longer suit and is forcing unless responder is a passed hand.
- A jump in a new suit (*jump shift*) shows about 17 or more points and is forcing to at least the game level.

Jordan 2NT (Truscott; Dormer)

When partner's 1 ♥ or 1 ♠ is doubled for takeout:

- A jump to 2NT shows four-card or longer support and the values for a limit raise or better in opener's major.
- A jump to the three level in opener's major suit is a *preemptive* (weak) *raise* showing four-card support but less than the values for a limit raise.

If the partnership uses *Jacoby 2NT* in response to a major-suit opening, *Jordan 2NT* takes precedence after a takeout double when the partnership use both conventions.

The following exercises assume you are using the methods outlined in the summary.

Exercise One — Opening a Major Suit

If you are in first or second position, what would be your opening call with each of the following hands? What would you call with the same hands if you have a chance to open in third position? Fourth position?

1) ♠ K J 9 8 4
   ♥ A K Q 9 6
   ♦ 7 3
   ♣ K

2) ♠ K 10 7 5 4
   ♥ Q 8 4
   ♦ K 5
   ♣ K 6 3

3) ♠ 4
   ♥ A K J 10
   ♦ Q 7 4 2
   ♣ K 8 5 2

4) ♠ A Q 8 7 3
   ♥ —
   ♦ K Q J 6 5 2
   ♣ Q 7

5) ♠ Q 10 6
   ♥ A K 10 8 3
   ♦ K 8 5
   ♣ K 9

6) ♠ 3
   ♥ Q 8 7 5 4 2
   ♦ A J 3
   ♣ K 9 5

Exercise Two — *Drury*

As West, what do you do with each of these hands after the auction has started:

WEST	NORTH	EAST	SOUTH
Pass	Pass	1 ♠	Pass
?			

1) ♠ Q 7 5
   ♥ K 9
   ♦ J 10 8 3 2
   ♣ Q 7 2

2) ♠ K 10 7 3
   ♥ A J 9 8
   ♦ Q 7
   ♣ J 6 2

3) ♠ J 9 5
   ♥ Q 7 6
   ♦ K 8 7 4 2
   ♣ A 5

4) ♠ Q 3
   ♥ J 9
   ♦ Q 8 7 4
   ♣ Q 9 6 4 2

5) ♠ J 4
   ♥ K Q 10 8 7
   ♦ A 9 6 4
   ♣ 6 2

6) ♠ Q 6
   ♥ 7 4
   ♦ A 7 3
   ♣ K J 10 9 7 4

Exercise One — Opening a Major Suit

1) 1st, 2nd, 3rd, and 4th: 1 ♠.

2) 1st and 2nd: Pass; 3rd: 1 ♠; 4th: 1 ♠. Apply the *Rule of 15* — 11 high-card points plus five spades.

3) 1st and 2nd: 1 ♦; 3rd: 1 ♥/1 ♦. Open a good four-card major suit occasionally in third position; 4th: Pass/1 ♥/1 ♦. The *Rule of 15* suggests passing — 13 high-card points plus one spade. If you do open, 1 ♥ might be the best choice.

4) 1st, 2nd, 3rd, and 4th: 1 ♦.

5) 1st, 2nd, 3rd, and 4th: 1NT. With a balanced hand, open 1NT even with a five-card major.

6) 1st and 2nd: Pass; 3rd: 1 ♥; 4th: Pass. *Rule of 15* suggests passing — 10 HCPs plus one spade; bidding may get the partnership too high.

Exercise Two — *Drury*

1) 2 ♠. A standard raise with three-card support and 8 high-card points.

2) 2 ♣ (*Drury*). Find out if partner has a full opening bid.

3) 2 ♣ (*Drury*). With a fit and 10 high-card points, this is better than 2 ♦, which might be passed.

4) 1NT. The standard response with no fit and not enough strength to bid at the two level.

5) 2 ♥. This is non-forcing since you are a passed hand; partner won't expect a fit in spades since you didn't use *Drury*.

6) 3 ♣. This is the standard way to show an invitational hand with clubs when using the *Drury* convention.

Exercise Three — Responding to *Drury*

As East and playing standard responses to *Drury*, what do you rebid with each of the following hands after the auction has begun:

WEST	NORTH	**EAST**	SOUTH
Pass	Pass	1♥	Pass
2♣	Pass	?	

1) ♠ Q 8 7 5
   ♥ K Q 10 6 4
   ♦ A 7
   ♣ 6 3 _____

2) ♠ 6
   ♥ A J 8 7 4
   ♦ A Q J 3 2
   ♣ Q 10 _____

3) ♠ K 5 2
   ♥ Q 10 8 7 3
   ♦ K 2
   ♣ A J 7 _____

Exercise Four — More about *Drury*

You hold the following hand as East:

♠ J 8 2
♥ K J 10 6 3
♦ A 9 4
♣ Q 3

What is your next call in each of the following auctions?

1)
WEST	NORTH	**EAST**	SOUTH
Pass	Pass	1♥	1♠
2♣	Pass	? _____	

2)
WEST	NORTH	**EAST**	SOUTH
Pass	Pass	1♥	2♣
Double	Pass	? _____	

3)
WEST	NORTH	**EAST**	SOUTH
Pass	Pass	1♥	Double
2♣	2♠	? _____	

4)
WEST	NORTH	**EAST**	SOUTH
Pass	Pass	1♥	Pass
2♦	Pass	? _____	

5)
WEST	NORTH	**EAST**	SOUTH
Pass	Pass	1♥	Pass
3♣	Pass	? _____	

Exercise Three — Responding to *Drury*

1) 2 ♦. This shows a substandard opening bid using standard responses to *Drury*. (Playing *reverse Drury,* you would rebid 2 ♥.)

2) 3 ♦/2 ♥/4 ♥. A rebid of 2 ♦ would show a substandard opening; you could rebid 2 ♥ showing a full opening bid or go directly to 4 ♥, but 3 ♦ is more descriptive. (Playing *reverse Drury,* you could rebid 2 ♦, since 2 ♥ would show a substandard opening.)

3) 2NT. This shows a full opening bid with a balanced hand. (Playing *reverse Drury*, you would make the same rebid.)

Exercise Four — More about *Drury*

1) 2 ♦. Partner's 2 ♣ bid is *Drury* and this is the standard response to show a substandard opening bid. (Playing *reverse Drury*, you would rebid 2 ♥ to show a minimum.)

2) 2 ♦. When the opponents overcall 2 ♣, double takes the place of *Drury*. (Playing *reverse Drury,* you would rebid 2 ♥ to show a minimum.)

3) Pass. 2 ♣ is still *Drury* after the double. Once North bids you can pass to show a substandard opening bid. With a full opening you would have to bid something after the 2 ♠ bid.

4) Pass. If partner is a passed hand, a new-suit bid is no longer forcing. With a heart fit, partner would have bid *Drury*.

5) Pass. Partner's 3 ♣ bid shows an invitational hand with a good club suit. You have no reason to bid again.

Exercise Five — Other Responses to a Major

As East, what do you respond with each of the following hands after the auction starts:

WEST	NORTH	EAST	SOUTH
1 ♠	Pass	?	

1)
♠ 3
♥ J 9 7 6 4 2
♦ K 9 7 3
♣ Q 3

2)
♠ K 3
♥ A 9 8
♦ 9 7
♣ A K Q J 7 3

3)
♠ 7 5
♥ A Q J 9 6
♦ K 10 7 3
♣ J 4

4)
♠ 8 6
♥ K Q 9
♦ A J 10 2
♣ K Q J 3

5)
♠ 3
♥ A K 8 7
♦ K J 9 7
♣ Q 9 6 3

6)
♠ Q 6
♥ A J 9
♦ Q 10 6 2
♣ A 10 7 3

Exercise Six — 2NT as a Limit Raise

As East, what do you respond with each of the following hands after the auction starts:

WEST	NORTH	EAST	SOUTH
1 ♥	Double	?	

1)
♠ A 8 6
♥ Q 9 3
♦ 10 8 7 6 2
♣ J 4

2)
♠ K 6
♥ A J 7 5
♦ Q 10 7 3
♣ 9 8 6

3)
♠ 7 5
♥ K J 9 6
♦ 8 3
♣ J 9 8 7 4

4)
♠ K J 3
♥ A 8
♦ Q 10 8 3
♣ J 10 7 2

5)
♠ 3
♥ K 10 8 7 4
♦ 9 8 7 4 2
♣ J 3

6)
♠ A 9
♥ K 10 9 7
♦ K Q
♣ J 8 7 4 2

Exercise Five — Other Responses to a Major

1) 1NT. This hand isn't strong enough to bid a new suit at the two level. A 1NT response doesn't promise a balanced hand.

2) 3♣. This is a *jump shift* showing a hand of about 17 or more points. You are forcing the partnership to at least game and suggesting interest in a slam level contract.

3) 2♥. A new suit at the two level shows about 11 or more points. To bid hearts, you need at least a five-card suit.

4) 3NT. This is the standard response to show a balanced hand with 15 to 17 points.

5) 2♣. You have enough to bid a new suit at the two level. With a choice of four-card suits, bid the suits up the line — a response of 2♥ would show a five-card or longer suit.

6) 2♣. Assuming the partnership is using the *Jacoby 2NT* convention, you can't respond with a natural 2NT. Instead, bid a new suit, planning to bid 3NT at your next opportunity.

Exercise Six — 2NT as a Limit Raise

1) 2♥. With enough to raise partner's suit to the two level, make the same bid over the takeout double.

2) 2NT (*Jordan*). After an opponent's takeout double, a jump to 2NT shows four-card support and the strength for a limit raise.

3) 3♥. Although the strength is right for a raise to the two level, a pre-emptive jump to the three level should be more effective in keeping the opponents out of the auction. After a takeout double, the jump raise is weak, since you could use 2NT to show the strength for a limit raise or more.

4) Redouble. With no fit and 10 or more high-card points, the standard way to start off is with a redouble.

5) 4♥. With a weak hand but an excellent fit, make a preemptive raise all the way to the four level.

6) 2NT (*Jordan*). The jump to 2NT after an opponent's takeout double shows a limit raise *or better* in partner's suit.

Bid and Play — Deal 1

(E–Z Deal Cards: #4, Deal 1 — Dealer, North)

Suggested Bidding

WEST	NORTH	EAST	SOUTH
	Pass	Pass	Pass
1♠	Pass	2♠	Pass
Pass	Pass		

After the first three players pass, West has a choice between opening the bidding or passing and moving to the next deal. With a borderline hand, West can apply the rule of 15. Adding 5 for the five-card spade suit to the 11 high-card points gives a total of 16, indicating that the hand could be opened. With four-card support and 9 points, East doesn't have enough for *Drury* but has enough for a straightforward raise to 2♠. That should end the auction.

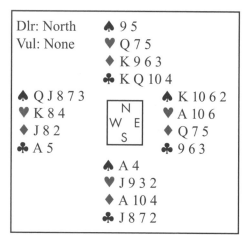

Dlr: North
Vul: None

```
           ♠ 9 5
           ♥ Q 7 5
           ♦ K 9 6 3
           ♣ K Q 10 4
♠ Q J 8 7 3              ♠ K 10 6 2
♥ K 8 4          N      ♥ A 10 6
♦ J 8 2       W     E   ♦ Q 7 5
♣ A 5            S      ♣ 9 6 3
           ♠ A 4
           ♥ J 9 3 2
           ♦ A 10 4
           ♣ J 8 7 2
```

Both North and South are close to competing for the contract, but neither have quite enough to take a chance. If North–South do find a way into the auction, their best partscore is in clubs. Over 2♠, they would have to compete to 3♣, and that contract can be defeated at least one trick.

Suggested Opening Lead

North is on lead and the most attractive card is the ♣K, top of a broken sequence.

Suggested Play

West wants to be sure of taking eight tricks and getting a plus score. There is a sure loser in spades, one in hearts, three in diamonds, and one in clubs. One too many. There's nothing that can be done about the spade loser or the club loser, and there is likely to be a heart loser unless there is a very lucky lie of the cards. Declarer needs to focus on the diamond suit.

There are a couple of possibilities in diamonds if declarer must lead the suit. A low diamond could be led toward dummy's ♦ Q, hoping North holds both the ♦ A and ♦ K. That isn't likely to be the case since North did not bid during the auction and the opening lead has marked North with at least the ♣ K and ♣ Q. An alternative would be to lead a low diamond from dummy toward the ♦ J, hoping South holds the ♦ A and ♦ K. There are other possibilities, but the only sure way to get a diamond trick is to have the defenders lead the suit. Recognizing this, declarer should manoeuver to force the defenders to lead diamonds.

After winning the ♣ A, declarer starts by drawing trumps. Suppose declarer leads a spade to dummy's ♠ K and South wins the ♠ A and leads a club. North wins and plays another club which West ruffs. West draws the remaining trump. This has worked well in that the defenders have no spades remaining and there are no clubs in the East–West hands. The stage is set. Rather than playing diamonds, declarer now takes the ♥ A, ♥ K, and leads a third round of hearts . . . giving up the heart loser. Declarer has now brought about the desired position. If the defenders lead a club or a heart, it gives declarer a ruff and a sluff. Declarer can ruff in one hand and sluff (discard) a diamond loser from the other hand. Declarer loses only two diamond tricks. If the defenders lead a diamond from either side, declarer plays low and can't be prevented from getting one trick with either the ♦ Q or ♦ J.

The challenge for declarer is to visualize this end position and then work to bring it about.

Suggested Defense

The defenders best chance to defeat the contract is to avoid giving declarer any help by leading the diamond suit themselves. After South wins the ♠ A and returns a club, it would be best for North not to play a third round of clubs, since that eliminates the clubs from the East–West hands and helps declarer bring about the desired end position. It will be difficult for North to see this, and declarer could later ruff a club anyway to achieve the same result. The defenders will have to hope that it is declarer who leads diamonds and they can then take three tricks in the suit.

Bid and Play — Deal 2

(E–Z Deal Cards: #4, Deal 2 — Dealer, East)

Suggested Bidding

WEST	NORTH	EAST	SOUTH
		Pass	Pass
Pass	1♠	Pass	2♦
Pass	Pass	Pass	

After three passes, it's up to North to decide whether to start the bidding. The *Rule of 15* guideline suggests opening 1♠ — 11 high-card points plus five spades. It would be dangerous for East to enter the auction at this point. The heart suit isn't very strong, partner has passed, and East has length in opener's suit. South responds 2♦ and the bidding returns to North. Since South passed originally, the 2♦ response is not forcing. North's best decision is to pass and hope

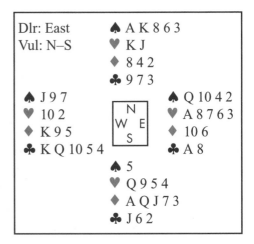

Dlr: East
Vul: N–S

♠ A K 8 6 3
♥ K J
♦ 8 4 2
♣ 9 7 3

♠ J 9 7
♥ 10 2
♦ K 9 5
♣ K Q 10 5 4

♠ Q 10 4 2
♥ A 8 7 6 3
♦ 10 6
♣ A 8

♠ 5
♥ Q 9 5 4
♦ A Q J 7 3
♣ J 6 2

that the partnership can make a partscore. If the partnership uses the *Drury* convention, there is an inference that South does not have support for spades — otherwise, South would have responded 2♣.

East has the final decision and might be tempted to "balance" with a bid of 2♥. This would be dangerous since North–South have not necessarily found a good fit. The length in spades is a warning to East that defending might be best. If East does bid, North–South can get a plus score by defending and South might choose to double.

Suggested Opening Lead

West is on lead and should lead the ♣K, top of a broken sequence.

Suggested Play

It is difficult for declarer to count losers. There are two heart losers, although it's unlikely that declarer will lose more than one trick. The ♥10 might appear, a heart could be ruffed in dummy, or a heart could be discarded on one of dummy's high spades. There are three club losers, so declarer's challenge will be to restrict the losers in the trump suit to one.

Declarer can avoid a trump loser if East holds the ♦K and the suit is divided 3–2. Even if the diamond finesse loses, there should be only one trump loser if the suit divides 3–2. So, the contract appears reasonable if the diamonds behave.

Suppose the defenders take the first three club tricks. West then leads a heart to East's ♥A and East leads back a heart which is won in dummy. It's tempting to take the diamond finesse but declarer might decide that it's unlikely that East holds the ♦K. East has already shown up with the ♣A and ♥A and might have opened the bidding or competed in the auction with the ♦K as well. If that's the case, declarer is best to play the ♦A and then the ♦Q. If the diamonds break 3–2 and West wins with the ♦K, the contract should make if the defenders can't get a heart ruff. On the actual layout, this will work and South will come home in the precarious 2♦ contract . . . but read on.

Suggested Defense

The defenders first challenge comes at trick one. When West leads the ♣K, East must overtake with the ♣A and lead back a club so that the defenders get their three club tricks. If East plays the ♣8 on the first trick, the suit becomes blocked and declarer will have an opportunity to discard a club loser on one of dummy's high spades.

Having overcome this hurdle, the defenders can actually defeat the contract. After winning the third round of clubs, West might see no future in leading a fourth round, since declarer can ruff. A fourth round of clubs will be very effective, however, if East ruffs with the ♦10. To win the trick, declarer must overruff with the ♦ J, and West now has two diamond tricks — one with the ♦ K and a second with the ♦ 9. This defensive maneuver is called an uppercut. It's difficult to visualize, but West might see the possibility of getting a second trump trick this way if partner holds the ♦ 10, ♦ J, or ♦ Q. East must also visualize the position and cooperate by ruffing with the ♦ 10, rather than the ♦ 6.

West might be afraid that leading a fourth round of clubs could cost the defenders a trick if partner holds the ♥ A Q, for example. Declarer can discard a heart from dummy on the fourth round of clubs, and if East doesn't have a high diamond, the defenders may have lost their chance to defeat the contract. West can probably work out from the auction that it is very unlikely that East holds both the ♥ A and ♥ Q, but it is likely that most defenders will lead a heart, rather than a fourth round of clubs. Defenders are aware that giving declarer a ruff and a sluff is not usually a good idea . . . but there are always exceptions. If West does lead a heart, East can still defeat the contract by ducking the ♥ A. On gaining the lead with the ♦ K, West can then lead a second heart to East's ♥ A and East can return a third round of hearts for West to ruff with the ♦ 9.

On the actual deal, West may get a second chance even if East doesn't duck the ♥ A. Suppose . . . on the actual deal, West may get a second chance. Suppose the defenders win the first three clubs and West then leads a heart. East wins the ♥ A and returns a heart, which declarer wins in dummy. If declarer takes the diamond finesse, West will have another chance to lead a fourth round of clubs. At this point, West may realize that there is no other chance for the defense.

This deal illustrates how finely tuned the struggle for a partscore can be. Playing in a social game, everyone might pass and get on to the next deal since none of the players has 13 points. A deal like this, however, can prove quite interesting — both during the play and in the analysis afterwards.

Bid and Play — Deal 3

(E–Z Deal Cards: #4, Deal 3 — Dealer, South)

Suggested Bidding

WEST	NORTH	EAST	SOUTH
			Pass
Pass	1♠	Pass	2♣
Pass	2♦	Pass	2♠
Pass	Pass	Pass	

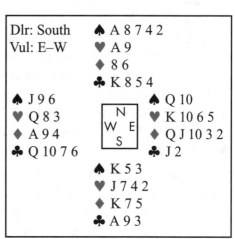

Dlr: South   ♠ A 8 7 4 2
Vul: E–W   ♥ A 9
              ♦ 8 6
              ♣ K 8 5 4

♠ J 9 6   ♠ Q 10
♥ Q 8 3   ♥ K 10 6 5
♦ A 9 4   ♦ Q J 10 3 2
♣ Q 10 7 6   ♣ J 2

              ♠ K 5 3
              ♥ J 7 4 2
              ♦ K 7 5
              ♣ A 9 3

After two passes, North opens with minimal values in third position. East's suit isn't good enough for an overcall at the two level, so the bidding comes back to South. With support for partner's suit and 11 high-card points, South's usual plan would be to create an invitational sequence to get the partnership to at least 3♠. With the *Drury* convention available, South can bid 2♣ to check on the quality of North's opening bid. North's 2♦ reply shows a sub-minimum opening, so South settles for a partscore of 2♠.

If the partnership uses *reverse Drury*, the auction would go like this:

WEST	NORTH	EAST	SOUTH
			Pass
Pass	1♠	Pass	2♣
Pass	2♠	Pass	Pass
Pass			

North's 2♠ rebid would show the sub-par opening bid and South would now pass. Either method of responses would allow the partnership to stop at the two level rather than the three level.

Suggested Opening Lead

East would lead the ♦Q, top of a sequence. North's 2♦ rebid has nothing to do with diamonds.

Suggested Play

The opening lead suggests that the ♦A is unfavorably placed, so declarer can expect two diamond losers. There is a heart loser, and even if the defenders' spades divide 3–2, there is a sure trump loser. North will have to limit the club suit to one loser. There are a couple of chances for eliminating a club loser. The suit might be divided 3–3, in which case North's fourth club will be a winner, or North may be able to trump a club loser in dummy.

Since it's more likely the clubs are divided 4–2 than 3–3, declarer should aim to ruff a club in dummy. To do this, declarer must plan the play carefully. Suppose the defenders start with three rounds of diamonds and declarer trumps the third round. North's first thought might be to play two rounds of trumps, with the ♠A and ♠K, leaving the defenders' high spade outstanding and leaving one spade in dummy to ruff the club loser. The problem with this line of play is that declarer must then give up a club trick before the fourth club can be ruffed. The defender who wins the third round of clubs may have the high trump and can draw dummy's last trump. That would happen on the actual layout.

Declarer's second thought might be to play the clubs before touching the trump suit. If declarer plays the ♣A, ♣K, and a third round of clubs, however, another problem might develop. If the clubs don't divide 3–3, the defender winning the third round of clubs might play a fourth round. If the other defender ruffs this and declarer has to overruff with dummy's ♠K, declarer might lose two trump tricks. Again, this would happen on the actual layout of the cards.

To counter both possibilities, declarer has to slightly modify the order of play. After ruffing the third round of diamonds, declarer should play a low club from both hands. Declarer gives up the club trick early, before the defenders can do any damage. Suppose the defenders win this trick and lead a heart.

Declarer takes the ♥A and plays the ♠A and ♠K, drawing two rounds of trumps and leaving the defenders with one high trump. Now declarer plays the ♣A and ♣K. If the defender with the last trump ruffs one of the club winners, there is still a trump left in dummy to take care of the club loser. If the clubs divide 4–2 and neither of the club winners is ruffed, declarer now ruffs the fourth round of clubs with dummy's remaining low trump. The defenders get one heart trick, two diamond tricks, one club trick, and their high spade — not enough to defeat the contract.

Suggested Defense

The defenders have a chance to defeat the contract if declarer doesn't handle the hand very carefully. If declarer plays two rounds of trumps early and then gives up a club trick, West can win and play a third round of spades. The defenders get two club tricks. If declarer plays three rounds of clubs early, West can win the third round and play a fourth round of clubs. East ruffs with the ♠10, and now declarer has no way to avoid two spade losers.

Bid and Play — Deal 4

(E–Z Deal Cards: #4, Deal 4 — Dealer, West)

Suggested Bidding

WEST	NORTH	EAST	SOUTH
Pass	Pass	1♥	Double
2♣	Pass	2♥ (4♥)	Pass
3♥	Pass	4♥	Pass
Pass	Pass		

East has a sound 1♥ opening bid in third position and South has the ideal hand for a takeout double. With support for partner's suit and 10 high-card points, West can use *Drury* to ask whether East has a full opening bid. With most partnerships, *Drury* still applies after the takeout double. By rebidding 2♥ rather than 2♦, East confirms a full opening bid. East might even jump directly to game, knowing West has a fit in hearts and 10 or more points. Either way, the partnership should reach game in hearts.

```
Dlr: West      ♠ J 10 7 3
Vul: Both      ♥ 7 5
               ♦ 9 7 6 3
               ♣ J 10 9
  ♠ A 6                      ♠ 8 4 2
  ♥ K 10 4         N         ♥ A Q J 8 6 3
  ♦ Q J 10 5    W     E      ♦ A
  ♣ 6 5 4 3        S         ♣ K 7 2
               ♠ K Q 9 5
               ♥ 9 2
               ♦ K 8 4 2
               ♣ A Q 8
```

Suggested Opening Lead

South has a difficult choice of leads but is likely to start with the ♠K, top of touching honors.

Suggested Play

East has two spade losers and three club losers. One spade loser can be trumped in the dummy. A club loser might be avoided by leading toward the ♣K, hoping North has the ♣A. This idea loses some of its appeal because South made a takeout double. It's more likely that South has the ♣A than North.

Looking for an alternative to the club finesse, declarer can plan to take advantage of dummy's diamonds. After taking the ♦A, declarer can cross to dummy and lead the ♦ Q. If North plays the ♦ K, East can ruff and later discard two club losers on dummy's established ♦ J and ♦ 10. If North doesn't play the ♦ K, East can discard a club loser. This is a variation of the loser on a loser play. If South wins the ♦ K, the ♦ J and ♦ 10 are still established for later club discards. If South leads a club, declarer will get a trick with the ♣ K.

The only danger to this line of play is if North ever gets the lead and plays a club, trapping East's ♣ K. To avoid this, declarer should duck the first round of spades. Suppose declarer ducks the first round of spades and South continues with a second spade. Declarer wins the ♠ A, crosses to the ♦ A, plays the ♥ A and a heart to dummy's ♥ 10. Declarer then leads the ♦ Q and discards a club when North plays a low diamond. South wins with the ♦ K but can't defeat the contract. In fact, if South doesn't take the ♣ A, declarer gets the rest of the tricks by discarding the remaining two clubs on dummy's diamond winners.

Suggested Defense

If South leads the ♠ K and declarer wins the first trick with dummy's ♠ A, the defenders have a chance. Suppose declarer unblocks the ♦ A, crosses to dummy with a heart, and leads the ♦ Q, discarding a club. On winning the ♦ K, South can defeat the contract by leading a low spade to North's ♠ 10. North then leads the ♣ J and the defenders take two club tricks.

How does South know to lead a low spade after winning the ♦ K? North can help on the first trick. When the ♠ A is played, North should play the ♠ J. The play of an honor in this situation promises the next lower honor and denies the next higher honor. By playing the ♠ J, North is showing the ♠ 10 and telling partner that it is safe to lead a low spade away from the ♠ Q.

This all requires good cooperation between the partners. North must realize the importance of the ♠ 10 as an entry so that clubs can be led through declarer's holding. South has to have the courage to believe North's signal. If North doesn't play the ♠ J on the first trick, South can still defeat the contract by leading a low spade upon winning the ♦ K, but it's much more difficult. Instead, South might take the ♠ Q and then lead clubs, hoping the defenders have two tricks to take in that suit.

Of course, declarer can simply duck the opening lead of the ♠ K to avoid all of these complications. (South can always defeat the contract by leading a low spade at trick one and then leading a second low spade after winning the ♦ K . . . but anyone who defends like that has already seen all four hands!)

CHAPTER 5

Minor-Suit Openings and Responses

MINOR-SUIT OPENINGS AND RESPONSES

Opening bids of 1♣ and 1♦ cover a wide range of hands. They can show an unbalanced hand with a long minor suit, a balanced hand that falls outside the range of a notrump opening bid, or a hand that can't be opened 1♥ or 1♠ because there is no five-card major suit. There's more variation in the responses to minor suits. The partnership rarely raises the minor suit directly — preferring to look for a major-suit fit or a notrump contract before settling on a minor suit.

OPENING BIDS OF 1♣ AND 1♦

For the most part, opening bids of 1♣ and 1♦ are natural, showing a four-card or longer suit. When partnerships use a style of *five-card majors*, however, occasionally the bidding is opened with a three-card minor suit.

Choosing a Minor

The only choice at the one level is to open with a minor suit when a hand doesn't have a five-card major suit and doesn't fall within the range to open 1NT. The longer minor suit is opened. The following guideline is used with minor suits of equal length:

- Open 1♦ with two equal-length minors of four cards or more.
- Open 1♣ with two three-card minor suits.

Here are sample hands for the opening bidder:

♠ K 7
♥ A 9 6 4   This is a typical opening bid of 1♣, since clubs is
♦ 4   the longest suit.
♣ A Q 8 7 6 3

♠ A J 7 4   Open 1♦. With no five-card or longer major suit,
♥ Q 9   open the longer minor suit.
♦ K J 5 3
♣ Q 5 2

♠ 5
♥ K 9 7 5
♦ Q 10 8 4
♣ A K J 5

Open 1 ♦. With four cards in both minors, the standard opening bid is 1 ♦. Some partnerships prefer to open the bidding 1 ♣ with this hand — the *better* minor — but the standard style is to start with 1 ♦.

♠ K 8 7 3
♥ Q 9 6 4
♦ A Q 4
♣ Q 3

Open 1 ♦. With no five-card major suit, open the bidding in the longer minor suit.

♠ A 9 3
♥ J 8 6 4
♦ A J 5
♣ K 10 4

Open 1 ♣. With no five-card major suit and a choice between two three-card minor suits, the standard guideline is to open the bidding 1 ♣. Even partnerships that open four-card majors avoid opening the bidding with a very weak four-card major suit and would usually open this hand 1 ♣.

♠ A K J 4
♥ A Q 7 3
♦ A J
♣ 7 6 3

Open 1 ♣. This is an extreme example of opening 1 ♣ as the longer minor. With 19 high-card points, the hand is too strong for 1NT but not strong enough for 2NT. With no five-card major, the longer minor is opened. Opener hopes the auction will not end there — but it might.

Not all hands with length in a minor suit are opened 1 ♣ or 1 ♦. Consider the following:

♠ K Q 5
♥ K J
♦ A J 8 7 6
♣ J 8 3

Open 1NT. A balanced hand that falls within the appropriate range for 1NT should be opened 1NT. This hand is worth 15 high-card points plus 1 point for the five-card suit.

♠ 4
♥ 9 8 6 3 2
♦ A 5
♣ A K Q 8 2

Open 1 ♥. Open the higher-ranking of two five-card suits regardless of the relative strengths in the suits.

♠ ~~~984
♥ K 2
♦ 5
♣ A Q 9 7 5

Open 1 ♠. There's no universal agreement on the best opening bid with five spades and five clubs. Some partnerships prefer to open 1 ♣ with a minimum-strength hand and five clubs and five spades — intending to rebid 1 ♠ if partner responds 1 ♦ or 1 ♥. With a maximum-strength hand, opener can jump shift to 2 ♠ after a response of 1 ♦ or 1 ♥. This is a matter of partnership style. For most partnerships, the recommendation is to keep things simple and use the guideline of opening the higher-ranking of two five-card suits. (See additional discussion under *reverses* in Chapter 6.)

The Short Club

There are times when a hand must be opened with a bid in a three-card minor suit. Many players refer to this concept as the *short club*. For the most part, this is a misnomer. Although a 1 ♣ opening bid is occasionally made on a three-card suit, most of the time it will be made on a four-card or longer suit. At times, the bidding can be opened on a three-card diamond suit.

The term *short club* often results in the mistaken impression that responder can't pass the opening bid of 1 ♣ — in case it's short! Some players go so far as to tell partner not to pass the opening bid of 1 ♣, even with no points — partner is expected to respond 1 ♦ with a weak hand and no four-card major suit. This isn't standard bidding. For example, suppose the opening bid is 1 ♣ and responder holds this hand:

♠ 9 7 6 5 3
♥ Q 8 4
♦ 10 7 6 3
♣ 3

Responder should pass! 1 ♣ may be the best contract for the partnership. There's nothing to stop opener from holding a good six-card or longer club suit. Even if 1 ♣ isn't the best contract, the auction isn't over. The opponents could overcall, taking your side out of the 1 ♣ contract. They might make a takeout double, giving both opener and responder a chance to find a better spot if necessary. Even if they leave opener to struggle in 1 ♣, they may get a poor result, since they can likely make a contract of their own. Responding to 1 ♣ only courts disaster. Opener, with a minimum-strength hand, must bid again, since a new suit response is forcing. Opener, with a medium- or maximum-strength hand, will likely make a jump rebid, getting the partnership too high.

Forcing partner to respond with the above hand isn't standard practice. Partnerships that want to treat the 1♣ opening as a forcing bid should switch to a *forcing club* system.

Some partnerships do play what can technically be considered a *short club*. If the partnership style is that an opening bid of 1♥ or 1♠ always shows a five-card or longer suit and an opening bid of 1♦ always shows a four-card or longer suit, the following hand would be opened 1♣:

♠ K 9 6 2
♥ Q 10 8 4
♦ A K J
♣ 7 3

That is unquestionably a *short club*. Using standard methods, this hand would be opened 1♦, the longer minor. Partnerships that open 1♣ must let the opponents know — since it isn't the standard bid with that type of hand — but the 1♣ opening bid is still not forcing. Responder can pass with fewer than 6 points.

FORCING CLUB SYSTEMS

Partnerships that treat the opening bid of 1♣ as forcing are playing a *forcing club system*. There are many such systems: *Precision Club*, *Blue Team Club*, and *Roman Club*, for example. Most of these systems use the opening bid of 1♣ as a strong, artificial bid, replacing the more standard strong bids, such as the 2♣ opening. These are nonstandard methods, beyond the scope of this book, and partnerships that use them must inform the opponents about the 1♣ opening bid and any other bids that have a special meaning.

Third and Fourth Positions

There are tactical reasons for deviating from the standard openings of 1♣ and 1♦ in third or fourth position. Once partner is a *passed hand*, new suit responses are no longer forcing, giving opener some latitude.

For example:

- In third position, you might (on occasion) open lighter . This allows you to compete for the contract or help your side on defense.

- In fourth position, you could pass with 13 or more points when you don't hold many cards in the majors. You don't want to give the opponents a chance to compete successfully in the major suits. The usual guideline is the *Rule of 15*. Add your high-card points to the number of spades you hold: if the total is fewer than 15, pass; if the total is 15 or more, open the bidding.

- In third or fourth position, you occasionally open a strong four-card major suit, rather than a three-card minor suit, especially when opening light. If you don't buy the contract, you'd like to direct partner to the best opening lead. You may also open a strong four-card minor suit ahead of a weak five-card minor suit.

Here are examples as East after the auction has started:

WEST	NORTH	**EAST**	SOUTH
Pass	Pass	?	

♠ 10 6 2
♥ K 6 3
♦ 9 3
♣ A K J 5 3

Open 1♣. With 11 high-card points plus 1 point for the five-card suit, you don't have enough for an opening bid in first or second position. It's not a bad idea to bid 1♣ in third chair, since it might help partner find the best lead if your side defends. It might also cause the opponents to misjudge their combined strength. If partner bids 1♥ or 1♠ — normally a forcing response — you can pass and hope for the best. Your side might make a small partscore. If partner responds 1♦, try 1NT or 2♣.

If you were in fourth position with this hand, you should probably pass. Opening the bidding could lead to a minus score if the opponents overcall in a major suit.

♠ A K J 10
♥ K 7 5
♦ 7 5 3
♣ 8 6 2

If you're going to open this hand in third or fourth position, 1♠ is a better tactical bid than 1♣. If your side defends, you'd prefer partner to lead a spade, rather than a club.

♠ 8 3
♥ 3 2
♦ A K Q 10
♣ J 7 6 4 3

There's nothing wrong with passing, but you might want to stir things up a little with an opening 1♦ bid in third position. This should leave you better placed than an opening bid of 1♣. If partner responds 1♥ or 1♠, you can rebid 2♣ to show your other suit. 1♣ is likely to get partner off to the wrong opening lead if the opponents buy the contract. You'll also find yourself awkwardly placed if partner responds 1♥ or 1♠. In fourth position, you'll usually do best by passing. It doesn't satisfy the *Rule of 15*.

RAISING PARTNER'S MINOR-SUIT OPENING

Although the priority is to look for a major-suit fit or possibly a notrump contract when the opening bid is 1♣ or 1♦, there are times when responder's best choice is to raise opener's suit.

The Single Raise

A raise of opener's minor to the two level shows 6 to 9 points. Opener will usually have a four-card or longer suit to open the bidding 1♦ — the exception is when opener has exactly two four-card major suits, three diamonds, and a doubleton club. Responder should be willing to raise 1♦ with four-card or longer support. Opener will more frequently have a three-card suit when opening the bidding 1♣ — with no five-card major and three cards in both minor suits. Responder, therefore, should have at least five-card support to raise an opening 1♣ bid. In a competitive situation, responder may have to raise with one fewer club when there's no suitable alternative.

WEST	NORTH	**EAST**	SOUTH
1♣	Pass	?	

♠ 6 2
♥ A 9 3
♦ 10 8 5
♣ Q J 6 5 3

Respond 2♣. The hand is worth 8 points — 7 high-card points plus 1 length point for the five-card suit or 1 dummy point for the doubleton spade. With five-card support, clubs will make a good trump suit even if opener has only a three-card suit.

♠ 5
♥ 9 4 2
♦ A Q 7 4
♣ J 9 8 6 3

Respond 2♣. You could respond 1♦ but the immediate raise lets partner know about the club fit and also leaves less room for the opponents to come into the auction.

♠ 8 6 3
♥ A 9 3
♦ Q 7 2
♣ Q 9 8 2

Respond 1NT. You usually have five-card support to immediately raise opener's club suit. With only four clubs and no other four-card or longer suit to bid, respond 1NT. Opener can infer that you have four clubs, since you didn't bid another suit at the one level. With a minimum-strength unbalanced hand, therefore, opener can always return to 2♣. If North had overcalled 1♠, you might raise to 2♣ rather than bid 1NT with no stopper in the opponent's suit. Sometimes, you have to make the best of what you are dealt.

♠ K J 9 7
♥ 6 4
♦ 8 3
♣ K 10 7 6 3

Respond 1♠. Looking for a major-suit fit takes priority over an immediate raise. You can return to clubs later if you don't find a fit in spades.

The Limit Raise

The partnership has a choice of how to treat a jump raise of a minor suit: forcing, limit, or weak. The standard approach is to use the double raise as a *limit raise* — an invitational bid.

A limit raise to the three level shows about 10 to 12 points. The exact range depends on the partnership style and the interpretation of *points*. It's standard practice to count dummy points when supporting a major suit, but it isn't as clear-cut when supporting a minor suit. Consider the following hand:

♠ 4
♥ K 8 3
♦ A 10 9 7 3
♣ J 7 6 3

Initially, there are 8 high-card points and one point for length, putting the hand in the 6 to 9 point range. If partner were to open 1 ♦, however, you could value the singleton spade as 3 dummy points, instead of counting the length points. That would give you a total of 11 points, putting the hand in the range for a limit raise to 3 ♦. That's fine if the partnership plays the contract with diamonds as the trump suit, but what if opener rebids 3NT? That's quite likely, since opener will usually prefer to go for nine tricks, rather than 11, when accepting your invitation. Now the singleton spade is a disadvantage, rather than an advantage. The hand is back to being worth about 9 points — 8 high-card points plus a point for the fifth diamond.

This makes it a challenge for responder to judge whether to count dummy points when deciding to raise partner's minor suit. Most partnerships do count dummy points when deciding between a single raise and a jump raise, but use a guideline of about 11 or 12 points as the strength for a limit raise. That way, you retain the tactical advantage of the limit raise — the jump raise may keep the opponents out of the auction — while leaving a measure of safety if opener puts the contract into 3NT. Having a little extra strength never hurts; if opener elects to play game in the minor suit — 5 ♣ or 5 ♦ — the partnership will need about 28 or 29 combined points anyway.

WEST	NORTH	**EAST**	SOUTH
1 ♦	Pass	?	

♠ J 8 5
♥ 6 4
♦ A Q J 10 5
♣ K 9 3

Respond 3 ♦. This is a limit — invitational — raise showing 11 or 12 points. If opener passes, the partnership should be in the best partscore. If opener accepts the invitation, the partnership will play the deal in 3NT or 5 ♦.

♠ J 3
♥ 7 4 2
♦ K Q 8 4
♣ A J 7 3

Respond 3 ♦. You need four-card or longer support to raise partner's diamonds. Partner will occasionally have a three-card diamond suit, but it isn't worth worrying about when you have a limit raise available that will nicely describe your hand.

♠ K 4 2
♥ 3
♦ A Q 8 7 5
♣ 10 8 6 3

Respond 3 ♦. Nine high-card points plus 3 dummy points puts this hand in the category for a limit raise. You'll be a little shy in terms of high cards if partner chooses to play in 3NT, but the hand is too strong for a single raise to 2 ♦.

The Forcing Raise

If a raise of opener's minor to the two level shows 6 to 9 points, and a jump raise to the three level is a limit raise showing 10 to 12 points, what does responder do to show a forcing raise? For example, suppose partner opens the bidding 1 ♦ and you hold the following hand:

♠ K 7 3
♥ 5
♦ A K 10 8 4
♣ K 9 6 3

The *Jacoby 2NT* convention (see Chapter 3) isn't used after a minor suit opening because responder's priorities tend to be searching for a major-suit fit or looking to play in a notrump contract. Notrump responses are usually played as natural bids. Some partnerships use a conventional forcing raise, but without any such tools, responder would simply start with a new suit, 2♣, intending to show diamond support later in the auction.

This works quite well, since responder usually has another four-card or longer suit to bid or will have a balanced hand and can respond at the appropriate level in notrump. Occasionally, there will be awkward hands, however, and responder might need to manufacture a suitable bid. For example, suppose partner opens the bidding 1♣, and you hold the following hand:

♠ K Q
♥ 7 3
♦ A 9 3
♣ K Q 10 8 7 5

With no forcing raise available, a response of 1 ♦ is probably the best choice. You intend to make another forcing bid and show the clubs later in the auction — although if opener rebids 1NT, you could simply raise to 3NT, never bothering to mention your club support. An immediate jump to 3NT would be another choice, but your hand is unbalanced and has no strength in the heart suit — even if partner holds some values in hearts, a notrump contract may play better when declared from opener's side of the table.

OTHER RESPONSES TO 1♣ OR 1♦

When the partnership uses a five-card major style, opener will frequently hold a four-card major suit when the opening bid is 1♣ or 1♦. Before raising opener's minor or bidding notrump, responder's first priority is to look for a major-suit fit. A new suit response is forcing — unless responder has already passed, limiting responder's hand to fewer than 13 points.

Up the Line

With a choice of suits to bid at the one level, responder bids:

- The longest suit first.
- The higher-ranking of two five-card or six-card suits.
- The lowest-ranking of four-card suits.

This last point is called bidding suits *up the line*. Here are examples of responding as East after the bidding starts:

WEST	NORTH	**EAST**	SOUTH
1♣	Pass	?	

♠ 9 2
♥ 10 6 5 3
♦ A 5
♣ A J 10 7 3

Respond 1♥. Although you have fine support for opener's suit, the first priority is to look for a major-suit fit. Any four-card or longer suit is biddable by responder. Opener could hold a strong four-card heart suit but wouldn't be able to open the bidding 1♥, since that would show a five-card suit. Someone has to mention hearts, and that job falls on responder's shoulders. If opener doesn't have support for hearts, the partnership can always return to clubs.

♠ J 9 8 6 3
♥ 10 4 2
♦ A Q 8 6
♣ 3

Respond 1♠. With a choice of suits to bid at the one level, bid the longer suit.

♠ K J 10 8 3   Respond 1 ♠. With a choice of suits, bid the higher-
♥ A K 10 8 4   ranking of two five-card suits. You plan to show the
♦ 8   hearts at your next opportunity if opener doesn't sup-
♣ 7 2   port spades.

♠ K 10 8 4   Respond 1 ♥. With a choice of four-card suits to bid
♥ Q 9 5 2   at the one level, bid the lower-ranking suit. If opener
♦ 10 5   holds four hearts, the major-suit fit will be found
♣ Q 8 3   right away. If opener holds four spades, opener will
show them on the rebid, and again the fit will be
found. That's how bidding *up the line* is expected to work.

♠ A 8 7 3   Respond 1 ♦. The principle of responding up the line
♥ 9 4   with four-card suits also applies when one of the suits
♦ A Q J 8   is diamonds. Although the priority is to find a ma-
♣ J 6 2   jor-suit fit, opener could hold a four-card diamond
suit and a five-card or longer club suit for the opening
1 ♣ bid. If responder starts with 1 ♠, the diamond fit may get lost. Some
partnerships prefer to bypass the diamond suit in certain situations, and
this style is discussed further at the end of this chapter.

Notrump Responses to 1 ♣ and 1 ♦

Notrump responses to a minor suit are usually played as natural, showing the following ranges:

- 1NT shows 6 to 10 points, and is non-forcing.
- 2NT shows 13 to 15 points, and is forcing.
- 3NT shows 16 or 17 points, and is non-forcing.

With 11 or 12 points and a balanced hand, responder bids a new suit,
intending to bid 2NT at the next opportunity to show an invitational-
strength balanced hand. If responder is a *passed hand*, then a jump to
2NT shows 11 or 12 points — since responder can't have 13 to 15 points.

Since the priority is to find a major-suit fit, notrump responses tend
to deny a four-card or longer major suit. Occasionally, players bypass a

major suit with a balanced hand, but it's not standard practice. More frequently, responder will bypass a four-card or longer minor suit with a balanced hand.

Here are examples as East after the bidding starts:

WEST	NORTH	**EAST**	SOUTH
1♦	Pass	?	

♠ Q 6 2
♥ K 9 6 3
♦ K 10 5
♣ J 9 5

Respond 1♥. Although you have a balanced hand, priority goes to showing the major suit, rather than showing the balanced hand pattern. Playing five-card majors, there's a reasonable possibility that opener has a four-card heart suit. If you don't find a fit in hearts, the partnership can still end in notrump.

♠ K J 8
♥ A J 9
♦ J 9 4
♣ K J 6 5

Respond 2NT. The response of 2NT shows a balanced hand with 13 to 15 points. It's forcing. Opener can raise to 3NT with no interest in going beyond the game level, and in the knowledge that responder doesn't have a four-card or longer major suit. Opener bids something other than 3NT with an unbalanced hand or interest in a slam contract.

♠ K 9 5
♥ A Q
♦ Q 10 7 4 2
♣ K Q 9

Respond 3NT. This shows a balanced hand with 16 or 17 points. It's non-forcing. With a minimum-strength balanced hand, opener can pass. With interest in a slam contract, opener can bid beyond 3NT. The 3NT response describes the balanced nature of the hand and the strength in a single bid. It's more descriptive than trying to find a suitable sequence to show a forcing raise in diamonds.

♠ 8 4
♥ J 9 3
♦ Q 5
♣ K 9 7 6 4 2

Respond 1NT. The response of 1NT doesn't necessarily guarantee a balanced hand. If responder has 6 to 10 points and can't bid a new suit at the one level or raise opener's diamonds, 1NT is the only option left.

♠ Q J 3 ♥ Q 9 7 ♦ A J 5 ♣ Q 10 8 5	Respond 2♣. With a balanced hand and 11 or 12 points, start with a new suit. You intend to rebid 2NT at your next opportunity as an invitational bid, although opener's next bid may not give you that opportunity — if opener raises to 3♣, for example.

For an alternative approach, see *2NT as a non-forcing response to a minor* in the Glossary.

Jump Shift

A jump response in a new suit — a *jump shift* — shows a strong hand with interest in reaching a slam contract. The treatment of a jump shift in response to a minor suit is identical to that discussed in Chapter 4.

Preemptive Jump Responses

A jump response that skips two or more levels — either a raise or a new suit — is normally treated as a preemptive (weak) bid. For example, consider the following hands as East after the auction starts:

WEST	NORTH	**EAST**	SOUTH
1♦	Pass	?	

♠ 10 6 ♥ J 4 ♦ Q 10 9 8 7 5 3 ♣ 5 2	Respond 4♦. A single raise to 2♦ would show 6 to 9 points, and a jump raise to 3♦ would be a limit raise showing 10 to 12 points. A raise of opener's minor suit to the four level is a weak, preemptive bid. Since this bid takes the partnership past 3NT, it should be used

only when the tactical advantage of keeping the opponents out of the auction outweighs the likelihood that your side can make game in notrump. The 4♦ response isn't forcing, and opener should bid again only with a very strong hand, as responder won't hold much in the way of high cards.

♠ K J 10 9 7 6 5 ♥ 3 ♦ 9 4 ♣ 10 8 3	Respond 3♠. A response of 1♠ would be natural and forcing, and a response of 2♠ would be a jump shift. A response of 3♠ shows the type of hand which you would have opened with a preemptive 3♠ bid if

partner had passed. This response is non-forcing. Opener should pass except when holding a hand that is likely to make a game contract opposite a long spade suit — either a very strong hand or a good fit with spades. Some partnerships prefer other methods to show a weak hand with a long suit (see *weak jump shifts* in the Appendix) and may assign a different meaning to the double jump in a new suit (see *splinter bids* in the Appendix).

♠ 3
♥ K Q 10 8 6 5 4 2
♦ 10 8
♣ 7 6

Respond 4♥. This is a weak, non-forcing response, but it shows an eight-card suit — the type of hand you would open the bidding 4♥. Opener should expect you to have this type of hand for the 4♥ response — you're only interested in play-ing at the game level with your suit as trump. Opener should bid again only with a very strong hand and slam aspirations. Preemptive jump responses are rarely used over a major suit since they take the partnership past 3NT. Most partnerships prefer to use *splinter bids* in place of preemptive jump responses over a major suit.

HANDLING INTERFERENCE

If the opponents come into the auction with a takeout double or an overcall after an opening bid of 1♣ or 1♦, many of responder's bids retain their original meaning, but there are some exceptions.

After a Takeout Double

When an opponent makes a takeout double of the opening bid of 1♣ or 1♦, responder can integrate the redouble and *Jordan 2NT* (as described in Chapter 4) into the responses as follows:

- A new suit at the one level is still forcing and shows 6 or more points.
- A single raise of opener's minor shows 6 to 9 points.
- A jump raise of opener's minor is treated as a *preemptive raise* rather than a limit raise.

- A response of *2NT*, instead of showing a balanced hand of 13 to 15 points, is used to show a limit raise or better (*Jordan 2NT*).
- A redouble shows a hand worth 10 or more points, usually without support for opener's suit.

For example, consider the following hands for responder (East) after the auction begins:

WEST	NORTH	**EAST**	SOUTH
1♣	Double	?	

♠ 8 4
♥ Q J 9 6 5
♦ 9 5
♣ K 10 7 3

Respond 1♥. The opponent's double hasn't taken away any bidding room, so responder can make the same response as if there were no double. A new suit at the one level is still forcing. If opener doesn't have a fit for hearts, responder can show the club support at the next opportunity.

♠ 9 6 4
♥ 8 4 3
♦ J 6 3
♣ A Q 7 3

Bid 2♣. Although responder prefers to have five clubs to raise — in case opener has a three-card suit — four-card support is acceptable in a competitive situation. No other bid is attractive, and if you don't show the club support at this point there may not be another chance once the opponents start bidding.

♠ 4
♥ 10 8 4
♦ Q 9 6 2
♣ Q J 8 7 5

Jump to 3♣. After the takeout double, a jump raise is preemptive rather than being a limit raise. If you pass, or raise only to the two level, the opponents are likely to find their best spot. Having opened 1♣, partner is unlikely to hold more than four cards in a major suit, so the opponents should have at least an eight-card fit in spades. By jumping to 3♣, you may keep the opponents out of the auction, or make it difficult for them to judge whether to play partscore or game. Partner won't expect you to have much. With 10 or more points, you would have redoubled or bid 2NT.

♠ K 9 4
♥ 7 3
♦ J 10 2
♣ A Q 9 7 5

Bid 2NT. A jump to 2NT is used to show at least the values for a limit raise. If you were to redouble with this hand, the opponents' subsequent bidding might make it difficult for you to show club support at an appropriate level. The 2NT bid shows club support, and at the same time, it shows an invitational-strength hand. With minimal values, opener can retreat to 3♣, or bid 4♣ or 5♣ with long clubs in an attempt to keep the opponents from their best contract. With extra strength, opener can raise to 3NT or bid a new suit to search for the best contract.

Some partnerships prefer to reverse the meanings of the jump raise and 2NT response after the takeout double of a minor suit — see *flip-flop* in the Appendix.

After an Overcall

If there is an overcall after the 1♣ or 1♦ opening, responder now has a *cuebid* of the opponent's suit available. This can be used to show a game-forcing hand worth 13 or more points. This frees up the response of 2NT to be used as a competitive bid.

- A new suit at the one level is still forcing and shows 6 or more points.
- A new suit at the two level is forcing and shows 10 or more points.
- A raise of opener's suit to the two level shows 6 to 9 points.
- A jump raise is invitational, showing 10 to 12 points.
- A response of 2NT is used as a natural, invitational bid — showing about 11 or 12 points — rather than as a game-forcing response showing 13 to 15 points.
- A *cuebid* of the opponent's suit is used as an artificial game force and usually shows a fit for opener's suit.

Here are some examples for responder (East) after the auction starts:

WEST	NORTH	**EAST**	SOUTH
1 ♦	1 ♠	?	

♠ 7 5
♥ 8 4 3
♦ K Q 8
♣ K 10 8 6 3

Raise to 2 ♦. You'd like to have four-card support for partner's minor suit, but three cards will have to do in a competitive situation. You don't have enough strength to bid a new suit at the two level, and a bid of 1NT is unattractive with two low cards in the opponent's suit. If you don't show diamond support now, you may not get another opportunity — if South raises to 2 ♠ for example.

♠ J 3
♥ A K 10 9 8 4
♦ K 8 3
♣ 6 4

Bid 2 ♥. You would have responded 1 ♥ without the interference, but you have enough strength to bid a new suit at the two level.

♠ K J 4
♥ Q J 5
♦ A 9 8 4
♣ J 7 5

Jump to 2NT. In a competitive situation, the 2NT response is only invitational. If North had passed, a jump to 2NT would be forcing, showing about 13 to 15 points. With strength in spades, 2NT is more descriptive than a limit raise to 3 ♦.

♠ J 4 2
♥ A 7
♦ K Q 8 7 5
♣ K 8 4

Cuebid 2 ♠. You are too strong to make a limit raise to 3 ♦ and 3NT would be risky with no sure stopper in the opponent's suit. A cuebid of the opponent's suit is forcing to game. You hope opener can bid notrump with some strength in spades. If not, you can show the diamond support at your next opportunity.

The use of the double after an opponent's overcall is discussed in the chapter on *negative doubles* in *More Commonly Used Conventions*.

SUMMARY

An opening bid of 1 ♣ or 1 ♦ usually shows a four-card or longer suit. It can occasionally be made on a three-card suit when opener has no five-card major and no four-card or longer minor. With a choice of four-card minor suits, open 1 ♦; with a choice of three-card minor suits, open 1 ♣.

Responder should look for a major-suit fit before raising opener's minor. With a choice of four-card suits to bid at the one level, responder bids the lowest-ranking suit first.

When raising opener's minor suit, use the following guidelines:

Raising Opener's Minor Suit

Except in competition, responder should have at least four-card support to raise diamonds and five-card support to raise clubs.

- With 6 to 9 points, raise to the two level.
- With 10 to 12 points, make a *limit raise* by jumping to the three level.
- With 13 or more points and an unbalanced hand, start by bidding a new suit.

Notrump Responses to a Minor Suit

- With 6 to 10 points, respond 1NT.
- With 11 or 12 points and a balanced hand, bid a new suit, intending to bid 2NT at the next opportunity.
- With 13 to 15 points and a balanced hand, bid 2NT, forcing.
- With 16 or 17 points and a balanced hand, bid 3NT.
- With 17 or more points and a good suit, responder can jump one level showing interest in reaching a slam contract. A double jump or triple jump in a new suit is preemptive, showing a long suit with a weak hand.

Responding to 1♣ or 1♦ after a Takeout Double

- A new suit at the one level is still forcing and shows 6 or more points.

- A single raise of opener's minor shows 6 to 9 points.

- A jump raise of opener's minor is treated as a *preemptive raise* rather than a limit raise.

- A response of 2NT is used to show a limit raise or better (*Jordan 2NT*), not a balanced hand of 13 to 15 points.

- A redouble shows a hand worth 10 or more points, usually without support for opener's suit.

Responding to 1♣ or 1♦ after an Overcall

- A new suit at the one level is still forcing and shows 6 or more points.

- A new suit at the two level is forcing and shows 10 or more points.

- A raise of opener's suit to the two level shows 6 to 9 points.

- A jump raise is invitational, showing 10 to 12 points.

- A response of 2NT is used as a natural, invitational bid — showing about 11 or 12 points — rather than as a game-forcing response showing 13 to 15 points.

- A *cuebid* of the opponent's suit is used as an artificial game force, usually showing a fit for opener's suit.

NOTE: See the Appendix (pages 316–325) for a discussion of these supplemental conventions and/or treatments.

Inverted Minor-Suit Raises

Jump Shift in Other Minor as a Forcing Raise

Splinter Bids

Bypassing Diamonds

1NT Response to 1♣

2NT as an Invitational Response to a Minor

Weak Jump shifts

Flip-Flop

The following exercises assume you are using the methods outlined in the summary.

Exercise One — Opening Minor Suits

What is your opening call with each of the following hands in first or second position? What would you call with the same hands if you have an opportunity to open in third or fourth position?

1) ♠ 4
   ♥ J 4
   ♦ K J 8 7 3
   ♣ A K 9 6 3
   _____

2) ♠ 7 5 4
   ♥ A Q 6
   ♦ K 3
   ♣ A Q J 8 5
   _____

3) ♠ 2
   ♥ A K J 3
   ♦ Q 9 7 4
   ♣ K 8 6 2
   _____

4) ♠ Q 8 7 3
   ♥ A 8 4
   ♦ A 9 6
   ♣ K 10 7
   _____

5) ♠ Q J 7 6
   ♥ K J 6 3
   ♦ Q 8 4
   ♣ A 7
   _____

6) ♠ A J 8 7 3
   ♥ A
   ♦ K J 9 6 5 3
   ♣ 3
   _____

Exercise Two — Bidding Up the Line

Partner opens the bidding 1 ♦, and the next player passes. What do you respond with the following hands?

1) ♠ Q 7 4 2
   ♥ 8 4
   ♦ A J 8 6 3
   ♣ 7 6
   _____

2) ♠ A K 9 4
   ♥ J 6 5 2
   ♦ 9 7 3
   ♣ Q 2
   _____

3) ♠ K 10 8 7 3
   ♥ Q J 9 4 2
   ♦ 8
   ♣ 10 5
   _____

4) ♠ 10 7 3
   ♥ K 9 4
   ♦ J 2
   ♣ A 10 8 7 4
   _____

5) ♠ Q 8 7 4
   ♥ Q 3 2
   ♦ 2
   ♣ K 10 7 6 2
   _____

6) ♠ K Q 6 3
   ♥ Q 4
   ♦ 8 7
   ♣ A Q 9 6 4
   _____

Exercise One — Opening Minor Suits

1) 1st/2nd: 1♦. Open the higher-ranking of two five-card suits.

    3rd: 1♦. Normal opening bid.

    4th: Pass. The *Rule of 15* — 12 high-card points plus one spade.

2) 1st/2nd: 1NT. With a balanced hand, open 1NT even with a five-card suit.

    3rd/4th: 1NT. No reason to change the opening bid.

3) 1st/2nd: 1♦. Open the higher ranking of two four-card minor suits.

    3rd: 1♥ or 1♦. Can open a good four-card major suit occasionally in third position.

    4th: Pass or 1♥ or 1♦. The *Rule of 15* suggests passing — 13 high-card points plus one spade. If you do open, 1♥ might be the best choice.

4) 1st/2nd: 1♣. With a choice between three-card minor suits, open 1♣.

    3rd: 1♣. Still open 1♣. The spades aren't robust enough to warrant opening the four-card suit.

    4th: 1♣. The *Rule of 15* — 13 high-card points plus four spades.

5) 1st/2nd: 1♦. Open the longer minor suit.

    3rd: 1♥ or 1♦. It might be more effective to open a four-card major suit. Opening 1♥ gives you the best chance of finding a major-suit fit.

    4th: 1♥ or 1♦. The *Rule of 15* — 13 high-card points plus four spades.

6) 1st/2nd: 1♦. Open the longest suit, even with a five-card major.

    3rd/4th: 1♦. Nothing has changed.

Exercise Two — Bidding Up the Line

1) 1♠. Showing the four-card major takes priority over raising diamonds.

2) 1♥. Bid four-card suits up the line. The quality of the suits is not important.

3) 1♠. With a choice of five-card suits, bid the higher-ranking.

4) 1NT. Not strong enough to bid a new suit at the two level.

5) 1♠. Although you aren't strong enough to bid 2♣, you can still show the four-card major.

6) 2♣. With enough strength to bid a new suit at the two level, bid the longer suit first; you can show the spades later.

Exercise Three — Raising Opener's Minor

Partner opens the bidding 1♣, and the next player passes. What do you respond with the following hands?

1) ♠ 10 8 2
    ♥ Q 9 3
    ♦ J 8 7 5 2
    ♣ 4 2

2) ♠ 9 5
    ♥ 7 4 3
    ♦ A 8 2
    ♣ K J 6 5 3

3) ♠ K 8 5
    ♥ Q 6 2
    ♦ J 9 5
    ♣ K 8 4 2

4) ♠ J 4
    ♥ K Q 9
    ♦ 6 5 3
    ♣ A J 8 7 5

5) ♠ 9 6
    ♥ J 9 8 2
    ♦ K 5
    ♣ A Q 8 6 3

6) ♠ 7 6
    ♥ A 8
    ♦ A 9 6 3
    ♣ K Q 10 8 2

Exercise Four — Responding in Notrump

Partner opens the bidding 1♦, and the next player passes. What do you respond with the following hands?

1) ♠ K J 9
    ♥ Q 10 4
    ♦ K 8 3
    ♣ A J 8 3

2) ♠ A Q
    ♥ K 10 5
    ♦ K 9 7 3
    ♣ K Q 6 5

3) ♠ Q J 7
    ♥ A J 5
    ♦ Q 6 3
    ♣ J 10 8 4

Exercise Three — Raising Opener's Minor

1) Pass. You don't have enough strength to respond. Don't be afraid that partner is short in clubs.

2) 2♣. With no major to bid, show the club support.

3) 1NT. With only four-card support for clubs and a balanced hand, 1NT is probably a better choice than 2♣.

4) 3♣. A jump raise is invitational, showing 11 or 12 points.

5) 1♥. Despite the good club fit, look for the major-suit fit first.

6) 1♦. You are too strong to make a limit raise of 3♣. Start with a new suit, intending to show the club support later.

Exercise Four — Responding in Notrump

1) 2NT. In response to a minor suit, 2NT is a forcing bid showing 13 to 15 points and a balanced hand.

2) 3NT. This shows a balanced hand with 16 or 17 points; it's more descriptive than starting with 1♦.

3) 2♣. With 11 points and a balanced hand, start by bidding a new suit, intending to make an invitational bid of 2NT at your next opportunity.

Exercise Five — Responding after a Takeout Double

As East, what do you do with each of these hands after the auction begins:

WEST	NORTH	**EAST**	SOUTH
1♣	Double	?	

1) ♠ 7 4
   ♥ 3
   ♦ Q 8 6 3 2
   ♣ K J 8 7 5

2) ♠ A Q 8
   ♥ 10 2
   ♦ 8 4 3
   ♣ A 10 8 7 6

3) ♠ 7 6
   ♥ K 9 6
   ♦ 8 5 4 3
   ♣ K J 10 8

Exercise Six — Responding after an Overcall

As East, what do you bid with each of the following hands after the auction starts:

WEST	NORTH	**EAST**	SOUTH
1♦	1♥	?	

1) ♠ J 8 5
   ♥ 7 3
   ♦ A Q 6 2
   ♣ K J 8 3

2) ♠ Q 10 8
   ♥ K J 7
   ♦ K Q 8
   ♣ 10 8 4 2

3) ♠ A 8 2
   ♥ 9 4
   ♦ K 10 9 7 4
   ♣ A Q 6

Exercise Five — Responding after a Takeout Double

1) 3♣. After the takeout double, this is a preemptive (weak) raise. With a stronger hand, you would redouble or bid 2NT.

2) 2NT (*Jordan*). After the takeout double, this shows a limit raise in partner's minor suit.

3) 2♣. This is likely to be a better choice than 1NT when you have so little strength in two suits. You'd prefer to have five-card support, but nothing's perfect.

Exercise Six — Responding after an Overcall

1) 3♦. The opponent's interference doesn't prevent you from making a limit raise.

2) 2NT. After the overcall, this is an invitational bid showing a balanced hand with 10 to 12 points and strength in the suit overcalled.

3) 2♥. The cuebid shows a game-forcing hand, usually with support for opener's suit.

Bid and Play — Deal 1

(E–Z Deal Cards: #5, Deal 1 — Dealer, North)

Suggested Bidding

WEST	NORTH	EAST	SOUTH
	1 ♦	Pass	1 ♥
Pass	1 ♠	Pass	3 ♠
Pass	Pass	Pass	

With a hand too weak to open 1NT and with no five-card major suit, North opens 1 ♦. With a choice of four-card suits to bid at the one level, South responds up the line by bidding the lower-ranking suit, 1 ♥. North continues bidding up the line by showing the four-card spade suit. South has uncovered an eight-card spade fit and has a hand of invitational strength — 10 to 12 points. To invite opener to game, South jumps to 3 ♠. With a minimum for the opening bid, North declines the invitation, and the partnership rests in partscore.

```
Dlr: North    ♠ A 7 5 4
Vul: None     ♥ 6 2
              ♦ A K 6 5
              ♣ Q 5 4
♠ Q 10 2            ♠ 9 8
♥ Q J 7 4     N    ♥ 10 9 8
♦ J 10 8   W   E   ♦ Q 9 4 2
♣ 9 7 2        S   ♣ A K J 6
              ♠ K J 6 3
              ♥ A K 5 3
              ♦ 7 3
              ♣ 10 8 3
```

Suggested Opening Lead

East is on lead and should select the ♣A, top of a broken sequence.

Suggested Play

Declarer has two diamond losers, three club losers, and at least one potential spade loser. There's not much that can be done about the club losers if the defenders are careful, but declarer can plan to trump two diamond losers in the dummy.

In the spade suit, with eight cards in the combined hands, the percentage play to avoid a spade loser is to play the ♠A and then take the spade finesse if the ♠Q doesn't appear — following the guideline 'eight ever, nine never.' On this deal, however, declarer can afford a spade loser and declarer has another use for dummy's spade — trumping diamond losers. After winning a trick, North should play the

♠A and ♠K. When the spades divide 3–2, declarer can go about trumping the two diamond losers in the dummy — ruffing dummy's hearts to get entries back to North's hand. Declarer loses a spade trick and three club tricks.

If the missing trumps were divided 4–1, declarer would still have a chance after taking the ♠A and ♠K. With two diamond tricks and two heart tricks to go along with the two top spades, declarer would have to hope to get three more spade tricks through ruffing diamonds and hearts.

On the actual deal, the defenders can defeat the contract if declarer tries the spade finesse. Taking the ♠A and ♠K is a form of safety play in a contract of 3♠. If North–South reach a contract of 4♠, declarer has little choice but to try the spade finesse and will likely be defeated two tricks.

Suggested Defense

The defenders must be careful to avoid letting declarer make 10 tricks in a spade contract. If East takes the first two tricks with the ♣A and ♣K, North's ♣Q will be established and the defenders will end with only one more trick, West's ♠Q. To prevent this, West should play the ♣2 on the first club trick — a discouraging signal — and East should respect West's signal and switch to another suit. The ♥10, leading through dummy's strength, would be a good choice for East.

After the heart switch, the defender's can't defeat the contract if declarer simply takes the ♠A and ♠K. West will eventually get a trick with the ♠Q and can lead a club to give the defenders the tricks they are entitled to in that suit.

If declarer takes the ♠A and then tries the spade finesse by playing a low spade to dummy's ♠J, the defenders can defeat the contract. For example, West can return a third round of spades to prevent declarer from getting enough tricks by ruffing losers. West can also lead back a club to defeat the contract. After the defenders win two more club tricks, East can lead the fourth round of clubs to promote West's ♠10 — if declarer doesn't ruff with dummy's ♠K, West can win the trick by ruffing with the ♠10; if declarer ruffs with dummy's ♠K, West gets the ♠10 later. Even if East returns a diamond, rather than the fourth round of clubs, the defenders will get another trick. (If East leads a heart after taking the club tricks, declarer can actually take the remainder of the tricks by ruffing a heart, ruffing a diamond, ruffing a heart, and taking the last trick with dummy's ♠K.)

Bid and Play — Deal 2

(E–Z Deal Cards: #5, Deal 2 — Dealer, East)

Suggested Bidding

WEST	NORTH	EAST	SOUTH
		1♦	Pass
3♦	Pass	3NT	Pass
Pass	Pass		

After East's opening bid of 1♦, West has a hand worth about 12 points — 10 high-card points plus 2 for distribution. West shows this hand by making a limit raise to 3♦. With 14 points and high cards in all of the other suits, East accepts the invitation by bidding 3NT. It should be easier to take nine tricks in notrump than 11 tricks in diamonds.

```
Dlr: East        ♠ Q J 9 5
Vul: N–S         ♥ K Q 9
                 ♦ Q 9 6
                 ♣ J 9 4
♠ K 6                      ♠ A 10 3
♥ 6 4 2          N         ♥ A 10 5
♦ K J 10 7 5 2  W   E      ♦ A 8 4 3
♣ K 3            S         ♣ Q 7 2
                 ♠ 8 7 4 2
                 ♥ J 8 7 3
                 ♦ —
                 ♣ A 10 8 6 5
```

Suggested Opening Lead

South is on lead and should lead the ♣6, fourth highest from the longest and strongest suit.

Suggested Play

The opening lead will establish a club trick for declarer and there should be nine more winners to take — two spades, one heart, and six diamonds — if the diamonds break 2–1, as one would normally expect. When the contract looks easy, however, declarer should be careful to guard against bad breaks. After winning the first club trick, if declarer leads the ♦A, the contract can no longer be made. With the diamonds dividing 3–0, North will have to get a trick with the ♦Q and can lead back a club. South will take four club tricks to defeat the contract.

East's first challenge comes at trick one. On the lead of the ♣6, declarer should play West's ♣K. This wins the trick and leaves East with the guarded

♣Q. It will now be safe to lose a trick to South, because South can't lead clubs again without giving East a trick with the queen. North has become the dangerous opponent because, if North gets the lead, East's ♣Q can be trapped. Since the only real danger now is that one of the opponents holds all three of the missing diamonds, declarer should start the diamond suit by playing dummy's ♦K. On the actual hand, South discards on the first round of diamonds and declarer can take a finesse against North's ♦Q. East ends up with 10 tricks.

If both opponents had followed suit to the first round of diamonds, taking 10 tricks would be easy, since the diamonds would have divided 2–1. What if South had all three of the missing diamonds? After winning the first trick with dummy's ♦K, East would now have to lose a trick to South's ♦Q. But that would be okay, since South isn't the dangerous opponent. South can't effectively lead clubs after winning the trick. The contract is still secure. Playing the ♦K first is a safety play, since it guarantees the contract.

If declarer had played the ♣3 from dummy on the first trick, North would play the ♣J to force East to win the trick with the ♣Q. With only the singleton ♣K left in dummy, now both opponents would be dangerous. If declarer loses a diamond trick to either opponent, the defenders are in a position to take all of their club tricks.

What if North held the ♣A rather than South? Dummy's ♣K would be taken by North's ace, and North would lead another club. Now East would have to hold up with the ♣Q until the third round of the suit. South would now become the dangerous opponent, so declarer should start diamonds by leading the ♦A to guard against South holding all three diamonds. If North has all three diamonds, there's no harm in losing a trick to North's ♦Q. North will probably have no clubs left to lead, and if North did have a fourth club, the clubs would have divided 4–4 so the contract would still be safe.

Suggested Defense

South gets the defenders off to the best start by leading a low club. If declarer subsequently loses a trick to North's ♦Q, North can return a club to defeat the contract. If declarer plays the hand correctly, there's nothing the defenders can do except be careful to hold on to the right cards to prevent East from taking more than 10 tricks.

Bid and Play — Deal 3

(E–Z Deal Cards: #5, Deal 3 — Dealer, South)

Suggested Bidding

WEST	NORTH	EAST	SOUTH
			1♣
1♥	2♥	Pass	2NT
Pass	3NT	Pass	Pass
Pass			

Playing five-card majors, South has to open the longer minor suit. With a choice between two three-card minor suits, South bids 1♣. West has a good six-card suit which can be overcalled at the one level. North has a fit with partner and enough strength to take the partnership to game. This can be shown by cuebidding the opponent's suit. North's cuebid shows the strength necessary to make a limit raise or to bid more in opener's suit.

Dlr: South
Vul: E–W

	♠ K 9 4	
	♥ J 4	
	♦ A 8 3	
	♣ A J 10 8 4	
♠ Q 8		♠ J 10 6 2
♥ A Q 10 8 5 2	N W E S	♥ 9 6
♦ Q J 7 2		♦ 10 6 4
♣ 7		♣ Q 5 3 2
	♠ A 7 5 3	
	♥ K 7 3	
	♦ K 9 5	
	♣ K 9 6	

With a minimum-strength balanced hand and a stopper in the opponent's suit, South rebids notrump at the cheapest available level. North now raises to game in notrump. It should be easier for the partnership to take nine tricks than 11.

Suggested Opening Lead

West is on lead and would lead the ♥8, fourth from longest and strongest.

Suggested Play

Declarer has two sure tricks in spades, two in diamonds, and two in clubs. With the heart lead, declarer is certain of a trick in that suit. Two more tricks are needed. The obvious source of the additional tricks is the club suit. It may be possible to take all five tricks in the club suit with the help of a successful finesse. Even if a trick is lost to the ♣Q, two additional tricks will be established in the suit.

There's the danger, however, that if a trick is lost to the ♣Q, the opponents can take enough heart tricks to defeat the contract. On the surface, it looks as though South will have to play the club suit by guessing which opponent has the ♣Q.

In situations like this, declarer should plan the play carefully before playing to the first trick. It may not appear to matter which heart is played from dummy — since declarer is sure to get one trick with the ♥K — but it makes all the difference to the play. Declarer should play dummy's ♥J on the first trick, with every expectation that it will win the trick! West has led the ♥8, fourth highest. With a holding such as ♥A 10 9 8 x or ♥Q 10 9 8 x, West would lead the ♥10, top of an interior sequence. Declarer can expect that the lead is from some holding such as ♥A Q 10 8 x or ♥A Q 9 8 x. If East doesn't have the ♥A or ♥Q, dummy's ♥J will win the first trick. This doesn't gain anything directly — declarer was always entitled to one, and only one, heart trick — but it secures the contract.

When the ♥J wins the first trick, East — not West — becomes the dangerous opponent. If East gets the lead, East can lead a heart, trapping declarer's remaining ♥K. West is no longer dangerous. If West gets the lead, West can't lead hearts without giving declarer a trick with the ♥K. That determines how declarer handles the club suit. After winning the ♥J, declarer should lead the ♣J from dummy, and when East produces a low club, declarer should play a low club from the South hand, taking the finesse. On the actual layout, the finesse succeeds. Declarer can now play a low club to the ♣9, repeating the finesse. The ♣K is played and South can cross to one of dummy's winners to take the ♣A and remaining club winner. South finishes with 10 tricks.

If the ♣Q had been in the West hand, the finesse would have lost but the contract would have been safe. West can't lead hearts without giving South a trick with the ♥K, and if West leads something else, declarer has four club winners to go with the other five winners. South makes at least nine tricks.

The finesse should be taken on the first round of the suit. If the ♣A is taken before finessing, declarer gets only three club tricks because of the unfortunate break in the suit. Declarer will then have a difficult time taking nine tricks without giving East the lead.

Suggested Defense

After an opening lead of the ♥8, the defense can't defeat the contract if declarer handles both the heart and club suits correctly. If East does get a trick with the ♣Q, a heart return will defeat the contract two tricks.

It may be interesting to speculate what would happen if West led a different heart at trick one. If West leads the ♥A and continues with the ♥Q after seeing dummy, declarer can make the contract with the hold up play. Now West becomes the dangerous opponent, and a club trick can safely be lost to East's ♣Q. More spectacular is the imaginative opening lead of the ♥Q. Declarer can still hold up on the first trick and make the contract, or declarer can make the contract by guessing where the ♣Q lies. If West is up to making such a sensational lead, then declarer may be up to finding an appropriate reply.

Bid and Play — Deal 4

(E–Z Deal Cards: #5, Deal 4 — Dealer, West)

Suggested Bidding

WEST	NORTH	EAST	SOUTH
1♣	Double	2NT	Pass
3♣	Pass	Pass	Pass

West has enough to open the bidding but no five-card major suit. With a choice of three-card minor suits, West opens 1♣. After West's opening bid, North has a reasonable hand for a takeout double — a hand worth an opening bid and support for all of the unbid suits. With 10 high-card points, East can redouble, but that may give North–South room to find their best contract. With five-card support for opener's minor and a hand worth a limit raise, East can make a conventional jump to 2NT — a jump to 3♣ over the takeout double would be preemptive.

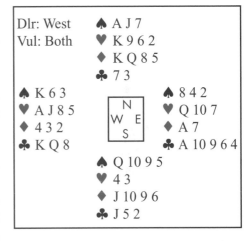

Dlr: West
Vul: Both

♠ A J 7
♥ K 9 6 2
♦ K Q 8 5
♣ 7 3

♠ K 6 3
♥ A J 8 5
♦ 4 3 2
♣ K Q 8

♠ 8 4 2
♥ Q 10 7
♦ A 7
♣ A 10 9 6 4

♠ Q 10 9 5
♥ 4 3
♦ J 10 9 6
♣ J 5 2

South, who would have responded 1♠ to the takeout double if East had passed or redoubled, doesn't have enough to come into the auction at the three level. West has a minimum-strength hand for the opening bid and returns to the agreed trump suit by bidding 3♣. Even with a balanced hand, West shouldn't pass partner's 2NT bid, since it's artificial and doesn't guarantee stoppers in the other suits.

North has nothing further to say, and East respects partner's decision to stop in partscore. The final decision is with South. Having passed over 2NT, South might consider competing at this point but will probably be dissuaded by the vulnerability. If South guesses to compete with 3♦, North–South will land on their feet, since that contract can be made. If South tries 3♠, the result will not be as cheerful, since East–West can defeat that contract at least one trick, and likely two tricks or more. North-South might have an easier time finding their best contract if the auction had proceeded a little differently. For example:

WEST	NORTH	EAST	SOUTH
1♣	Double	Redouble	1♠
Pass	Pass	2♣	2♦
Pass	Pass	3♣	Pass
Pass	3♦	?	

Aggressive bidding by North-South, but now East-West are likely to end with a poor result.

Suggested Opening Lead

North doesn't have a particularly attractive choice of leads but will probably start with the ♦K, top of touching honors.

Suggested Play

In 3♣, West has three potential spade losers, a heart loser, and two diamond losers — assuming the club suit behaves reasonably. One of the diamond losers can be trumped in dummy and one of East's spade losers can be discarded on West's extra heart winner after the ♥K has been driven out. In effect, West hopes to take five club tricks, a diamond trick, and three heart tricks. There's also the possibility that South holds the ♠A, but that's unlikely in light of North's takeout double.

There is a danger. If South can gain the lead, the defenders may be able to take three spade tricks — by trapping West's ♠K — to go along with a heart trick and a diamond trick. The only suit in which South might get the lead is diamonds. To prevent this, West should duck the opening lead of the ♦K, letting North win the trick. Now the contract is not in danger since North can't profitably attack spades. Assuming North leads another diamond, West wins with dummy's ♦A, draws trumps, and leads the ♥Q. If North doesn't win the first heart trick with the ♥K, declarer continues with the ♥10. North must take the ♥K on the first or second round of the suit or the defenders won't get a heart trick. After winning the ♥K, North still can't play spades without giving West a trick with the ♠K. Whether North leads a diamond or a heart, declarer wins the trick and discards one of dummy's spades on the fourth round of hearts. Declarer's only losers are two spade tricks, a heart trick, and a diamond trick.

Suggested Defense

If North leads the ♦K against West's 3♣ contract, the defenders have a chance if declarer takes the first trick with East's ♦A. On this trick, South should play the ♦J. Signaling with an honor in this situation tells partner that you don't have the next higher-ranking card — the ♦Q — but do hold the next lower-ranking card — the ♦10. This is valuable information for North. Suppose declarer now draws trumps and takes the heart finesse. North wins the ♥K and, with the knowledge that South holds the ♦10, leads a low diamond. South wins this trick and can lead a spade — the ♠10, top of an interior sequence — trapping West's ♠K. The defenders get three spade tricks, a heart trick, and a diamond trick.

If declarer ducks North's ♦K, the best North–South can do is defend carefully to hold declarer to nine tricks. If East–West end in a notrump contract, the defenders can hold declarer to seven tricks by leading a diamond. If declarer tries to develop an extra trick, the defenders can trap West's ♠K after taking their diamond winners.

CHAPTER 6

The Subsequent Auction

THE SUBSEQUENT AUCTION

After the opening bid and initial response, the auction can continue in many different directions. It is important for the partnership to distinguish between forcing and non-forcing bids. In practice, no bid is 100% forcing. You can always "take a view" and pass a theoretically forcing bid. This is poor practice, however, because it will start to undermine the partnership confidence in its bidding methods.

It would be comfortable to have simple guidelines to decide whether a bid is forcing. Even a straightforward agreement, however, such as "a new suit by responder is forcing," runs into exceptions. Most partnerships treat a new-suit bid by responder as non-forcing, if responder is a *passed hand.* You'll need some agreement. Here are common understandings about forcing and non-forcing bidding sequences.

OPENER'S NON-FORCING REBIDS

After a new-suit bid at the one level, the following rebids by opener are not forcing:

- A new, lower-ranking suit.
- A raise or rebid of an "old" suit.
- A bid of notrump.

WEST	NORTH	**EAST**	SOUTH
1♥	Pass	1♠	Pass
2♣	Pass	?	

West's 2♣ rebid is non-forcing. West is showing an unbalanced hand with at least five hearts and four or more clubs. It will usually be a minimum-strength hand of 13 to 16 points, but it could also be a medium-strength hand of 17 or 18 points — not quite strong enough to *jump shift.* Although 2♣ isn't forcing, East will only pass with a minimum-strength hand for the 1♠ response and a preference for clubs as the trump suit.

WEST	NORTH	**EAST**	SOUTH
1 ♥	Pass	1 ♠	Pass
3 ♥	Pass	?	

West's 3 ♥ rebid shows a medium-strength hand with a six-card or longer heart suit. East can pass with a minimum-strength hand of 6 to 8 points. The situation would be similar if West rebid 3 ♠. East could decline the invitation by passing. Even a jump to 4 ♥ or 4 ♠ by West would be non-forcing, although it would show a maximum-strength hand of 19 to 21 points.

WEST	NORTH	**EAST**	SOUTH
1 ♥	Pass	1 ♠	Pass
2NT	Pass	?	

Following the notrump structure in Chapter 1, West's rebid shows a balanced hand of 18 or 19 points — too strong for an opening 1NT (15 to 17) and too weak for an opening 2NT (20 or 21). East can pass with a bare minimum for the 1 ♠ response. (A partnership that uses this rebid to show a balanced hand of 19 to 21 points would treat this rebid as forcing.) Similarly, a 1NT or 3NT rebid by West would be non-forcing.

A popular style after a new-suit bid at the two level is to treat all bids as forcing until game is reached (see the chapter on *Two-Over-One* in *More Commonly Used Conventions*). There are other possible agreements. Some partnerships treat any rebid by the opener below the level of 2NT as forcing once responder bids a new suit at the two level.

WEST	NORTH	**EAST**	SOUTH
1 ♠	Pass	2 ♥	Pass
2 ♠	Pass	?	

Since the 2 ♠ rebid shows a minimum-strength hand, East could pass at this point. A raise to 3 ♥ by West would be non-forcing. If West had rebid 3 ♠, showing a medium-strength hand, the partnership would be forced to the game level. That makes sense since opener would be showing 17 or 18 points and responder has shown at least 10 with the 2 ♥ response.

WEST	NORTH	**EAST**	SOUTH
1♠	Pass	2♣	Pass
2NT	Pass	?	

In standard methods, North's 2NT rebid shows a minimum-strength balanced hand and is non-forcing.

OPENER'S FORCING REBIDS

Opener's Jump Shift

When responder bids a new suit at the one level, a jump rebid by opener in a new suit — a *jump shift* — is forcing to the game level. Opener's jump shift shows a hand worth about 19 or more points. Since responder is expected to have 6 or more points for the initial response, the partnership should have enough combined strength for a game contract. Consider the following hands for opener after the auction starts:

WEST	NORTH	EAST	SOUTH
1♦	Pass	1♥	Pass
?			

♠ A
♥ 10 4
♦ A K Q 10 4
♣ A Q 10 9 3

Rebid 3♣. This is a classic jump shift. Opener's hand is worth 21 points — 19 high-card points plus 1 point each for the five-card suits. Assuming responder has at least 6 points, the partnership has the combined strength for a game contract. A rebid of 2♣ would not be forcing, so opener has to jump shift to make sure that the auction keeps going.

♠ A K 10 4
♥ K J 3
♦ A Q 9 6 4
♣ 3

Rebid 2♠. There are only 17 high-card points, but the hand is worth more because of the good heart support and singleton club. With only three-card support for hearts, it's difficult to show the fit right away — a jump raise to game would promise four-card support. Instead, jump shift, intending to show the heart support at the next opportunity.

♠ Q 8 3
♥ 2
♦ A K 10 9 7
♣ A K 6 3

Rebid 2♣. This hand isn't strong enough to commit the partnership to game with a jump shift. 2♣ shows either a minimum- or medium-strength hand. If responder doesn't have enough to bid again, the partnership is unlikely to belong in game.

If responder bids a new suit at the two level, *any new suit by opener is forcing* at least one round. There's no need for opener to jump shift with a strong hand. Responder has 10 or more points and must bid again.

WEST	NORTH	EAST	SOUTH
1♠	Pass	2♣	Pass
?			

♠ A Q 8 7 4
♥ K 7 3
♦ A Q 9 5
♣ 4

Rebid 2♦. Once responder shows enough strength to bid a new suit at the two level, opener, with 16 total points, knows the partnership has enough combined strength for game. It's not necessary for opener to guess the best contract right away. A new-suit bid is forcing and leaves room for the partnership to explore.

♠ A K J 8 5
♥ A K 9 3
♦ 8 4
♣ Q J

Rebid 2♥. With 18 high-card points plus 1 for length, opener has enough strength to jump shift. A jump shift is not necessary, however, since the 2♥ rebid is forcing. Responder's 2♣ bid guarantees another bid unless opener specifically limits the hand to a minimum opening bid — by rebidding 2♠, 2NT, or 3♣. Some players still use the jump shift in this situation, but partnerships that use *splinter bids* (see the Appendix) would treat a jump to 3♥ as a splinter bid, rather than a jump shift.

Opener's Reverse

When responder bids a new suit, opener's rebid of a new suit without a jump that prevents responder from returning to opener's original suit at the two level is called a *reverse*.

Compare these two auctions:

1) WEST	NORTH	EAST	SOUTH
1 ♦	Pass	1 ♠	Pass
2 ♣	Pass	?	

2) WEST	NORTH	EAST	SOUTH
1 ♦	Pass	1 ♠	Pass
2 ♥	Pass	?	

In the first auction, opener — West — hasn't reversed. If responder — East — prefers diamonds to clubs, responder can return to opener's original suit at the two level by bidding 2 ♦ . In the second auction, West's bidding is a *reverse*. If East wants to return to diamonds, East will have to bid 3 ♦ , not 2 ♦ .

To reverse, opener needs a medium or maximum-strength hand — 17 or more points — since responder might be forced to go to the three level with as few as 6 points. Suppose this is responder's (East) hand in the above sequences:

♠ K 8 6 3 2   Given the first auction above, responder prefers dia-
♥ 8 2   monds to clubs and can return to opener's first suit
♦ Q 9 6   by bidding 2 ♦ — this is called *giving preference*.
♣ 8 4 2   This takes the auction no higher than the two level.
If opener has a minimum-strength hand, the partner-
ship can stop in its best fit at a low level. Given the second auction above, responder prefers diamonds to hearts but can only return to opener's first suit by bidding 3 ♦ . If opener were to reverse with a minimum hand of about 13 points, the partnership could wind up at the three level with as few as 19 combined points — less than half the high cards in the deck. For this reason, opener shouldn't reverse with a minimum. If opener has 17 or more points, even if responder has as few as 6 points, the partnership will have at least 23 combined points — which should be enough for a three-level contract.

Most partnerships treat opener's reverse as *forcing for one round*. It doesn't commit the partnership to the game level — unlike a jump shift — but responder must bid again and opener must make at least one more bid unless the partnership has reached a game contract.

Consider the following hands for opener after the bidding has started:

WEST	NORTH	EAST	SOUTH
1♦	Pass	1♠	Pass
?			

♠ K 3
♥ A K 8 4
♦ A Q J 10 8
♣ 8 2

Rebid 2♥. With a medium-strength hand, opener is strong enough to reverse to show the heart suit. Responder is forced to bid again, but the partnership should be safe at the three level even if responder has a minimum hand.

♠ J 3
♥ A 8 4 2
♦ A Q J 10 8
♣ 8 2

Rebid 2♦. With a minimum-strength hand, opener doesn't have enough to reverse by rebidding 2♥. That would be a forcing bid and might push the auction to the three level when both partners have minimum hands. Instead, opener must be content with rebidding the diamond suit. If responder has enough to bid again, the partnership can still find a heart fit if one exists. Otherwise, the partnership can rest safely at the two level.

♠ K Q 5
♥ A Q J 8
♦ A K 9 6 2
♣ 4

Rebid 2♥. With fine support for responder's spade suit, this is a maximum-strength hand. An immediate raise to 4♠ would show strength, but would also promise four-card support — since responder may have only a four-card spade suit. Instead, opener can start with a *reverse*, which is forcing. At the next opportunity, opener can show spade support and a strong hand with only three-card support. Opener doesn't need to jump shift to 3♥ with this hand — which would technically be a "jump shift reverse" — because the 2♥ rebid is forcing. A jump to 3♥ in this sequence is usually reserved for some conventional meaning, such as a *splinter bid*.

♠ K Q 5
♥ 4
♦ A K 9 6 2
♣ A Q J 8

Rebid 3♣. This hand is similar to the one above, but with the clubs and hearts exchanged. It shows one difference between a jump shift and a reverse. With a lower-ranking second suit and a maximum-strength hand, opener has to jump shift to 3♣ to force responder to bid again, since a simple rebid of 2♣ wouldn't be forcing. In the previous example, the second suit was higher-ranking than the original suit, so opener could use the reverse as a forcing bid. The other difference between a jump shift and a reverse is that the jump shift is forcing to game. The reverse is only forcing for one round — although opener may subsequently force the partnership to the game level.

Responder's Rebid after a Reverse

The modern style is to treat a reverse as forcing. Responder needs a way to show a weak hand. Some partnerships treat any bid of an old suit by responder — a rebid of responder's suit at the two level or a raise of one of opener's suits to the three level without a jump — as a minimum-strength hand, but the modern style is as follows:

- A rebid of responder's suit at the two level shows a five-card or longer suit and is forcing for one round. If opener rebids 2NT, raises responder's suit, or rebids an old suit at the three level, responder can now pass with a minimum hand.

- A rebid of 2NT is artificial (conventional) and denies five or more cards in responder's suit. If opener rebids a suit at the three level, responder can now pass with a minimum hand.

- Any other rebid by responder shows more than minimum strength and commits the partnership to at least the game level.

This agreement is sometimes referred to as *Ingberman* — after Monroe Ingberman of White Plains, New York, who made several contributions to bidding theory — but is more popularly known as *lebensohl over reverses*. Here are examples for responder after the auction begins:

WEST	NORTH	**EAST**	SOUTH
1♣	Pass	1♠	Pass
2♥	Pass	?	

♠ Q 10 8 6 3
♥ 8 2
♦ A 9 6 4
♣ 7 6

Rebid 2♠. The rebid of responder's suit at the two level promises nothing more than a minimum-strength hand, but shows at least a five-card suit. With a medium-strength hand, opener can raise to 3♠ with three-card support, or rebid 2NT, or return to 3♣ without a fit for spades. None of these bids would be forcing. With a maximum-strength hand, opener can raise to 4♠ with three-card support, jump to 3NT with no fit, or rebid 3♥ to show at least five hearts and at least six clubs — since opener bid clubs first.

♠ K J 8 4
♥ 9 7
♦ Q 10 8 7 2
♣ 5 3

Rebid 2NT. With only a four-card spade suit, responder rebids 2NT to show a minimum hand. The 2NT rebid is artificial (conventional) and doesn't promise a balanced hand; it merely shows a weak hand without five or more spades. Opener must bid again, but responder can then pass if opener simply rebids 3♣.

♠ K 9 7 4
♥ Q 8
♦ J 5 3
♣ A 8 6 3

Rebid 3♣. Playing *lebensohl over reverses*, any bid other than a rebid of responder's suit or 2NT is forward-going and commits the partnership to at least the game level. Without this agreement, a simple preference to 3♣ would be interpreted as a weak hand.

RESPONDER'S NON-FORCING REBIDS

Suppose the auction starts off like this:

WEST	NORTH	**EAST**	SOUTH
1♦	Pass	1♥	Pass
1♠	Pass	?	

At this point, most of responder's bids are non-forcing. The usual partnership agreement is the following:

- A bid of 1NT or an old suit at the two level — 2 ♦, 2 ♥, or 2 ♠ — shows a minimum-strength hand of 6 to 10 points.

- A bid of 2NT or an old suit at the three level — 3 ♦, 3 ♥, or 3 ♠ — shows an invitational-strength hand of 11 or 12 points.

- A bid at the game level — 3NT, 4 ♥, 4 ♠, or 5 ♦ — shows a game-going hand of 13 to 16 points.

Consider the following hands for East after the above auction:

♠ Q 6
♥ K 10 8 4
♦ J 9
♣ Q 10 8 3 2

Rebid 1NT. This shows a hand of 6 to 10 points with no preference for either of opener's suits. East shouldn't bid 2♣ at this point, since that would be a forcing bid and is likely to get the partnership too high. The 1NT bid isn't forcing; opener can pass with a minimum-strength balanced hand.

♠ 8 3
♥ K J 10 8 6 5
♦ 8 4
♣ Q 6 2

Rebid 2 ♥. The rebid of an old suit at the two level shows a minimum-strength hand for responder, 6 to 10 points. Opener is expected to pass with a minimum-strength hand, leaving the partnership in responder's choice of partscore. Opener should bid again only with a very unbalanced hand or extra strength.

♠ K 8 7 3
♥ Q J 9 4
♦ 4 2
♣ Q 6 2

Rebid 2♠. The raise of opener's second suit to the two level shows a minimum-strength hand for responder. Although the raise theoretically shows 6 to 10 points, with a bare 6 or 7 points responder could pass 1 ♠ — since it's not a forcing rebid by opener. Responder will have 8 to 10 points to raise opener's second suit.

♠ J 7 4
♥ A 8 6 2
♦ J 9 6 5
♣ 8 2

Rebid 2 ♦. Having failed to find a heart fit, responder returns to opener's original suit at the two level, showing a minimum-strength response. Returning to opener's original suit is referred to as *giving preference*. Giving preference at the cheapest available level doesn't show any extra values for responder.

♠ 10 8 3
♥ K J 10 5
♦ Q 4
♣ A J 10 3

Rebid 2NT. A jump to 2NT is invitational, showing 11 or 12 points. It shows a hand too strong to rebid 1NT, but not strong enough to go all the way to 3NT. With a minimum-strength hand, opener can pass.

♠ J 3
♥ K Q 7 2
♦ A J 8 4 3
♣ 9 5

Rebid 3 ♦. An old suit at the three level is invitational, showing 11 or 12 points. This is sometimes referred to as a *jump preference*; it shows a better hand than a simple preference to 2 ♦, but not enough to commit the partnership to game.

♠ A 10 9 4
♥ A Q 8 6
♦ K 8 3
♣ 7 2

Rebid 4♠. A jump to 3 ♠ — an old suit at the three level — would be invitational. With a game-going hand and a fit with one of opener's suits, responder should take the partnership to game.

RESPONDER'S FORCING REBIDS

Fourth-Suit Forcing

Since most of responder's available rebids are non-forcing after three suits have been bid, responder needs a way to make a forcing bid when more information is needed to settle on a contract. For example, consider East's rebid with the following hand after the auction has started:

WEST	NORTH	EAST	SOUTH
1 ♦	Pass	1 ♥	Pass
1 ♠	Pass	?	

♠ 5 3
♥ A K J 8 3
♦ A J 10 8
♣ 7 4

East is awkwardly placed for a rebid. The partnership has the combined strength needed for game, but the best contract isn't clear. The partnership may belong in 3NT, 4♥, 5♦, or even 6♦. East doesn't want to jump to 3NT without any high cards in clubs, the unbid suit. A jump to 3♥ — an old suit — is invitational and promises at least a six-card suit since opener hasn't shown support. A jump to 4♥ could put the partnership in a poor contract — opener may not have any hearts. A rebid of 2♦ shows a minimum-strength response of 6 to 10 points, and a jump to 3♦ — an old suit — is invitational, showing 11 or 12. A jump to 4♦ or 5♦ would take the partnership beyond 3NT, which could be the best spot.

In such a situation, most partnerships agree to play the bid of the fourth suit as artificial (conventional) and forcing. This is commonly referred to as *fourth suit forcing*, but this is a misnomer since the bid of the fourth suit by responder would be forcing — but natural — when playing standard methods. The real significance of the agreement is that the bid of the fourth suit is *artificial* — it says nothing about the actual holding in the fourth suit. With the above hand, responder would rebid 2♣ as a forcing bid. This has nothing to do with clubs; it only requests that opener make a further descriptive bid.

Partnerships can have different agreements about whether fourth suit is forcing for only one round, or whether it's forcing to the game level. If the fourth suit is bid at the two level or higher, the most popular style is to treat it as a *game-forcing* bid — since responder has other ways to show hands of invitational strength.

Opener's Rebid after Fourth-Suit Forcing

When responder bids the fourth suit, opener should bid notrump only when holding some strength in the fourth suit, since responder hasn't promised anything in the suit. Opener can raise with four cards in the suit — since there is the possibility that a fit exists — but not if it would take the partnership beyond 3NT. Otherwise, opener rebids an old suit or shows belated support for responder's first suit. Here are some examples of how the auction might continue after responder bids the fourth suit:

West			East
♠ Q J 10 8	**WEST**	**EAST**	♠ 5 3
♥ 7	1 ♦	1 ♥	♥ A K J 8 3
♦ K Q 6 4 2	1 ♠	2 ♣	♦ A J 10 8
♣ K Q 10	2NT	3 ♦	♣ 7 4
	3NT	Pass	

After responder bids the fourth suit, opener rebids 2NT to show the values in clubs. West doesn't need a balanced hand to bid notrump at this point, only some strength in the fourth suit. East's 3 ♦ bid shows diamond support and is forcing — with diamond support and a hand of only invitational strength, responder would have jumped to 3 ♦ over opener's 1 ♠ rebid. West, with no interest in trying for 11 or 12 tricks in a diamond contract, suggests a final contract of 3NT, and responder has no reason to disagree.

West			East
♠ A K J 4	**WEST**	**EAST**	♠ 5 3
♥ Q 7 2	1 ♦	1 ♥	♥ A K J 8 3
♦ K 6 4 2	1 ♠	2 ♣	♦ A J 10 8
♣ 10 6	2 ♥	4 ♥	♣ 7 4
	Pass		

Without any strength in the fourth suit, opener shows belated support for responder's hearts. This can't be four cards, since opener would have raised immediately with four-card support. Having found a heart fit, responder doesn't need to show diamond support and can simply put the partnership in game.

West			East
♠ A K 10 6	**WEST**	**EAST**	♠ 5 3
♥ 9 4	1 ♦	1 ♥	♥ A K J 8 3
♦ K Q 7 5 3	1 ♠	2 ♣	♦ A J 10 8
♣ 10 6	2 ♦	3 ♦	♣ 7 4
	3 ♠	5 ♦	
	Pass		

Without any strength in the fourth suit or support for hearts, opener rebids diamonds. Responder now shows diamond support. This is a forcing bid, since responder would not bid the fourth suit before raising diamonds with an invitational-strength hand. Opener shows spade strength, in case the partnership belongs in 3NT. With neither partner holding strength in clubs, responder settles for game in diamonds.

West	WEST	EAST	East
♠ A Q J 6	1 ♦	1 ♥	♠ 5 3
♥ Q	1 ♠	2 ♣	♥ A K J 8 3
♦ K 9 7 5	3 ♣	3 ♦	♦ A J 10 8
♣ J 10 6 3	3NT	Pass	♣ 7 4

West raises the fourth suit to finish describing the hand. East shows diamond support and opener suggests playing in notrump. East, knowing opener has at most one heart — opener bid diamonds, spades, and clubs — can't see a better contract.

West	WEST	EAST	East
♠ K Q J 6	1 ♦	1 ♥	♠ 5 3
♥ 2	1 ♠	2 ♣	♥ A K J 8 3
♦ K Q 7 6 5 2	2 ♦	3 ♦	♦ A J 10 8
♣ A 3	4NT	5 ♥	♣ 7 4
	6 ♦	Pass	

West rebids the six-card diamond suit after responder's 2 ♣ bid. When responder shows diamond support — and at least game-going values — opener uses the *Blackwood* convention (see *More Commonly Used Conventions*) to get the partnership to the excellent slam contract.

If the fourth suit is bid at the one level, most partnerships don't treat the sequence as forcing to game. Suppose the auction starts this way:

WEST	NORTH	**EAST**	SOUTH
1 ♣	Pass	1 ♦	Pass
1 ♥	Pass	1 ♠	Pass
?			

In this sequence, responder's 1♠ bid is forcing for one round, but it could be either a natural bid looking for a fit in spades or it could be artificial (conventional). East might hold either of these hands:

♠ K 10 8 3	East is simply looking for a spade fit. East intends to
♥ 9 4	pass West's next bid, unless West jumps to show some
♦ A J 8 6 2	extra strength. For example, if West now bids 1NT,
♣ 10 3	2♣, 2♦, or 2♠, East will pass. If West bids 3♠,
	East will accept the invitation and continue to 4♠.

♠ 9 6	East has a forcing raise in clubs but doesn't have a
♥ 4 2	way to show it right away. An initial raise to 3♣
♦ A Q 6 2	would be a limit raise, so East starts by responding
♣ A K J 8 7	1♦. Over the 1♥ rebid by opener, East still doesn't

have a way to show the strong club support. A bid of 2♣ would show 6 to 10 points, and a jump to 3♣ would be invitational, showing 11 or 12 points. East has to bid the fourth suit as a conventional forcing bid, intending to show club support on the next round. If West rebids 1NT or raises to 2♠, for example, East will bid 3♣. This would now be forcing, since East could have shown an invitational hand with clubs by jumping to 3♣ on the previous round.

After a 1NT Rebid by Opener

When opener rebids 1NT, responder can sign off by passing or by bidding an old — previously bid — suit at the two level. Responder can invite game by raising to 2NT or by jumping to the three level in an old suit. With a game-going hand, responder may need to make a forcing bid if the best final contract is still in doubt. Since only two suits have been bid, *fourth suit forcing* is unavailable. While some partnerships play that any new suit bid by responder at this point is forcing, the more common agreement is that a new suit by responder is forcing only if it's a *reverse* or a *jump shift*.

For example, consider the following hands for East after the auction begins:

WEST	NORTH	**EAST**	SOUTH
1 ♦	Pass	1 ♥	Pass
1NT	Pass	?	

♠ 3
♥ K Q 8 7 5
♦ 7 3
♣ A K J 5 4

Bid 3♣. If the partnership treats 2♣ as non-forcing, then responder has to bid 3♣ — a *jump shift by responder* — as a forcing bid. Opener must bid again, and the partnership is committed to at least game.

♠ A 8 4
♥ A 10 8 6 3
♦ K Q 7 2
♣ 6

Bid 2♠. The partnership may belong in 3NT, but might also belong in 4 ♥, 5 ♦, or 6 ♦. A bid of 2 ♦ at this point would be a sign off, and a jump to 3 ♦ would only be invitational. To force opener to bid again, responder can bid 2♠. This is referred to as a *reverse by responder* because opener would have to go to the three level — 3 ♥ — to show support for responder's first suit. Responder's 2♠ bid isn't looking for a spade fit, since opener has already denied a four-card spade suit by rebidding 1NT rather than 1♠. Instead, it's an artificial (conventional) forcing bid, committing the partnership to the game level and telling opener that responder needs more information to determine the best contract. Responder can show diamond support on the next round of bidding — if opener rebids 2NT or 3♣, for example. Opener will have a chance to show three-card support for hearts, having denied four cards by failing to raise on the previous round.

♠ 3
♥ K 9 6 4 2
♦ J 10 8 6 3
♣ Q 4

Bid 2 ♦. By returning to an old suit at the two level, responder is showing a minimum-strength hand and opener is expected to pass.

♠ 8 4
♥ K J 10 8 7 3
♦ Q 8 2
♣ K 5

Bid 3♥. A jump to the three level in a previously bid suit is invitational, showing 11 or 12 points. With a minimum, opener can pass. Otherwise, opener can accept the invitation by bidding game.

♠ K Q 9 5
♥ A J 8 6
♦ 7 3
♣ K 10 4

Bid 3NT. Opener hasn't supported hearts and would have rebid 1♠ with a four-card spade suit — bidding up the line. Without the possibility of an eight-card major suit fit, responder can take the partnership directly to the best game.

♠ 4
♥ Q 9 7 5 2
♦ 4 2
♣ K J 8 6 3

Bid 2♣. Leaving partner to play in 1NT when responder holds an unbalanced hand doesn't appear to be a good choice, but rebidding 2♥ may put the partnership in a 5–2 fit. The best option is to rebid 2♣, giving opener the choice of passing and playing with clubs as trump or returning to 2♥ with three-card support for that suit. Although 2♣ is a new suit by responder, most partnerships do not treat this as a forcing bid after a 1NT rebid by opener, because opener doesn't have to go to the three level to show preference for responder's first suit. For alternative ways of handling the auction after opener's 1NT rebid, see *new minor forcing* and *checkback Stayman* at the end of this chapter.

After a 2NT Rebid by Opener

Consider the following auction:

WEST	NORTH	**EAST**	SOUTH
1♦	Pass	1♠	Pass
2NT	Pass	?	

If the partnership opens 1NT with 15 to 17 points and 2NT with 20 or 21 — as recommended in Chapter 1 — then the above sequence shows only 18 or 19 points and a balanced hand. Using this approach, most partnerships treat opener's 2NT rebid as non-forcing. Responder can pass with only 6 or 7 points. Any further bid by responder below the game level, however, is treated as forcing — even an old suit at the three level.

Here are some hands for East after the auction has started as above:

♠ K 9 6 5
♥ Q 3
♦ 5 4
♣ 10 8 7 5 2

Pass. Having scraped up a 1♠ response, it's best to leave partner in 2NT at this point. Even if partner has 19 points, there is little chance for a game contract. Wish partner luck when you put down the dummy!

♠ K J 8 7 4
♥ A 8 2
♦ 9 4 2
♣ 7 3

Bid 3♠. Opener's 2NT rebid denies four-card support for spades, but opener could hold three spades. The 3♠ rebid is forcing, asking opener to choose between 3NT and 4♠.

♠ A 8 6 3 2
♥ K J 7 4
♦ 3
♣ 9 5 4

Bid 3♥. Opener may have four hearts or three-card spade support. Opener can rebid 3NT with a doubleton spade and only three hearts.

♠ A Q 6 3 2
♥ 4
♦ K J 8 3
♣ 10 7 2

Bid 3♦. There could be a slam in diamonds or spades. The 3♦ bid is forcing. Opener can show belated spade support or bid 3NT with no interest in slam. With a good hand for diamonds, opener can raise to 4♦ or make a cuebid.

SUMMARY

Opener's Forcing and Non-Forcing Rebids

After a response at the one level:

- Opener can force responder to bid again by making a *jump shift* — a jump bid in a new suit. A jump shift shows 19 or more points and commits the partnership to game.

- Opener can force responder to bid again by making a *reverse* — the bid of a new suit that prevents responder from returning to opener's original suit at the two level. A reverse shows 17 or more points and is forcing for at least one round.

- Other rebids by opener are non-forcing.

After a response at the two level using standard methods:

- A new suit by opener is forcing for one round.

- A jump rebid is forcing to game.

- A simple rebid of opener's suit, a raise of responder's suit, or a rebid of 2NT is non-forcing.

Responder's Rebid after Opener's Reverse (lebensohl over reverses)

After a reverse by opener:

- A rebid of responder's major suit at the two level shows a five-card suit but doesn't promise any extra strength.

- A rebid of 2NT by responder shows a minimum hand.

- Any other bid by responder commits the partnership to game.

Responder's Forcing and Non-Forcing Rebids

After the partnership has bid three suits (without a jump shift or reverse):

- A bid of 1NT or an old suit at the two level is non-forcing, showing a minimum-strength hand of 6 to 10 points.

- A bid of 2NT or an old suit at the three level is invitational, showing a medium-strength hand of 11 or 12 points.

- A bid to the game level shows a game-going hand of 13 to 16 points.

- A bid of the fourth suit is forcing and may be artificial (conventional). If the fourth suit is bid at the two level or higher, it commits the partnership to at least a game contract.

After opener rebids 1NT:

- A jump shift or a reverse by responder is forcing.

- Any other rebid by responder is non-forcing.

After opener rebids 2NT:

- Any subsequent bid by responder is forcing.

NOTE: See the Appendix (pages 325–328) for a discussion of these supplemental conventions and/or treatments.

New Minor Forcing

Checkback Stayman

Wolff Sign-off

The following exercises assume you are using the methods outlined in the summary.

Exercise One — Opener's Rebid

As West, what do you rebid with each of the following hands after the auction starts:

	WEST	NORTH	EAST	SOUTH
	1♦	Pass	1♠	Pass
	?			

1) ♠ 4
   ♥ A 5
   ♦ K Q 9 7 2
   ♣ A Q 8 6 3 _____

2) ♠ 3
   ♥ K 9 6 3
   ♦ A J 10 8 4
   ♣ A 6 2 _____

3) ♠ Q 7
   ♥ J 9 4
   ♦ K J 6 3
   ♣ A Q 5 4 _____

4) ♠ K J
   ♥ A K 10 5
   ♦ A Q 9 8 3
   ♣ 7 3 _____

5) ♠ Q 5
   ♥ 8 2
   ♦ A K Q 7 5
   ♣ A K J 7 _____

6) ♠ K 5
   ♥ Q J 7
   ♦ A K J 8 7
   ♣ A 8 3 _____

Exercise Two — Responding to a Reverse

As East, what do you bid with each of the following hands after the auction starts:

	WEST	NORTH	**EAST**	SOUTH
	1♦	Pass	1♠	Pass
	2♥	Pass	?	

1) ♠ Q 10 9 5 4
   ♥ 8 6 5
   ♦ J 3
   ♣ K 6 4 _____

2) ♠ K 10 8 4
   ♥ Q 6 3
   ♦ 5 2
   ♣ Q 8 5 3 _____

3) ♠ A J 10 5 3
   ♥ K J 9 6
   ♦ 6 4
   ♣ 9 2 _____

Exercise One — Opener's Rebid

1) 2♣. Show the second suit at the two level. The hand isn't strong enough for a jump shift — 15 high-card points plus 1 point for each of the five-card suits puts it in the medium-strength category.

2) 2♦. With a minimum-strength opening, you aren't strong enough to reverse. Rebid the first suit.

3) 1NT. Showing a balanced hand takes priority over bidding a second suit at the two level.

4) 2♥. 17 high-card points plus 1 point for the five-card suit puts this in the medium-strength category. That's strong enough for a reverse, forcing for one round.

5) 3♣. Make a jump shift with a maximum-strength hand, committing the partnership to game. A rebid of 2♣ would be non-forcing.

6) 2NT. This shows a balanced hand of 18 or 19 points, too strong to open 1NT.

Exercise Two — Responding to a Reverse

1) 2♠. Partner's reverse is forcing for one round. A rebid of 2♠ shows a five-card or longer suit but doesn't promise any extra strength.

2) 2NT. With a minimum-strength response, no five-card suit, and no particular fit with partner's suit, 2NT is the weakest bid you can make.

3) 3♥. Raising partner's suit after a reverse commits the partnership to game. It isn't necessary to jump to the game level — partner may have more to say.

Exercise Three — Responder's Rebid after Bidding a New Suit at the One Level

As East, what do you rebid with each of the following hands after the auction starts:

WEST	NORTH	**EAST**	SOUTH
1♦	Pass	1♠	Pass
2♣	Pass	?	

1) ♠ K 10 8 7 4
   ♥ 6 3
   ♦ J 8 2
   ♣ Q 9 3 _____

2) ♠ A J 10 7
   ♥ K J 8
   ♦ 8 6 4
   ♣ Q 3 2 _____

3) ♠ A 10 7 4 2
   ♥ 9 5
   ♦ Q J 8 3
   ♣ K 3 _____

4) ♠ A K 10 9 5
   ♥ 8 3
   ♦ Q 4
   ♣ A J 6 2 _____

5) ♠ J 8 6 5 3
   ♥ K 7 5
   ♦ 5
   ♣ Q 9 7 3 _____

6) ♠ K Q J 9 7 5
   ♥ J 3
   ♦ A J
   ♣ K 6 2 _____

Exercise Four — Responder's Rebid after Bidding a New Suit at the Two Level

As East, what do you rebid with each of the following hands after the auction starts:

WEST	NORTH	**EAST**	SOUTH
1♥	Pass	2♣	Pass
2♦	Pass	?	

1) ♠ 9 3
   ♥ J 5
   ♦ Q 7 4
   ♣ A Q J 7 6 4 _____
   _____

2) ♠ K Q 7
   ♥ 8 3
   ♦ Q 4 2
   ♣ K J 10 7 5 _____

3) ♠ Q 9
   ♥ 6 4
   ♦ A 9 7 5
   ♣ K Q 10 8 4

4) ♠ A Q 9
   ♥ J 6
   ♦ 10 7 4
   ♣ A Q J 9 5 _____

5) ♠ 9 6 2
   ♥ 5
   ♦ A J 4
   ♣ A K J 9 7 4 _____

6) ♠ 6 4 2
   ♥ K 8 3
   ♦ Q 7
   ♣ A J 8 6 2 _____

Exercise Three — Responder's Rebid after Bidding a New Suit at the One Level

1) 2 ♦. Give preference to partner's first suit. Partner might have spades, but partner should have at least five diamonds.

2) 2NT. This is invitational, showing 11 or 12 points.

3) 3 ♦. Jump preference to opener's first suit shows an invitational-strength hand of about 11 or 12 points.

4) 2 ♥ (fourth suit forcing). A raise to 3 ♣ would only be invitational and a jump to 4 ♣ would get the partnership beyond 3NT making it difficult to uncover a spade fit. The bid of the fourth suit commits the partnership to game and allows you to show club support on the next round of bidding.

5) Pass. A raise would be invitational so it's best to settle for partscore right here.

6) 2 ♥. A jump to 3 ♠ would be invitational and a jump to 4 ♠ might get the partnership to the wrong spot. Start with the fourth suit; you can then show the good spade suit on the next round of bidding.

Exercise Four — Responder's Rebid after Bidding a New Suit at the Two Level

1) 3 ♣. A new suit by opener is forcing after a two-level response. Rebid the clubs, promising nothing extra.

2) 2NT. This is an invitational bid, showing 11 or 12 points.

3) 3 ♦. Raising opener's second suit shows an invitational-strength hand of about 11 or 12 points.

4) 3NT. A rebid of 2NT or 3 ♣ would not be forcing. Make sure the partnership gets to game.

5) 2 ♠ (fourth suit forcing). A rebid of 3 ♣ would not be forcing and a jump to 4 ♣ would get the partnership beyond 3NT. Bid the fourth suit. This is an artificial game-forcing bid. After hearing opener's rebid, you will be better placed to know what to do. If opener rebids 2NT, you can now bid 3 ♣ as a forcing bid.

6) 2 ♥. You've already promised 10 or more points by bidding a new suit at the two level. You don't need to jump to the three level to show an invitational hand with support for partner's major suit.

Exercise Five — Responder's Rebid after Opener Rebids 1NT

As East, what would you rebid with each of the following hands after the auction starts:

WEST	NORTH	**EAST**	SOUTH
1♦	Pass	1♥	Pass
1NT	Pass	?	

1) ♠ 7 5
   ♥ K J 7 6 4 3
   ♦ J 9 2
   ♣ Q 5 _____

2) ♠ Q 9 3
   ♥ A 10 7 3
   ♦ K J 8 4 2
   ♣ 4 _____

3) ♠ 6
   ♥ A J 9 6 3
   ♦ K 4
   ♣ K Q 8 7 2 _____

4) ♠ A Q 8 5
   ♥ K Q 9 6 3
   ♦ Q 8 5
   ♣ 2 _____

5) ♠ A K J 7
   ♥ K J 9 3
   ♦ 6
   ♣ J 8 6 5 _____

6) ♠ K 6
   ♥ A J 10 8 6 3
   ♦ 9 4
   ♣ K 8 3 _____

Exercise Six — Responder's Rebid after Opener Rebids 2NT

As East, what would you rebid with each of the following hands after the auction starts:

WEST	NORTH	**EAST**	SOUTH
1♣	Pass	1♠	Pass
2NT	Pass	?	

1) ♠ Q 9 7 5
   ♥ J 8 3
   ♦ K 5 4
   ♣ 7 4 2 _____

2) ♠ K Q 8 7 4
   ♥ 9 4 2
   ♦ 6 5
   ♣ K 9 5 _____

3) ♠ Q 10 8 5 4
   ♥ K 9 6 3
   ♦ 6 4
   ♣ Q 6 _____

Exercise Five — Responder's Rebid after Opener Rebids 1NT

1) 2♥. The bid of an old suit at the two level is a sign-off.

2) 3♦. This is invitational, showing 11 or 12 points.

3) 3♣. A jump in a new suit is forcing.

4) 2♠. This is forcing since it is a reverse by responder; opener would have to go to the three level to give preference to hearts.

5) 3NT. There's no point in making a forcing bid. Opener didn't raise hearts and didn't show a four-card spade suit.

6) 4♥. Opener should have at least two hearts for the 1NT rebid.

Exercise Six — Responder's Rebid after Opener Rebids 2NT

1) Pass. Opener's rebid shows a balanced hand of 18 or 19 points and is non-forcing.

2) 3♠. Any bid over 2NT is forcing. 3♠ shows the five-card suit and asks opener to choose between 3NT and 4♠.

3) 3♥. A new suit over the 2NT rebid is forcing. With 7 high-card points plus 1 length point for the five-card heart suit, you have enough to commit the partnership to game. Opener will know you have at least five spades and four hearts.

Bid and Play — Deal 1

(E–Z Deal Cards: #6, Deal 1 — Dealer, North)

Suggested Bidding

WEST	NORTH	EAST	SOUTH
	Pass	1♦	Pass
1♥	Pass	3♣	Pass
3NT	Pass	Pass	Pass

East opens the higher-ranking of two five-card suits. South doesn't have enough to enter the auction. With a choice of four-card suits, West responds up the line by bidding 1♥. North passes and the auction comes back to East. East wants to show the second suit but can't afford to bid only 2♣. West could pass that rebid — and might do so on the actual hand. With 18 high-card points plus 1 point for each of the five-card suits, East has enough to commit the partnership to the game level by making a jump shift to 3♣.

Dlr: North
Vul: None

```
              ♠ Q 10 8 3
              ♥ K 9 3
              ♦ Q 2
              ♣ J 9 4 2
♠ K 7 5 2              ♠ J 6
♥ J 10 8 4     N        ♥ A
♦ 8 4        W   E      ♦ A K 9 5 3
♣ K 6 3        S        ♣ A Q 10 7 5
              ♠ A 9 4
              ♥ Q 7 6 5 2
              ♦ J 10 7 6
              ♣ 8
```

Despite holding only 7 points, West is forced to bid again over the 3♣ rebid by opener. With some strength in spades and hearts, West's best choice is 3NT. East could rebid the clubs to show a five-card suit, but there's no reason to believe that 5♣ or 5♦ will be a better spot than 3NT. Having described the hand with reasonable accuracy, East should pass 3NT.

Suggested Opening Lead

North is on lead and should elect to lead spades, the unbid suit. With no sequence, North starts with the ♠3, fourth highest.

Suggested Play

Declarer has one sure winner in hearts, two in diamonds, and three in clubs.

With the spade lead, West is sure to get a trick with the ♠K. Two more tricks are needed. These should come from the club suit, if the missing clubs divide 3–2 or the ♣J can be trapped.

Declarer should play the ♠J from the dummy. This may win the trick if North has both the ♠A and ♠Q. South wins with the ♠A and returns a spade. West can hold up winning the ♠K, but the defenders can continue leading spades to drive it out.

If the missing clubs divide 3–2, declarer will have no difficulty making the contract. When taking winners, it's usually a good idea to play the high card from the short side first. However, the clubs are not necessarily all winners in this situation since the ♣J is missing. Declarer can't do anything if South holds four or more clubs including the ♣J, but declarer can take a precaution against North holding four clubs headed by the ♣J.

West should start by playing one of dummy's high clubs, then winning the second round with the ♣K. If both opponents follow suit, it doesn't matter whether the ♣J has appeared. The defenders clubs are divided 3–2 and West can simply take the rest of the tricks in the suit. On the actual hand, South discards on the second round of the suit. West now knows that the clubs have divided 4–1 and North holds the ♣J. By winning the second round of clubs in the West hand, declarer can lead a low club toward dummy and take the finesse. North's club holding doesn't prevent declarer from making the contract.

If North were to play the ♣K and then win the second round of clubs in the dummy, it would be too late to do anything when South discards. There's no entry back to the West hand to take the finesse. Declarer will have to give up a club trick to North's ♣J and can no longer make the contract.

Suggested Defense

When North leads a low spade, South should win the ♠A — third hand high — and lead back the ♠9, top of the remaining doubleton in partner's suit. The defenders should establish three winners in the spade suit without difficulty. Then there's not much for the defenders to do but sit back and hope that declarer doesn't find the winning play in the club suit. If declarer does give up a trick to North's ♣J, South should eventually get a diamond trick to defeat the contract.

Bid and Play — Deal 2

(E–Z Deal Cards: #6, Deal 2 — Dealer, East)

Suggested Bidding

WEST	NORTH	EAST	SOUTH
		Pass	1 ♦
Pass	1 ♠	Pass	2 ♥
Pass	2 ♠	Pass	2NT
Pass	3NT	Pass	Pass
Pass			

After East passes, South starts the auction by bidding the longest suit, 1 ♦. West doesn't have enough strength to introduce the club suit at the two level. North shows the spade suit and the bidding comes back to South. South rebids 2 ♥. This is a reverse, showing at least a medium-strength hand with longer diamonds than hearts. It's forcing for one round.

North's most descriptive rebid is to show the good five-card spade suit. Using the *Ingberman* style of re-

```
Dlr: East      ♠ K Q J 7 5
Vul: N–S       ♥ 6 4 2
               ♦ 6 3
               ♣ Q 10 8
♠ 8 2                        ♠ 10 9 6 4 3
♥ K J 8 3         N          ♥ Q 9
♦ 10 4         W   E         ♦ K J 9 8
♣ A J 9 5 2        S         ♣ 6 4
               ♠ A
               ♥ A 10 7 5
               ♦ A Q 7 5 2
               ♣ K 7 3
```

sponses to a reverse, a rebid of 2NT would show a weak hand and deny a five-card spade suit. With no real fit for spades, South now tries 2NT. Knowing South has at least a medium-strength hand of 17 or 18 points, North takes the partnership to game.

Suggested Opening Lead

West's opening lead would be the ♣5, fourth highest from the longest and strongest suit.

Suggested Play

The play to the first trick is often crucial, and this hand is a typical example. If the ♣8 is played from dummy, East can't produce a higher card.

Declarer's first instinct might be to win the trick as cheaply as possible by playing a low club from the South hand, but appearances can be deceiving. Before deciding what to do, declarer should plan the entire play.

Declarer can count four sure tricks in spades, one in hearts, and one in diamonds. Declarer will get one club trick for sure after the opening lead and can establish a second winner in that suit. There will be an extra trick from the spade suit if the defender's spades divide 4–3, and there's always the possibility of a successful diamond finesse if East has the ♦ K.

The complication in all this is that there's no sure entry to the dummy. The spade suit is *blocked*. North's ♣ Q is the only possible entry, and South must be careful to make use of it. From the opening lead and East's inability to play a club higher than the ♣ 8, it would appear that West has the ♣ A. Consequently, declarer should win the first trick with the ♣ K, keeping two low clubs in the South hand. After winning the ♣ K, declarer plays the ♠ A to unblock the suit, and then leads a low club toward dummy. West can't prevent declarer from getting to dummy with the ♣ Q to take the spade winners. When the spades fail to divide favorably, declarer has to take the diamond finesse for nine tricks — four spades, one heart, two diamonds, and two clubs.

What happens if declarer lets dummy's ♣ 8 win the first trick? After the ♠ A is played, West can prevent declarer from getting to dummy. If declarer leads the ♣ K, West can duck. That gives declarer a second club trick but no entry to dummy. If instead South tries leading a low club, West can win the ♣ A and lead a third round, forcing declarer to win with the ♣ K. Without the spade winners, declarer can't make the contract if the defenders hold on to the right cards.

Suggested Defense

The defenders' best chance of defeating the contract is to prevent declarer from reaching dummy. If declarer does win the first trick with dummy's ♣ 8 or ♣ 10, West can work out that South holds the ♣ K. If South tries the tricky play of leading a low club toward dummy's ♣ Q after unblocking the ♠ A, West must hop up with the ♣ A to prevent declarer from reaching dummy. West needs to be alert to find this play.

It's a little easier if South leads the ♣ K after playing the ♠ A. West should see the importance of ducking this trick so that the ♣ Q doesn't become an entry. Ducking the club won't cost a trick, since declarer is always entitled to two tricks in the suit.

Bid and Play — Deal 3

(E–Z Deal Cards: #6, Deal 3 — Dealer, South)

Suggested Bidding

WEST	NORTH	EAST	SOUTH
			1 ♦
Pass	1 ♥	Pass	1 ♠
Pass	2 ♣	Pass	2 ♦
Pass	3 ♦	Pass	4 ♦
Pass	5 ♦	Pass	Pass
Pass			

After South's opening bid of 1 ♦, North's priority is to look for a major suit fit. North bids the heart suit, and South continues bidding up the line by showing the spade suit. North now has to find a rebid. North has the values to take the partnership to game, but the best contract is unclear. A preference to 2 ♦ would show a minimum-strength response of 6 to 10 points, and a jump to 3 ♦ would be invitational, showing 11 or 12 points. To make a forcing bid, North bids the fourth suit, 2 ♣.

```
Dlr: South    ♠ K 4
Vul: E–W      ♥ A 9 6 2
              ♦ A Q 10 7 2
              ♣ 6 3
♠ J 9 7              ♠ 10 8 5 2
♥ Q 8 7 5      N     ♥ J 10 4
♦ 6 5        W   E   ♦ 9
♣ K J 9 2      S     ♣ A Q 10 7 4
              ♠ A Q 6 3
              ♥ K 3
              ♦ K J 8 4 3
              ♣ 8 5
```

North's 2 ♣ bid is artificial (conventional), so South can't bid notrump without some strength in clubs. Instead, South rebids the diamonds. North now shows diamond support by raising to the three level. This is a forcing bid — with an invitational-strength hand and a diamond fit, North would have bid 3 ♦ on the previous round. Still unable to bid notrump, South can continue in diamonds. North, with no strength in clubs, will settle for game.

Alternatively, over 3 ♦ South might bid 3 ♥ to show some help for hearts, having previously denied four-card or three-card support by failing to raise hearts on either of the last two rounds of bidding. North could make one more try for 3NT by showing some strength in spades, but South would return to diamonds and North would settle for game with diamonds as trump. Neither partner has strength in clubs.

Suggested Opening Lead

West is on lead. Having listened to the auction, West should choose a club, the suit in which neither North nor South has shown any strength — North's 2♣ bid was artificial, saying nothing about clubs. West should lead the ♣2, fourth best.

Suggested Play

There is little to the play in 5♦ after the defenders take the first two club tricks. Declarer can win the next trick, draw trumps, and ruff the spade loser in the dummy.

Suggested Defense

The defense can't do anything to defeat 5♦. If West doesn't find an initial club lead, declarer can discard one of dummy's clubs on the third round of spades and take 12 tricks.

If North–South wander into 3NT, the defenders can defeat that contract by taking the first five club tricks. After the opponents have bid diamonds, hearts, and spades, it shouldn't be too difficult to find a club lead no matter which defender makes the opening lead.

Bid and Play — Deal 4

(E–Z Deal Cards: #6, Deal 4 — Dealer, West)

Suggested Bidding

WEST	NORTH	EAST	SOUTH
Pass	1♦	Pass	1♥
Pass	1♠	Pass	2♣
Pass	2♥	Pass	4♥
Pass	Pass	Pass	

With no five-card major suit, North opens the longer minor. South responds 1♥. North chooses to show the spade suit rather than raise hearts with only three-card support. This is the correct approach, since South could have four hearts and four spades and be responding up the line.

South now has to find a suitable rebid. South knows the partnership has enough combined strength for game but doesn't know the best

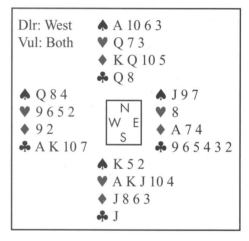

Dlr: West
Vul: Both

♠ A 10 6 3
♥ Q 7 3
♦ K Q 10 5
♣ Q 8

♠ Q 8 4
♥ 9 6 5 2
♦ 9 2
♣ A K 10 7

♠ J 9 7
♥ 8
♦ A 7 4
♣ 9 6 5 4 3 2

♠ K 5 2
♥ A K J 10 4
♦ J 8 6 3
♣ J

choice of game. A jump to 3♥ would be non-forcing and show a six-card suit. A jump to 4♥ would be a wild guess, since North could be short in hearts. A jump to 3♦ would also be only invitational. Holding a singleton club, South doesn't want to jump to game in notrump. South needs more information from North before deciding on the best contract. So, South bids 2♣, fourth-suit forcing. It says nothing about clubs. Instead, it asks North for a further descriptive bid. When North shows belated support for hearts, South knows where the contract belongs and bids the game.

Suggested Opening Lead

South's 2♣ bid is artificial and doesn't promise any length or strength in clubs. West can treat clubs as the 'unbid' suit and lead the ♣A, top of touching honors.

Suggested Play

The contract looks fairly straightforward. There's one loser in spades, one in diamonds, and one in clubs. Whenever the contract looks easy, declarer should consider what might go wrong. There is the danger that the defenders can get a diamond ruff before trumps are drawn if the missing diamonds divide 4–1. There's not much declarer can do if that's the case. A more subtle danger is if the defenders' trumps divide 4–1.

Suppose West continues with the ♣K after winning the first trick and declarer ruffs. Declarer starts to draw trumps and gets the unfortunate news that West started with four trumps. If all of the trumps are drawn, South will have none left when it comes time to establish the diamonds. When the defenders win the ♦A, they can take all of their club winners. On the other hand, if declarer doesn't draw all of the trumps, West may be able to get a diamond ruff when declarer tries to knock out the ♦A. The defenders don't have to win the ♦A on the first round, so West may get a ruff even though the diamonds divide 3–2.

To avoid this dilemma, declarer shouldn't trump the second round of clubs. Instead, declarer can discard a spade loser. A spade trick must be lost anyway, so this doesn't cost anything. It does make a big difference, however. If West leads another club, declarer can ruff this in dummy and retain five trumps in the South hand. Declarer can then draw all of West's trumps and still have one left when the defenders get a trick with the ♦A.

Discarding a spade on the second round of clubs risks going down if the diamonds are divided 4–1 while the trumps are divided 3–2. It's still the best play, however. The defenders may not find the diamond ruff if South discards a spade — West may lead another club or switch to a spade. If there is an immediate diamond ruff, the defenders could always have defeated the contract anyway. Finally, if West held a singleton diamond, West may have led it instead of continuing with the ♣K.

Suggested Defense

If declarer does ruff the second round of clubs, the defenders will have to be careful to take advantage of their opportunity. If declarer draws all of the trumps, the defenders should have no difficulty taking their club winners when East wins the ♦ A. If declarer stops drawing trumps after playing two rounds and discovering the 4–1 break, the defenders must be more careful.

When declarer leads diamonds, East must duck the first round and win the second round. East then leads a third round of diamonds for West to ruff. How does East know to do this? On the first round of diamonds West should play the ♦ 9, starting a high-low sequence to show an even number. East may be able to figure out what's going on from the way declarer is playing the hand. In that case, East can give West a diamond ruff to defeat the contract.

It's not easy to find the winning defense if declarer makes a slight misstep, but at least the defenders have a chance.

CHAPTER 7
Weak Two-Bids

WEAK TWO-BIDS

Most hands are opened at the one level, so the partnership has as much room as possible to search for the best contract. Opening bids at the two level have traditionally been used as *strong two-bids*, showing a hand too strong to open at the one level. Opening bids in a suit at the three level or higher are commonly used to show hands with a long suit, too weak to open at the one or two level. These are called *preemptive opening bids*, or *preempts*. They can make the bidding difficult for the opponents. This tactic has proven so successful that many players today prefer to use methods that allow them to preempt more frequently.

You are the dealer:

♠ A Q 10 7 5 2　　You don't have enough strength to open the bidding
♥ 9 7　　　　　　at the one level. With a six-card suit, it would be ad-
♦ Q 6 5　　　　　venturesome to open at the three level. Are you com-
♣ 7 5　　　　　　fortable passing? Probably not. You might like to tell
partner about your spades, and at the same time make the auction more difficult for the opponents.

Many club and tournament players like to open 2♠ on this type of hand. This is a *weak two-bid*. Here is a complete deal:

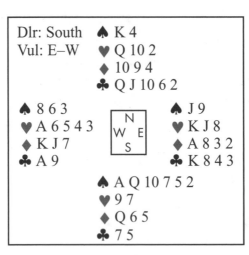

```
Dlr: South    ♠ K 4
Vul: E–W      ♥ Q 10 2
              ♦ 10 9 4
              ♣ Q J 10 6 2
  ♠ 8 6 3           N        ♠ J 9
  ♥ A 6 5 4 3    W     E     ♥ K J 8
  ♦ K J 7          S        ♦ A 8 3 2
  ♣ A 9                      ♣ K 8 4 3
              ♠ A Q 10 7 5 2
              ♥ 9 7
              ♦ Q 6 5
              ♣ 7 5
```

If South were to pass, West would open the bidding 1 ♥, and East has enough strength to make sure the partnership reaches the game level. East–West can make a contract of 4 ♥. If South opens the bidding 2 ♠, West is faced with more of a challenge. With only 12 high-card points and a five-card suit, West would be taking a chance by overcalling 3 ♥. If West passes and North passes, East has a problem. With 12 high-card points and only three-card support for hearts, a takeout double isn't attractive — it might result in the partnership playing in a seven-card fit at the three level.

An opening bid of 2 ♠ by South makes the auction much less comfortable for the opponents. South could play the contract in a partscore when the opponents can make a game. Even if the opponents double the 2 ♠ contract, it will probably be defeated two tricks, not enough to compensate East–West for their game bonus.

The 2 ♠ bid has other advantages as well. It will get North off to the best lead if the opponents play the contract. Because the bid has taken away a lot of bidding room, it makes bidding accurately difficult for the opponents. They may even get too high.

Opening a Weak Two-bid

The partnership can use 2 ♦, 2 ♥, and 2 ♠ as *weak two-bids*. One opening bid at the two level, 2 ♣, is reserved for strong hands, and this will be discussed in the next chapter. The general guideline for opening a *weak two-bid* of 2 ♦, 2 ♥, and 2 ♠ is the following:

- 5 to 11 high-card points.

- a good six-card suit.

If you and your partner agree to play *weak two-bids*, you don't have to open at the two level because your hand fits the requirements.

Here are additional considerations:

- The opening two-bid shows a weak hand, and your opponents know that as well as your partner. This gives them the option of doubling your contract for penalties. Having a good suit reduces the risk that you'll go down more tricks than you can afford. The interpretation of *good* suit varies with the vulnerability. If you are vulnerable, you should probably have a suit headed by three of the top five honors, e.g., A K J x x x , A Q 10 x x x, K J 10 x x x. If you aren't vulnerable, your suit could be less robust, e.g., K J 9 x x x, Q J 9 x x x, A 10 9 x x x.

- Consider your position at the table. In first or second position, follow the requirement for a good six-card suit, with most of the hand's strength concentrated in your suit. Partner has not yet passed and could hold a strong hand. You want to have the type of hand partner is expecting, so that partner can make an informed decision about how high to compete. In third position, you have more latitude because partner has already passed. For example, you might open at the two level with a good five-card suit on occasion (K Q J x x). In fourth position, you rarely open with a *weak two-bid*, since you could simply pass the deal out. A *weak two-bid* in fourth position should be made with a sound hand, with the expectation that you are going to take at least eight tricks.

- The *weak two-bid* is made with the intention of interrupting the opponents' auction but will sometimes make the bidding difficult for partner. Partner might have a good hand and you have taken away some of the room needed to explore for the best contract. Most players avoid opening a *weak two-bid* with a side four-card major suit or a void. Those types of features make it difficult for partner to estimate the potential of the deal.

Here are examples:

♠ 9 4
♥ A J 10 8 7 3
♦ K 9 5
♣ 6 4

With a good six-card heart suit and only 8 high-card points, this would be a good hand for a weak 2 ♥ bid.

♠ Q 10 7 6 4 2
♥ 8
♦ 10 5 3
♣ K 8 2

With 5 high-card points and a poor six-card suit, this hand shouldn't be opened with a *weak two-bid* if your side is vulnerable. Even non-vulnerable, it's a risky bid in first or second position. It's more acceptable to open 2 ♠ with this hand in third position, non-vulnerable.

♠ 10 7 3
♥ 4
♦ K Q J 10 7 5
♣ 9 6 2

Although you have only 6 high-card points, you could open this hand 2 ♦ at any vulnerability if you are playing *weak two-bids*.

♠ A K J 10 9 5
♥ 3
♦ Q J 8 3
♣ 10 2

This hand falls within the parameters for an opening bid of 2 ♠, but most players would open with 1 ♠. The hand has 11 high-card points plus 2 points for the six-card suit, which meets the requirements for an opening bid at the one level. This is the type of hand which could be opened 2 ♠ in fourth position, with the intention of making the contract.

♠ 4
♥ A Q 10 9 7 6 3
♦ J 6 2
♣ 8 3

With a seven-card suit, open this hand with a pre-emptive 3 ♥, rather than 2 ♥. Some players would treat this hand as a *weak two-bid*, especially when vulnerable, but a three-level opening bid with a good seven-card suit is usually more effective.

♠ K 9 7 5
♥ 10 8 7 5 4 2
♦ A 8 3
♣ —

This hand is unsuitable for a *weak two-bid*, despite the six-card heart suit. The suit is poor, and there is a four-card spade suit as well as a void. If you open 2♥, you might miss a game contract in spades or suffer a large penalty when the opponents can make only a partscore. Instead, pass.

♠ A Q J 9 8
♥ 6 2
♦ 10 9 7 3
♣ 7 4

With only a five-card suit, this hand should probably not be opened 2♠ in first or second position. Once partner is a passed hand, however, opening 2♠ with this hand in third position would be a reasonable gamble.

RESPONDING TO A WEAK TWO-BID

The *weak two-bid* is primarily a defensive type of opening. It gives responder a good description of opener's hand. The partnership needs to agree on the meaning of responder's bids. Here are commonly accepted agreements.

The response can be straightforward:

• A raise of opener's suit to any level is to play and could be preemptive. Opener is expected to pass.

• A jump to 3NT or game in a new suit is to play. Opener is expected to pass.

Sometimes, responder wants more information and can get it in one of these ways:

• A response in a new suit below the game level is forcing for one round, showing a five-card or longer suit. Opener rebids as follows:

  • With three-card support, or a doubleton honor, opener raises responder's suit.

- With no fit for responder's suit, opener rebids the original suit with a minimum (5 to 8 points) and bids a new suit or notrump with a maximum (9 to 11 points).

- A response of 2NT is artificial (conventional) and forcing, showing game interest and asking opener for a further description. Opener rebids as follows:

  - With a minimum for the *weak two-bid* (5 to 8 points), opener rebids the original suit at the three level.

  - With a maximum for the *weak two-bid* (9 to 11 points), opener bids another suit to show a *feature* — usually an ace or king — in that suit; with no outside feature, opener rebids 3NT to show a maximum.

Since a response of 2NT or a new suit is forcing, this style of responses is usually referred to as *RONF* — **R**aise is the **O**nly **N**on-**F**orcing bid — although this is a bit of a misnomer, since jumps to game are also non-forcing.

Here are some examples for responder after the auction starts:

WEST	NORTH	**EAST**	SOUTH
2 ♥	Pass	?	

♠ K 10 8 7 6 5
♥ 3
♦ K Q 3
♣ Q 5 2

Pass. Partner has described a weak hand of 5 to 11 points with a six-card heart suit. The partnership belongs at the partscore level, and there's no point in looking for a better spot. A new suit response would be forcing and is likely to get the partnership into further trouble. The auction isn't yet over; the next opponent may enter the auction, and you'll be happy to defend.

♠ A K 9 5 2
♥ K 8 3
♦ 3
♣ K J 9 3

Bid 4 ♥. Even if partner has a minimum hand for the *weak two-bid*, you should expect to make ten tricks with your fit for partner's six-card heart suit. With little else besides a good heart suit (A Q x x x x), partner will probably lose only one diamond trick and two club tricks. There's no guarantee your side will take ten tricks, but it's certainly worth a try.

♠ 3
♥ Q 10 5
♦ 10 9 4 2
♣ K 9 7 5 3

Bid 4♥. It's unlikely partner can take ten tricks opposite this hand, but your purpose in jumping to game is as a further preemptive action. Since partner has a weak hand, it's doubtful that your side can take more than two tricks on defense. If you pass, the opponents are almost certain to enter the auction and reach a game contract. By raising to 4♥, you may keep the opponents out of the auction, or they may misjudge and bid too much or too little.

When you jump to 4♥, the opponents can't be certain whether you are taking a preemptive action — as on this hand — or bidding with a strong hand expecting to make the contract — as on the previous example. This is one reason *weak two-bids* are effective. You can keep the opponents guessing!

♠ 9 7
♥ Q 4
♦ Q 8 4 2
♣ A J 7 5 2

Bid 3♥. This isn't an invitational bid. It's a further preemptive maneuver, designed to make it difficult for the opponents to enter the auction. Holding only 9 high-card points opposite a weak opening bid, it's likely the opponents have the balance of strength. If you pass, the opponents will have an easier time coming into the auction than if you raise to the three level.

This type of action is part of the tactical considerations following a *weak two-bid*. A raise to the three level, like a raise to the game level, is a two-way bid. It could be made on a very weak hand — furthering the preemptive effect of partner's opening bid — or it could be made on a reasonably strong hand — with good defensive prospects should the opponents come into the auction. Neither opener nor the opponents can be certain which type of hand responder holds. For this reason, opener shouldn't bid again, leaving all further decisions to responder. This tactic also keeps the opponents off balance. They will be taking a risk when they enter the auction following responder's action. Responder may be laying a trap, waiting to double any opposing contract.

♠ Q J 3
♥ 5
♦ A K Q J 9 7 5
♣ A J

Bid 3NT. An immediate jump to 3NT shows a desire to play in that contract. Responder isn't asking for any further input from opener and may, or may not, have a fit with partner's suit. With this hand, you should have a good chance for nine tricks opposite partner's weak hand and long heart suit.

♠ A Q J 10 9 7 5
♥ —
♦ 7 5
♣ A K J 8

Bid 4♠. Like the jump to 3NT, an immediate jump to game in a new suit tells opener that you would like to play there. If you had interest in other contracts, you would start by bidding a new suit at the minimum level or 2NT.

♠ A 10 9 3
♥ K 7 2
♦ A Q 7
♣ 10 4 2

Bid 2NT. It's difficult to judge whether the partnership belongs at the game level. The 2NT response is artificial (conventional) and forcing, asking for further information from opener. If opener rebids 3♥, showing a minimum-strength hand, you can pass, leaving the partnership in partscore. If opener rebids 3♣, showing a maximum-strength hand with a feature in clubs, either the ace or king, you can bid game — 4♥ would be reasonable, but you might try for nine tricks in a contract of 3NT. If opener rebids 3♦ or 3♠ — showing a maximum with a feature in that suit — or 3NT — showing a maximum with no outside feature — 4♥ should be the best spot. 3NT is unlikely to fare well if neither partner has strength in clubs.

OPENER'S REBID

Opener's Rebid after a 2NT Response

The response of 2NT is artificial (conventional) and asks opener for further information. Opener rebids the original suit at the three level with a minimum (5 to 8 points). With a maximum (9 or more points), opener shows a side feature or bids 3NT. Here are examples after the auction has started:

WEST	NORTH	EAST	SOUTH
2♠	Pass	2NT	Pass
?			

♠ K Q 10 7 6 3
♥ 10 5
♦ J 8 3
♣ 9 2

Rebid 3♠. Holding only 6 high-card points, this is a minimum-strength *weak two-bid*. Rebidding your suit sends this message to partner.

♠ A Q 9 7 5 3
♥ 6
♦ K 8 4
♣ 8 7 5

Rebid 3♦. With a good hand, show your feature in diamonds. This should help partner choose the best contract.

♠ A K Q 8 6 3
♥ 9 4
♦ J 4
♣ 6 5 2

Rebid 3NT. With a maximum *weak two-bid* and no outside feature, opener rebids 3NT. This usually shows a "solid" suit. With 9 or more points and no feature in the other suits, your high cards must be in your own suit. Partner may elect to play in 3NT with some strength in the other three suits.

♠ A J 10 7 5 3
♥ 5
♦ J 2
♣ Q J 5 2

Awkward. You have a maximum *weak two-bid*, but 3NT tends to show a very good suit and 3♣ tends to show the ♣A or ♣K as an outside feature. Some partnerships allow opener to rebid 3♣ with this hand, treating the club holding as a *feature*. That's reasonable, but if your partner wouldn't appreciate such an exercise in judgment, rebid

3NT to show a maximum-strength hand with no outside feature.

Some players may choose to use the *Ogust convention* after opener's rebid following the 2NT response.

Opener's Rebid after a New Suit Response

If responder bids a new suit below the level of game, opener must bid again — unless responder passed originally. With a fit, opener can raise responder's suit. Otherwise, opener rebids the original suit with a minimum or finds another bid with a maximum. Here are examples after the auction starts:

WEST	NORTH	EAST	SOUTH
2 ♦	Pass	2 ♥	Pass
?			

♠ J 4
♥ 10 8 5
♦ A Q J 8 6 3
♣ 9 5

Raise to 3 ♥. East's response promises at least a five-card heart suit. Your raise lets partner know you have a fit.

♠ 6 5 3
♥ K 6
♦ A J 10 9 6 3
♣ 10 4

Raise to 3 ♥. You'd like to have three-card support, but a doubleton honor will do. You have a good *weak two-bid* and showing support for partner's suit is probably the most descriptive thing you can do.

♠ J 8 3
♥ 8
♦ K Q 10 9 7 4
♣ 8 4 2

Rebid 3 ♦. You have a minimum *weak two-bid* and you can't support partner's suit. You have little choice but to rebid your suit.

♠ Q 10 3
♥ 5 4
♦ A J 9 8 4 2
♣ K 4

Rebid 2NT. You don't have a good fit with partner, but you do have a maximum-strength hand for your *weak two-bid*. 2NT suggests that notrump might be the best spot for the partnership.

♠ 8 5 3
♥ 6
♦ A Q 10 8 6 3
♣ K J 4

Rebid 3♣. You don't have support for partner's suit, but you do have a maximum hand. 3♣ lets partner know about your strength and outside feature. Based on this information, partner can bid 3NT with strength in hearts and spades.

HANDLING INTERFERENCE

Since the *weak two-bid* doesn't promise much strength, the opponents will frequently enter the auction. If the *weak two-bid* is doubled for take-out, all of responder's choices remain the same. In addition, responder can redouble if interested in doubling the opponents for penalty. For example:

WEST	NORTH	**EAST**	SOUTH
2♠	Double	?	

♠ K 10 7 4
♥ 5
♦ K 9 8 7 2
♣ 10 7 5

Jump to 4♠. After the double, it's important to further partner's preemptive action by raising to as high a level as you're willing to compete. With your spade fit and lack of defense outside of spades, it's likely that North–South can make at least a game and perhaps a slam. Your jump to the four level should make it difficult for them to judge their best result. Even if they double your contract, they are unlikely to get a sufficient penalty to compensate for their own contract.

♠ 10 6 4
♥ K 4
♦ Q J 7 5 2
♣ A Q 10

Respond 2NT. The 2NT response is still artificial (conventional) and forcing. If opener rebids 3♠ to show a minimum, you can pass. If opener rebids anything else, showing a maximum, 4♠ should be a reasonable contract.

♠ 5
♥ K J 10 8
♦ K Q 6 3
♣ A Q 9 5

Redouble. It looks as though the opponents are in trouble. The redouble sends the message to partner that you're interested in doubling the opponents' contract. Wherever they rest, you should have enough to defeat their contract. If the opponents pass, leaving West in 2♠ re-doubled, you can probably provide more than enough tricks for partner to make that contract.

If there is an overcall of the *weak two-bid*, responder can still make the normal response, if there is room available. Responder also has the option of doubling for penalty or *cuebidding* the opponent's suit to show slam interest. Here are examples:

WEST	NORTH	**EAST**	SOUTH
2♥	2♠	?	

♠ 10 6 2
♥ Q 8 5
♦ A K J 2
♣ K 7 3

Bid 2NT. When available, 2NT is still an artificial (conventional) forcing bid. An immediate raise to 3♥ could be preemptive and opener would be expected to pass. With an invitational-strength hand, start with 2NT. If opener has a minimum and rebids 3♥ that should be high enough. If opener has a maximum, the partnership should have a reasonable chance at a game contract.

♠ K J 10 8 5
♥ 8
♦ A K 7
♣ J 9 6 3

Double. This is a penalty double of the opponent's contract, and partner is expected to pass.

♠ A 7 3
♥ Q J 7 3
♦ A K J 6 2
♣ 3

Cuebid 3♠. The bid of the opponent's suit shows a strong hand and slam interest. If partner has the right hand, slam is a possibility.

If an opponent bids after the artificial 2NT response, opener can make the normal rebid if there is room available. If not, opener has the option of passing with a minimum-strength hand and doubling or rebidding the original suit with a maximum-strength hand. For example:

WEST	NORTH	EAST	SOUTH
2♠	Pass	2NT	3♦
?			

♠ K Q 10 8 7 3
♥ A 5
♦ 9 6 2
♣ 5 3

Bid 3 ♥. With a maximum-strength hand, opener can conveniently show the outside feature after the overcall. This is the same response West would have made if there were no overcall.

♠ A J 10 7 5 4
♥ 9 3
♦ 8 7
♣ J 7 5

Pass. With a minimum-strength hand, you would have rebid 3♠ without the interference. After the overcall, you can pass to show a minimum.

♠ A Q 9 8 6 3
♥ 4
♦ Q J 5
♣ 10 9 2

Double. A double of the opponent's overcall shows a maximum with some strength in the opponent's suit. The double is optional. Responder can pass and defend for penalties or bid on if 3 ♦ doubled is unlikely to be the best spot for the partnership.

♠ A Q J 10 8 3
♥ 9 3
♦ 6 4
♣ K 8 2

Rebid 3♠. Without the interference, you would have bid 3♣, showing your club feature and maximum-strength *weak two-bid*. The 3 ♦ overcall hasn't left you enough room to conveniently show the feature, but you can show the strength by bidding instead of passing.

THE SUBSEQUENT AUCTION

Following the *weak two-bid,* the auction can proceed in several directions, depending on responder's hand and the actions of the opponents. Here are examples.

West
♠ K J 10 8 6 3
♥ 7
♦ Q 10 6 2
♣ J 4

WEST	NORTH	EAST	SOUTH
2♠	Pass	4♠	5♥
Pass	Pass	Dbl	Pass
Pass	Pass		

East
♠ A 9 5 2
♥ A K 8 3
♦ 8 5
♣ K 6 2

After West's *weak two-bid*, East raises to the game level, expecting that the partnership should have a reasonable chance of taking ten tricks. When South overcalls 5 ♥, West passes. West doesn't know what type of hand East holds, so any further bidding is up to East. With excellent defense against the opponents' contract, East doubles for penalty and West respects that decision.

West					East
♠ 6					♠ A J 9 8
♥ 9 3 2					♥ K Q 7 4
♦ K Q 10 8 6 3					♦ A 7
♣ A 8 3					♣ 9 7 2

WEST	NORTH	EAST	SOUTH
2 ♦	Pass	2NT	Pass
3 ♣	Pass	3NT	Pass
Pass	Pass		

East uses the conventional 2NT response to get more information from partner. West shows the club feature, and this is all East needs to know to put the partnership in game.

West					East
♠ 7 3					♠ K Q 8 4
♥ A 10 9 8 7 4					♥ Q 6 5
♦ Q 9					♦ A K 6 3
♣ 9 8 5					♣ J 7

WEST	NORTH	EAST	SOUTH
2 ♥	Pass	2NT	Pass
3 ♥	Pass	Pass	Pass

West shows a minimum-strength hand for a *weak two-bid* in response to East's inquiry. East leaves the partnership at the partscore level.

West					East
♠ A 6 2					♠ K Q 8 4
♥ K J 10 8 4 2					♥ Q 6 5
♦ J 9					♦ A K 6 3
♣ 9 8					♣ J 7

WEST	NORTH	EAST	SOUTH
2 ♥	Pass	2NT	Pass
3 ♠	Pass	4 ♥	Pass
Pass	Pass		

West's rebid shows a maximum-strength hand with a spade feature. East puts the partnership in the excellent game contract.

West					East
♠ 5					♠ A Q J 10 3
♥ 10 7 2					♥ A K Q 8 3
♦ A K 10 8 7 2					♦ 3
♣ 9 6 3					♣ Q 5

WEST	NORTH	EAST	SOUTH
2 ♦	Pass	2 ♠	Pass
3 ♦	Pass	3 ♥	Pass
4 ♥	Pass	Pass	Pass

West's 2 ♦ bid gets the auction off to an awkward start for East. East's 2♠ response is forcing and West rebids 3 ♦ with no fit and nothing extra. East shows the second suit, and this time finds West with some support. West's raise ends the auction.

West		East
♠ A 6 5		♠ K Q J 9 4
♥ Q 7 2		♥ 3
♦ 9 3		♦ J 8 6 2
♣ K 10 9 7 5		♣ Q 8 3

WEST	NORTH	EAST	SOUTH
Pass	Pass	2♠	Pass
3♠	Pass	Pass	Pass

After West passes, East opens in third position with a *weak two-bid* on a good five-card suit. West's raise to 3♠ is designed to further the preempt, making it more difficult for North–South to enter the auction. The combined effort lets East–West buy the contract on a hand where North–South might be able to make a game in a heart contract.

West		East
♠ 9 3		♠ A 10 7 4
♥ A J 10 8 4 3		♥ K Q 2
♦ K 4		♦ A Q J 8 5
♣ J 8 2		♣ 6

WEST	NORTH	EAST	SOUTH
2♥	Pass	2NT	Pass
3♦	Pass	4NT	Pass
5♦	Pass	6♥	Pass
Pass	Pass		

When West shows a diamond feature in reply to East's 2NT response, East can visualize the possibility of a slam. After using the *Blackwood* convention to find out that West has one ace, East puts the partnership in the fine slam contract.

OPENING SUIT BIDS AT THE THREE LEVEL OR HIGHER

Preemptive Opening Bid

An opening suit bid at the three level or higher is weak and preemptive, usually showing less than the values for an opening bid at the one level. An opening bid at the three level usually shows a good seven-card suit. With an eight-card suit, you can open at the four level. With a nine-card suit, you can open at the game level.

You need to look at the vulnerability when deciding whether to open with a preemptive bid. The standard guideline is the *Rule of 500* or the *Rule of two and three* — you don't want to suffer a penalty of more than 500 points if you are doubled (down two vulnerable; down three non-vulnerable). Most players don't stick too closely to this guideline, especially in third position. Here are some examples:

♠ 3
♥ K Q J 9 7 6 3
♦ 9 4 3
♣ J 4

Open 3 ♥. This is a typical opening preempt — a good seven-card suit with less than the values for an opening bid at the one level. In theory, you might suffer a penalty of 800 points or more if you are vulnerable and are doubled. Nevertheless, that wouldn't deter most players from opening this hand 3 ♥ at any vulnerability.

♠ 9 4
♥ 3
♦ 10 8 7 3
♣ A K J 10 7 3

An opening bid at the three level usually shows a seven-card suit, but many players would open this hand 3♣, especially non-vulnerable in third position. Once partner has passed, you have a little more leeway. Also, even if you play *weak two-bids*, you can't open 2♣ to show this type of hand.

♠ A 4
♥ Q 8 7 6 4 3 2
♦ Q 3
♣ J 4

Pass. This hand isn't worth an opening bid at the one level, and it isn't the right type of hand for a preemptive opening bid either. Your suit is weak and most of your strength lies in the other suits. If you were to open 3 ♥, even non-vulnerable, you could suffer a large penalty, and the opponents might not be able to make a game because of your high cards in the other suits. This hand isn't right for a *weak two-bid* either. 2 ♥ tends to show a decent six-card suit, and that's not a very accurate description of your suit.

♠ A Q J 10 8 6 4 3
♥ 3
♦ 10 8 5
♣ 2

Open 4♠. With an eight-card suit, an opening preempt at the four level is more effective than an opening bid at the three level. Most players would open this hand 4♠ at any vulnerability.

♠ 3
♥ A K J 9 7 5 3
♦ K J 10 4
♣ 4

Open 1♥ in first or second position. This hand has the values for an opening bid at the one level and there might be a slam if partner holds the right cards. You want to leave room to explore for the best contract. In third or fourth position — once partner has passed — the prospect of a slam contract is slight. Many players would open this hand 4♥, taking a chance that partner has enough to help you take ten tricks. At the same time, you'd prefer not to leave the opponents any room to explore, since they can probably take a lot of tricks in their best trump suit.

♠ —
♥ 8
♦ K Q J 9 7 6 5 3 2
♣ J 8 4

Open 5♦, non-vulnerable with your nine-card suit. You could do the same thing vulnerable, although many players might not be willing to take that big a risk and would settle for an opening bid of 4♦. An opening bid of 3♦ is a little timid — you can almost take nine tricks in your own hand.

RESPONDING TO A PREEMPTIVE OPENING BID

When partner opens the bidding with a preemptive bid, the most important thing for you to do is to form a picture of partner's hand. Partner has a long suit, with little or no strength outside that suit. Partner's hand will provide a lot of tricks only if the long suit is trump. Unless you have a source of tricks in your own hand or a good fit with partner's suit, you don't want to play in a notrump contract — partner is unlikely to have any entry to the long suit outside the suit itself. A new suit by responder is forcing — if it's below the level of game and if responder hasn't passed originally — but it's unusual to look for another trump suit after an opening preempt. Your usual choice is between passing or raising partner's suit. Raise opener's suit either in the expectation of making the contract or as a further preemptive move.

Here are examples after the auction starts:

WEST	NORTH	EAST	SOUTH
3 ♥	Pass	?	

♠ K Q 9 7 5 3
♥ 3
♦ K Q J
♣ Q J 3

Pass. Although there are a lot of points, they are likely to be of little use opposite partner's hand. Even with a good suit, partner will have trouble taking nine tricks when you put this hand down as dummy. There's no point in bidding 3NT, since you have no source of tricks. Even if you could establish winners in partner's heart suit, it would be unlikely that you could reach them. Responding 3 ♠, which is a forcing bid, would lead the partnership into more trouble. Pass without hesitation — perhaps the opponents will bid, and you'll get to defend.

♠ A K 9 3
♥ 7
♦ A J 8 5 2
♣ A 7 2

Bid 4 ♥. This hand should provide the extra winners partner needs to take ten tricks in a heart contract. Don't worry about raising partner's suit with a singleton. Partner has shown a good seven-card suit. You don't want to play this sort of hand in notrump — you won't get many tricks from partner's suit, and you don't have enough tricks on your own.

♠ 3 2
♥ Q 7 3
♦ 9 6 4
♣ K J 7 5 2

Bid 4 ♥. You certainly don't expect partner to be able to take ten tricks. Nonetheless, you should raise to the game level out of fear that the opponents can make at least a game contract, if not a slam. Partner has little or no strength outside the heart suit, so you can't expect to take more than one or two tricks on defense. Don't wait for the opponents to reach their best contract. Bid now, before it's too late. Maybe they'll think you hold the hand from the previous example!

SUMMARY

The weak two-bid *is a useful form of preemptive opening bid.*

Opening Weak Two-Bid — 2♦, 2♥, and 2♠

- 5 to 11 high-card points.
- a good six-card suit.

Responses to a Weak Two-Bid

- A raise of opener's suit to any level is to play and could be preemptive (weak). Opener is expected to pass.
- A jump to 3NT or game in a new suit is to play. Opener is expected to pass.
- A response in a new suit below the game level is forcing for one round, showing a five-card or longer suit. Opener rebids as follows:
    - With three-card support, or a doubleton honor, opener raises responder's suit.
    - With no fit for responder's suit, opener rebids the original suit with a minimum (5 to 8 points) and bids a new suit or notrump with a maximum (9 to 11 points).
- A response of 2NT is artificial (conventional) and forcing, showing game interest and asking opener for a further description of the hand. Opener rebids as follows:
    - With a minimum for the *weak two-bid* (5 to 8 points), opener rebids the original suit at the three level.
    - With a maximum for the *weak two-bid* (9 to 11 points), opener bids another suit to show a *feature* — usually an ace or king — in that suit; with no outside feature, opener rebids 3NT to show a maximum.

With a weak hand and a good seven-card or longer suit, an opening preemptive bid can be made at the three level or higher using the following guideline:

Rule of 500 (Rule of Two and Three)

To open a preemptive bid you need enough playing tricks to prevent a penalty of more than 500 points if you are doubled (down two vulnerable; down three non-vulnerable).

When responding to a three level or higher preemptive opening, visualize the type of hand partner holds and use the following guidelines:

Responding to a Preemptive Opening Bid

- You should usually choose between passing or raising partner's suit. You can raise in expectation of making the contract or as a further preemptive move.

- Avoid playing in notrump unless you have your own source of tricks or a fit with partner's long suit.

- A new suit by responder below the level of game is forcing.

The following exercises assume you are using the methods outlined in the summary.

Exercise One — Opening a Weak Two-bid

Your side is non-vulnerable. What call would you make with each of the following hands in first or second position? What would you call with the same hands in third or fourth position?

1) ♠ 6 5
   ♥ A Q J 8 7 3
   ♦ J 9 4
   ♣ 8 3

2) ♠ 5
   ♥ 7 6
   ♦ A J 10 8 7 4
   ♣ Q 9 6 3

3) ♠ Q 8 7 6 5 2
   ♥ K J 8 3
   ♦ Q 9
   ♣ 2

4) ♠ A K J 8 7 3
   ♥ 4
   ♦ K 9 4
   ♣ 8 6 2

5) ♠ 10 7 6
   ♥ K Q J 9 3
   ♦ 8 5 4
   ♣ Q 7

6) ♠ J 7
   ♥ 9 7 6
   ♦ 10 3
   ♣ K Q J 8 7 3

Exercise Two — Responding to a Weak Two-bid

Your side is non-vulnerable. Partner opens the bidding 2 ♦, and the next player passes. What do you respond with the following hands?

1) ♠ K J 9 7 4
   ♥ K Q 8 3
   ♦ 6 4
   ♣ K J

2) ♠ A K J 8 4 2
   ♥ 10 2
   ♦ Q 3
   ♣ A Q 7

3) ♠ A J 10
   ♥ A Q 2
   ♦ K 9 8
   ♣ Q 10 8 5

4) ♠ A K 6
   ♥ 9 6 4
   ♦ Q 8 3
   ♣ K J 5 4

5) ♠ J 7 4
   ♥ Q 2
   ♦ Q J 2
   ♣ Q 10 7 5 2

6) ♠ 3
   ♥ 10 8 7 6 4
   ♦ K 9 7 3
   ♣ K 6 3

Exercise One — Opening a Weak Two-Bid

1) 1st/2nd/3rd: 2 ♥. Ideal weak two-bid.
    4th: Pass. Doesn't qualify under the *Rule of 15*.

2) 1st/2nd/3rd: 2 ♦. Ideal weak two-bid.
    Some players might open 3 ♦ in 3rd position.
    4th: Pass. Doesn't qualify under the *Rule of 15*.

3) 1st/2nd: Pass. Suit isn't good enough and there's a four-card major.
    3rd: Pass or 1 ♠ or 2 ♠. The danger of getting your side into trouble is
    reduced once partner is a passed hand. You might open a *light* 1 ♠ or an
    off-center weak 2 ♠.
    4th: Pass. Doesn't qualify under the *Rule of 15* and the spades are poor.

4) 1st/2nd/3rd: 1 ♠. 11 high-card points plus 2 for the six-card suit. Some
    might open 2 ♠ in third position.
    4th: 2 ♠ or 1 ♠. 1 ♠ is acceptable but a sound weak two-bid in fourth
    position more accurately describes this hand. After partner has passed,
    it's unlikely your side has game, and you can make it difficult for the
    opponents to compete.

5) 1st/2nd/3rd: 2 ♥. Ideal weak two-bid.
    4th: Pass. Doesn't qualify under the *Rule of 15*.

6) 1st/2nd/3rd: Pass. Ideal for a weak two-bid but you can't open a weak
    two-bid in clubs. You might consider 3 ♣, despite the six-card suit.
    4th: Pass.

Exercise Two — Responding to a Weak Two-Bid

1) Pass. Game is unlikely and bidding is likely to get your side into trouble.

2) 2 ♠. This is forcing. A spade game is reasonable if partner has a fit; if
    not, there may be game in notrump or diamonds.

3) 3NT. You should be able to take nine tricks.

4) 2NT. This is artificial (conventional) and forcing.

5) 3 ♦. The hand likely belongs to the opponents but raising to the three level
    will make it more difficult for them to enter the auction.

6) 5 ♦. This is preemptive. You have little defense outside of diamonds.

Exercise Three — More Responses to a Weak Two-bid

Both sides are vulnerable. Partner opens the bidding 2♠, and the next player passes. What do you respond with the following hands?

1) ♠ Q 10 7 2
   ♥ 9 3
   ♦ K 10 7 5 2
   ♣ 6 3

2) ♠ —
   ♥ A K Q 10 8 7 4
   ♦ A Q J
   ♣ J 6 3

3) ♠ Q 8
   ♥ A Q J 2
   ♦ 9 5 3
   ♣ K Q 6 2

4) ♠ J 5
   ♥ Q 9 3
   ♦ K 6 5 3
   ♣ A Q 8 4

5) ♠ Q 6 2
   ♥ 9 8 2
   ♦ K Q 8 5
   ♣ Q 9 2

6) ♠ 7
   ♥ A K J 8 3
   ♦ A K 9 6 3
   ♣ K 6

Exercise Four — Opener's Rebid

As West, what do you rebid with each of the following hands after the auction starts:

WEST	NORTH	EAST	SOUTH
2♥	Pass	2NT	Pass
?			

1) ♠ J 3
   ♥ K Q 10 8 7 5
   ♦ 8 4
   ♣ 10 8 3

2) ♠ J
   ♥ K J 10 9 6 5
   ♦ 9 7 3
   ♣ A 10 4

3) ♠ 7 3
   ♥ A K Q 9 7 5
   ♦ J 9 4
   ♣ 8 2

Exercise Three — More Responses to a Weak Two-bid

1) 4♠. Raise to game as quickly as possible to try to keep the opponents from their best contract. It's likely they can make at least a game if not a slam.

2) 4♥. This tells partner you want to play game in hearts and aren't interested in spades. Partner is expected to pass.

3) 2NT. Game is possible if partner has a maximum. If not, you can stop in 3♠.

4) Pass. Game is unlikely for your side and you have good defense if the opponents come into the auction. Hopefully, you have enough for partner to make the 2♠ contract.

5) 3♠. The opponents can likely make something and your raise may make it more difficult for them to find their best spot. A jump to 4♠ could be too much if the opponents choose to double for penalty.

6) 3♥. This is forcing. You may make game in hearts if partner has a heart fit or game in diamonds or notrump without a heart fit. Even 4♠ may make if partner has a very good spade suit.

Exercise Four — Opener's Rebid

1) 3♥. Partner's 2NT is forcing and the rebid of your suit shows a minimum-strength weak two-bid.

2) 3♣. This shows a feature in clubs and more than a minimum for the weak two-bid.

3) 3NT. This shows a maximum weak two-bid with no side feature.

Exercise Five — Opener's Second Bid

    You hold the following hand as West:

            ♠ K Q 10 9 6 4
            ♥ J 8 3
            ♦ 9 3
            ♣ 7 4

    What is your next bid in each of the following auctions?

1)

WEST	NORTH	EAST	SOUTH
2♠	Pass	3♠	Pass
?			

2)

WEST	NORTH	EAST	SOUTH
2♠	Pass	3♥	Pass
?			

3)

WEST	NORTH	EAST	SOUTH
2♠	Double	2NT	3♦
?			

4)

WEST	NORTH	EAST	SOUTH
2♠	Pass	3NT	Pass
?			

5)

WEST	NORTH	EAST	SOUTH
2♠	3♣	4♠	5♣
?			

Exercise Six — Higher-Level Openings

    What is your opening call with each of the following hands?

1)	♠ 6	2)	♠ A Q J 9 7 6 4 3	3)	♠ —
	♥ A K J 9 8 5 3		♥ 3		♥ 7 2
	♦ J 7 4		♦ 9 4		♦ K Q J 9 8 7 5 4 3
	♣ 9 3		♣ J 8		♣ 10 8

Exercise Five — Opener's Second Bid

1) Pass. Partner's raise isn't invitational. You've already described your hand with the weak two-bid.

2) 4 ♥. A new suit by responder is forcing. Raise to show support.

3) Pass. You would have rebid 3 ♠ to show a minimum if South had passed, but the 3 ♦ bid gives you the option of passing to show nothing extra.

4) Pass. Partner has heard your descriptive opening bid and decided that 3NT is the best contract for your side. Partner hasn't promised a fit for spades.

5) Pass. Partner is the captain. Partner's 4 ♠ bid may have been made with a weak hand or a strong hand. Pass, and leave any further decision to partner.

Exercise Six — Higher-Level Openings

1) 3 ♥. With a seven-card suit, open a preemptive (weak) bid at the three level.

2) 4 ♠. An eight-card suit can be opened at the four level.

3) 5 ♦. With a weak hand but a good nine-card minor suit, you can open at the five level . . . to make things interesting!

Bid and Play — Deal 1

(E-Z Deal Cards: #7, Deal 1 — Dealer, North)

Suggested Bidding

WEST	NORTH	EAST	SOUTH
	Pass	2♥	Pass
Pass	Pass		

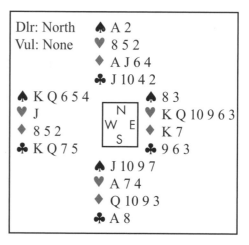

Dlr: North
Vul: None

♠ A 2
♥ 8 5 2
♦ A J 6 4
♣ J 10 4 2

♠ K Q 6 5 4
♥ J
♦ 8 5 2
♣ K Q 7 5

♠ 8 3
♥ K Q 10 9 6 3
♦ K 7
♣ 9 6 3

♠ J 10 9 7
♥ A 7 4
♦ Q 10 9 3
♣ A 8

After North's pass, East has a perfect hand for a weak two-bid. The opening bid of 2♥ shows a good six-card suit and less than values for an opening bid at the one level. South's hand is unsuitable for either an overcall or a takeout double. West doesn't much care for partner's choice of trump suit but should not attempt to *improve* the contract. West's hand is unsuitable for notrump, and a response in a new suit would be forcing, likely getting the partnership too high. West should pass, hoping partner can make eight tricks or that the opponents will enter the auction. North has the values for a balancing bid, but neither a takeout double nor an overcall is attractive. North passes, leaving East as declarer in 2♥.

North–South can make at least eight tricks in diamonds, and even a contract of 3♦ down one would be a good result. East's weak two-bid makes it difficult for North–South to enter the auction. If they do, West will get off to the best lead of the ♥ J.

Suggested Opening Lead

South is on lead and should choose the ♠J, top of a sequence.

Suggested Play

Declarer has a spade loser, a heart loser, two diamond losers, and two club losers. East should plan to draw trumps and then try finesses in both diamonds and clubs. East can lead twice toward dummy's ♣K and ♣Q, hoping that South has the ♣A. East can also lead a low diamond from dummy toward the ♦K, hoping North has the ♦A.

There's not much difficulty on the actual deal, since both the ♣A and the ♦A are favorably placed for declarer. The defenders can probably get a club ruff (see "Suggested Defense" below), but East should finish with at least eight tricks.

Suggested Defense

On the layout of the cards, there's nothing the defenders can do to prevent East from making the contract of 2♥. The best they can do is get a club ruff and prevent declarer from making an overtrick. This isn't easy. With a sequence to lead from, South is unlikely to start by leading the ♣A, hoping to get a ruff. On the lead of the ♠J, North will win the first trick with the ♠A but is unlikely to lead back a club. Unless one of the defenders switches to clubs before East can drive out the ♥A and draw trumps, declarer will take nine tricks.

If North–South find a way into the auction and play in a diamond partscore, East–West can probably take five tricks after the lead of the ♥J — one spade, two hearts, one diamond, and one club. If South plays in a notrump contract and West leads the ♥J, East must be careful to overtake this with the ♥Q and continue leading hearts. If East doesn't overtake and South holds up the ♥A, East–West won't be able to establish their heart winners while East still has a potential entry with the ♦K.

Bid and Play — Deal 2

(E-Z Deal Cards: #7, Deal 2 — Dealer, East)

Suggested Bidding

WEST	NORTH	EAST	SOUTH
		Pass	2♦
Pass	2NT	Pass	3♥
Pass	3NT	Pass	Pass
Pass			

With only a five-card heart suit, East does not have the right type of hand for a weak two-bid in first position. South, however, has an ideal hand for opening 2♦ — a good six-card suit and 9 high-card points. With a balanced hand, 15 high-card points and an honor in partner's suit, North is interested in reaching a game contract after hearing South's opening bid of 2♦. With no strength in hearts, it would be dangerous for

```
Dlr: East    ♠ A K 7 4
Vul: N–S     ♥ 10 6 2
             ♦ K 5
             ♣ K Q 10 4
♠ Q 10 9 5         ♠ J 6 2
♥ A 8       N      ♥ Q J 9 7 3
♦ J 6 2   W   E    ♦ 9 4
♣ J 9 7 3     S    ♣ A 8 2
             ♠ 8 3
             ♥ K 5 4
             ♦ A Q 10 8 7 3
             ♣ 6 5
```

North to insist on a contract of 3NT, especially since South could have as few as 6 points. North asks for more information by making the artificial (conventional) response of 2NT.

With close to a maximum for the weak two-bid, South shows a side feature in hearts. This is all North needs to know to put the partnership in a contract of 3NT. Opposite good diamonds and a feature in hearts, North expects to have a play for nine tricks. South respects North's decision.

Suggested Opening Lead

East is on lead. Although South has shown some values in hearts, that suit still looks best for the defense. Presumably, North has some strength in clubs and spades for the 3NT bid. South would start with the ♥ Q, top of the broken sequence.

Suggested Play

Declarer has two sure winners in spades and three in diamonds. If the missing diamonds divide 3–2 or the ♦ J appears on the first round, declarer will get three more tricks from that suit. Declarer can promote a ninth trick in clubs and may get a trick from the heart suit.

North has one hurdle to overcome, the opening heart lead. North wants to make sure that the defenders don't take four or five heart tricks and defeat the contract. There's no danger if East holds the ♥ A since the ♥ K will then be a trick. There is a danger if West holds the ♥ A. To decide whether to play the ♥ K on the first trick, North needs to look carefully at the layout of the suit. East's lead of the ♥ Q implies that East also holds the ♥ J. East could be leading from a holding such as ♥ A Q J x or ♥ Q J 9 x.

The ♥ 10 in North's hand is a critical card. As long as East holds the ♥ J, North can secure the contract by playing *low* on the first trick. East's ♥ Q may win the first trick, but now the defenders are helpless. If East continues with the ♥ J, declarer can cover with dummy's ♥ K and the ♥ 10 will become a trick if West wins the ♥ A. If East continues with a low heart, declarer plays low from dummy and will win the trick with the ♥ 10 unless West plays the ♥ A. If West does play the ♥ A on the second trick, South's ♥ K is a winner.

By playing a low heart from dummy on the first trick, declarer effectively freezes the suit. If the defenders lead the suit a second time, declarer is sure to get a heart trick. If the defenders lead anything else, declarer can establish a club trick to make the contract. There are many such positions where the suit is frozen for one side or the other or both. Whichever side leads the suit, that side will lose a trick.

Look at what happens if declarer, hoping East has the ♥ A, plays the ♥ K on the first trick. West wins and returns a heart, trapping North's ♥ 10. The defenders take the first five heart tricks and the ♣ A to defeat the contract two tricks.

If declarer negotiates the heart suit correctly, the only remaining challenge is the diamond suit. When the defenders' diamonds divide 3–2, six tricks roll home in the suit and declarer makes the contract.

Suggested Defense

If East starts with the ♥Q, the defenders can defeat the contract if dummy's ♥K is played on the first trick. If declarer plays a low heart from dummy on the first trick, there's nothing the defenders can do. If the ♥Q wins the first trick, East's best continuation is the ♥J, hoping that West holds the ♥10 or that North started with a doubleton ♥10.

Interestingly enough, if declarer does duck the first heart, West's best play is to overtake with the ♥A and return a heart. That gives declarer a trick with the ♥K but establishes the heart suit for the defense. Declarer cannot afford to let East win a trick with the ♣A and is restricted to nine tricks. If West doesn't overtake the first heart and East continues with a small heart, declarer is likely to come to ten tricks — getting a heart trick and having time to establish a club trick.

It's interesting to speculate what might happen if East leads a low heart rather than the ♥Q. Declarer should play low from dummy and not risk everything by playing the ♥K on the first trick. Then declarer will make the contract. If declarer plays the ♥K on the first trick, then the defenders can defeat the contract two tricks.

Bid and Play — Deal 3

(E-Z Deal Cards: #7, Deal 3 — Dealer, South)

Suggested Bidding

WEST	NORTH	EAST	SOUTH
			Pass
Pass	2♠	Double	3♠
Pass	Pass	Pass	

After South and West pass, this is the perfect time for North to open a weak two-bid. Since South has already passed, the partnership is unlikely to make a game contract but East–West could have most of the strength and might make a game. Also, North–South are not vulnerable. With a good suit, North is unlikely to get into much trouble even if doubled for penalties.

East has the right hand for a takeout double — a hand worth an opening bid or more with support

```
Dlr: South      ♠ A J 10 7 4 3
Vul: E–W        ♥ 6
                ♦ K J 8 4
                ♣ 7 2
♠ Q 8 5                      ♠ 9
♥ K 8 3 2        N           ♥ A Q 10 5
♦ 6 5 2        W   E         ♦ A 10 7 3
♣ A 10 6         S           ♣ K J 9 5
                ♠ K 6 2
                ♥ J 9 7 4
                ♦ Q 9
                ♣ Q 8 4 3
```

for all of the unbid suits. Now it's up to South. Although partner has been doubled at the two level, the double was not for penalties. If South passes, East–West will likely bid to their best contract. With three-card support for partner's suit, South should raise to the three level. North–South should have a nine-card fit, making it difficult for the opponents to double for penalty, and the raise will make it awkward for East–West to find their best spot.

Had South passed, West would be able to comfortably respond 3♥ to the takeout double, and East–West would likely land in their best contract. After the 3♠ bid, West has a tough decision. West has some high cards but not really enough to bid 4♥ and not enough to double 3♠. West's best choice is probably to pass and hope to defeat the contract. If West passes, that should end the auction. East doesn't have enough to compete any further.

Suggested Opening Lead

East has a difficult choice of opening leads. Anything could be right. It's usually best to avoid leading a singleton trump when there's no expectation that declarer will be ruffing losers in dummy. Instead, East should pick an unbid suit. The ♥A is quite reasonable. North has shown a weak hand and is unlikely to hold the ♥K. East will have a better idea of what to do next after seeing the dummy.

Suggested Play

North has a potential spade loser, a heart loser, two diamond losers, and two club losers. A diamond loser can be ruffed in dummy or the ♦10 might drop, so declarer's main concern should be the trump suit.

Declarer has a choice between playing the ♠A and ♠K, hoping the ♠Q will fall, or taking a finesse. The standard guideline in this situation is 'eight ever, nine never,' indicating that with nine or more cards you 'never' finesse. This is a guideline, however, not a rule. Declarer should also be guided by the auction. East's takeout double showing support for all of the unbid suits indicates that East is probably short in spades. Declarer should take this into account before deciding what to do in spades.

Suppose the defenders lead the ♥A and another heart which is ruffed by North. Before playing any trumps, declarer should lead diamonds next to drive out the ♦A. This will allow declarer to ruff a diamond loser even if the missing trumps divide badly. Suppose the defenders take their club winners after winning the ♦A and declarer regains the lead. Now it's time for the trump suit. Declarer plays a low spade to dummy's ♠K and leads a low spade back toward the North hand. West follows on the second round with a low spade and North is at the crossroads. Follow the guideline or take the finesse based on the inference from the auction?

As can be seen from the actual layout, North can make the contract by finessing. Is that the *right* play? In this situation, there is no right or wrong. That's what makes the game interesting. Going down one trick in a contract of 3♠ is no disaster. Making 3♠ will be an excellent result. North may still be pondering.

Suggested Defense

The defenders should avoid giving declarer any help. If the defenders lead spades, they will solve declarer's problem in that suit. Meanwhile, they should be careful to collect the tricks to which they are entitled — one heart, one diamond, and two clubs. Then they'll have to sit back and see if declarer gives them a second diamond trick or a spade trick.

If East–West bid to a heart contract, they are unlikely to take ten tricks even if they guess how to play the club suit. North–South should get at least one spade trick, one heart trick, and two diamond tricks, maybe more. If East–West get pushed to 4♥, they are likely to get a poor result if they go down two tricks (or get doubled and go down one trick). Vulnerable undertricks can be expensive.

Bid and Play — Deal 4

(E-Z Deal Cards: #7, Deal 4 — Dealer, West)

Suggested Bidding

WEST	NORTH	EAST	SOUTH
2 ♥	Pass	4 ♥	Double
Pass	Pass (?)	Pass	

West has an ideal hand for an opening weak two-bid in first position. North doesn't have enough strength to enter the auction at this point, so East has an opportunity to make the auction more difficult for North–South. With a weak hand but good support for partner's suit, East should raise to the game level. East doesn't expect partner to make a contract of 4 ♥ but, with little or no defensive strength, suspects the opponents can make a game or slam.

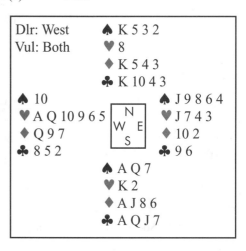

Dlr: West
Vul: Both

```
              ♠ K 5 3 2
              ♥ 8
              ♦ K 5 4 3
              ♣ K 10 4 3
♠ 10                        ♠ J 9 8 6 4
♥ A Q 10 9 6 5    N         ♥ J 7 4 3
♦ Q 9 7        W     E      ♦ 10 2
♣ 8 5 2           S         ♣ 9 6
              ♠ A Q 7
              ♥ K 2
              ♦ A J 8 6
              ♣ A Q J 7
```

East's bid creates a challenge for South. Holding 21 high-card points, South didn't anticipate that the auction would be at the four level before getting an opportunity to bid. With too much to pass, South has to double and hope for the best. After West's pass, it's now North that has a tough decision. Partner's double shows a good hand, but South is unlikely to hold a lot of strength in hearts. North–South can probably get a better score by bidding and making a game contract than by defeating the opponents' contract one or two tricks. With only four cards in each of the unbid suits, North's safest action is probably to pass and hope to get enough of a penalty to compensate for any North–South contract. Still, many North's would be tempted to bid 4 ♠ — and now South might push higher.

If East–West were not in the bidding, North–South would probably find a reasonable contract through some auction such as:

WEST	NORTH	EAST	SOUTH
Pass	Pass	Pass	2NT
Pass	3♣	Pass	3♦
Pass	3NT	Pass	Pass
Pass			

South would open 2NT showing a balanced hand of 20 or 21 points. North would use the *Stayman* convention to check for a major-suit fit and then settle for game in notrump. If West leads a heart, South will make at least 10 tricks. North–South can also make a contract of 5♣ or 5♦ — losing only one heart and one diamond.

East–West's bidding makes it very difficult for North–South to reach a makeable contract. If North bids and the partnership winds up in their 4–3 spade fit, they will fare poorly when the trumps break 5–1. Even if North–South do manage to find a minor suit fit, they may get too high, reaching a slam contract.

Suggested Opening Lead

If North–South decide to defend, North's best lead is probably a trump. When North–South have most of the strength, it's a good idea to lead trumps to try to prevent declarer from ruffing losers. On the actual hand, it won't make much difference. North could lead a low card in any suit and the defense should still come to the same number of tricks.

Suggested Play

West has a spade loser, a heart loser, three diamond losers, and three club losers. In a doubled contract, West can't afford to be defeated too many tricks or the penalty will be larger than any score the opponents could make in their best contract. West should plan to trump a diamond loser and a club loser in dummy. West should also plan to take a finesse in the trump suit, hoping to trap South's ♥K.

If the defenders don't lead a trump initially, West should give up two tricks in one of the minor suits, planning to ruff the third round in the dummy. West can then take the trump finesse and eventually ruff another loser in dummy. Playing carefully, West should finish with one spade loser, no heart losers, two diamond losers, and two club losers. Down two.

Since both partnerships are vulnerable, East–West will lose 500 points for being defeated two tricks doubled in a contract of 4 ♥. This is less than the value of a vulnerable game for North–South in 3NT, 5 ♣, or 5 ♦. East–West might do even better than this if North–South get to a spade contract or get too high in another denomination.

Suggested Defense

Although a trump lead is usually best against this type of auction, it won't do the defense much good on this deal. The defenders are entitled to only five tricks. If declarer doesn't take the heart finesse, the defenders may get a sixth trick, giving them a penalty of 800 points, but that's unlikely.

NOTE: See the Appendix (pages 328–332) for a discussion of these supplemental conventions and/or treatments.

Ogust Responses to Weak Two-Bids

Flannery 2♦

Namyats

CHAPTER 8
Strong 2♣ Opening

STRONG 2♣ OPENING

The partnership agrees to play *weak two-bids*, and this is your hand.

♠ A K J   This hand is too strong for an opening bid of 1 ♥,
♥ A K Q 10 7 6   which responder could pass. You can no longer open
♦ K 8   2 ♥, since that would show 5 to 11 points. The com-
♣ A 9   mon duplicate approach is to use an opening bid of
                    2♣ for all strong hands and to open *weak two-bids*
in diamonds, hearts, and spades. This is referred to as the *strong artificial
2♣ opening*. The 2♣ opening is artificial (conventional), and forcing. It's
used for strong opening hands whether they are balanced or unbalanced.

OPENING 2♣ WITH A STRONG UNBALANCED HAND

The opening bid of 2♣ can show a hand of about 22 or more points,
or a strong playing hand that can take nine or more tricks. For example:

♠ A K Q 10 7 5 3   It's likely that you can take ten tricks without any
♥ A K 8   help from partner. Using the *strong artificial 2♣
♦ A Q   opening*, this hand would be opened 2♣. The 2♣
♣ 4   bid is artificial and partner is forced to make a re-
                    sponse. You'll show the spade suit at your next turn
                    to bid.

♠ A Q 6   There is no guarantee you can make a game-level
♥ A K Q 9 3   contract with this hand, but it's too strong to open
♦ 7   1 ♥. You have 22 high-card points plus 1 for the five-
♣ A K 7 5   card suit. Start with 2♣, planning to show your dis-
                    tribution with your rebids.

♠ A K Q J 10 5   There are 17 high-card points in this hand, but the
♥ 5   distribution is so strong that you expect to take at
♦ A K 10 9 3   least nine — and probably ten — tricks in a spade
♣ 3   contract. Open 2♣, intending to show the spade suit
                    at your next opportunity and then the diamonds, if
                    necessary.

♠ K Q 5
♥ J
♦ A K J 8 5
♣ A Q 8 5

This is a strong hand, but not strong enough to open 2♣. Bid 1♦. If partner doesn't have enough to respond, it's unlikely that your side belongs at the game level.

OPENING 2♣ WITH A STRONG BALANCED HAND

Using the *strong artificial 2♣ opening*, balanced hands of 22 or more points are started with 2♣. Opener plans to rebid 2NT with a balanced hand of 22 to 24 points and 3NT with a balanced hand of 25 to 27 points.

As a consequence of using 2♣ for strong balanced hands of 22 or more points, an immediate opening bid of 2NT can be used to show a balanced hand of 20 or 21 points. This fits well with a 15 to 17 point range for an opening 1NT bid. With 18 or 19 points and a balanced hand, opener starts with one-of-a-suit, planning to jump to 2NT on the rebid.

The partnership uses the *strong artificial 2♣ opening*. You're the dealer.

♠ A K J 8
♥ K Q 7
♦ A Q 9
♣ K 8 3

With 22 high-card points, bid 2♣. After the response, opener plans to rebid 2NT, showing a balanced hand of 22 to 24 points.

♠ A Q J
♥ A K 10
♦ 10 7
♣ A K Q 9 5

With 5–3–3–2 distribution, this is a balanced hand. There are 23 high-card points plus 1 for the five-card suit. Open 2♣, intending to rebid 2NT. Most players today aren't deterred from bidding notrump by a small doubleton in one of the suits.

♠ K Q J
♥ A J 8 7 5
♦ A K J
♣ A Q

This is a balanced hand with 25 high-card points plus 1 point for the five-card suit. Open 2♣, intending to rebid 3NT to show a balanced hand of 25 to 27 points. A balanced hand can have a five-card major suit.

♠ K 6
♥ K J 10 8
♦ A Q J 7
♣ A Q 4

With a balanced hand of 20 high-card points, open 2NT. This shows a hand of 20 or 21 points, not strong enough to open with 2♣ and rebid 2NT.

RESPONDING TO 2♣

The opening 2♣ bid is artificial (conventional), responder is not allowed to pass. Responder bids as follows:

- With 8 or more points and a good five-card or longer suit, responder bids 2♥, 2♠, 3♣, or 3♦ (not 2♦). This is a *positive* response and commits the partnership to game. The definition of a *good* suit varies from partnership to partnership but is frequently interpreted as a five-card suit containing two of the top three honors (K Q x x x, A Q x x x, A K x x x) or any six-card or longer suit (K x x x x x, Q J x x x x, J x x x x x x). Some partnerships lower this requirement, but most would agree that a five-card suit headed by the jack isn't good enough.

- With 8 or more points and a balanced hand, responder bids 2NT. This is a positive response, committing the partnership to game.

- With all other hands, responder makes the artificial (conventional) response of 2♦, which is referred to as a *waiting* bid. It includes all hands with fewer than 8 points as well as those with 8 or more that are unsuitable for a positive response. This bid is not forcing to game.

On most hands, responder will bid 2♦. This gives opener the maximum amount of room to describe the hand. You are East.

WEST	NORTH	**EAST**	SOUTH
2♣	Pass	?	

♠ 10 8 4 2
♥ J 9 6 3
♦ 6 4
♣ J 6 5

Respond 2♦. The opening 2♣ bid is forcing, so responder can't pass even with a weak hand. The artificial (conventional) response of 2♦ is used for hands not strong enough for a positive response.

♠ J
♥ K J 8 4
♦ A 5 2
♣ J 8 7 5 3

Respond 2♦. Although the 2♦ response usually shows a weak hand of fewer than 8 points, it's also used with a hand unsuitable for a positive response. This hand has enough strength for a positive response, but it isn't balanced and doesn't have a good five-card suit. This illustrates why 2♦ is referred to as a waiting bid, rather than a negative response. With this hand, wait for opener's rebid to learn the nature of opener's hand. You'll make sure that the partnership keeps bidding to at least game.

♠ A Q 10 7 3 2
♥ 4 2
♦ 9 8
♣ 6 4 2

Respond 2♠. There are only 6 high-card points, but you can add 2 length points for the six-card suit, making this hand worth a positive response. The spade suit is strong enough to qualify.

♠ 7 3
♥ K Q 10 8 5
♦ 8 7 2
♣ K 5 2

Respond 2♥. This is a positive response, showing a five-card or longer suit with at least 8 points. Since opener has a hand worth about 22 or more points, the partnership is committed to at least game and will be interested in exploring slam possibilities.

♠ Q 8
♥ J 9 6 5
♦ K 10 8 3
♣ K 7 5

Respond 2NT. 2NT shows a balanced hand with 8 or more high-card points. There is no need to jump with a strong balanced hand, since the positive response commits the partnership to game. The partnership wants to leave some bidding room available to explore the possibility of a slam.

♠ 8 6 2
♥ 10 9 3
♦ A K J 8 6 3
♣ 3

Respond 3♦. With a positive response in diamonds, responder has to jump to the three level. The 2♦ response is reserved for the artificial (conventional) waiting bid.

OPENER'S REBID

If responder makes the waiting response of 2 ♦, opener then makes a rebid that describes the nature of the hand.

- Opener's rebid in a suit shows an unbalanced hand and is still forcing.

- A notrump rebid shows a balanced hand and is not forcing.

For example:

WEST	NORTH	EAST	SOUTH
2♣	Pass	2♦	Pass
?			

♠ 6
♥ A K J 10 8 5
♦ A K Q 6
♣ A Q

Rebid 2 ♥. This sequence shows the same type of hand that would be opened 2 ♥ if the partnership uses *strong two-bids*. Opener doesn't need to jump, since a rebid in a suit is forcing after the 2♣ opening. Notice that no bidding room has been lost through the use of the artificial (conventional) 2♣ opening bid when opener has a major suit. The partnership is still at the two level by the time opener has described the hand.

♠ —
♥ A K Q
♦ K Q 3
♣ A Q J 10 8 7 3

Rebid 3♣. With a strong minor-suit hand, opener has to show the suit at the three level after the 2 ♦ response. The initial 2♣ bid said nothing about clubs. This shows the slight disadvantage of using the artificial (conventional) 2♣ opening — when opener has a minor suit, the partnership will be at the three level before opener can describe the hand. For most partnerships, however, this disadvantage is more than offset by the benefit of freeing up the opening bids of 2 ♦, 2 ♥, and 2 ♠ for other uses, such as *weak two-bids*.

♠ A K J 10 7
♥ A
♦ A K Q 6 3
♣ J 4

Rebid 2♠. After the 2♦ response, opener starts showing suits in the usual order — starting with the higher-ranking of two five-card suits. The 2♠ rebid is forcing, so opener could show the diamond suit at the next opportunity, if necessary.

♠ A K J
♥ K Q 9 5
♦ K Q 7 3
♣ A 4

Rebid 2NT. The rebid of 2NT describes a balanced hand with 22 to 24 points. Unlike the rebid in a suit, the notrump rebid isn't forcing. It shows an upper limit of 24 points, so responder can pass without enough to take the partnership to the game level.

♠ K Q
♥ A Q 8
♦ A K Q 9 7
♣ A J 10

Rebid 3NT. 3NT describes a balanced hand with 25 to 27 points. It's a more descriptive rebid than 3♦, which would show an unbalanced hand with a long diamond suit. Since the partnership is already at the game level, the 3NT rebid isn't forcing.

If responder makes a positive response in a suit, the partnership is committed to the game level. Opener bids naturally, describing the hand and looking for a suitable trump fit. For example:

WEST	**NORTH**	EAST	SOUTH
	2♣	Pass	2♠
Pass	?		

♠ 4
♥ A K J 3
♦ K 3
♣ A K Q J 7 3

Rebid 3♣. The partnership is headed to at least game but has yet to find a suitable trump suit. Start by showing your club suit. Partner may be able to support that suit, or you might find a fit in hearts.

♠ Q 5
♥ A K J
♦ A K 7 3
♣ K Q 6 2

Rebid 2NT. This is the rebid you were planning to make if partner had responded 2♦. It's still the most descriptive bid you can make at this point. In this auction, your 2NT rebid is forcing — partner's positive response has committed the partnership to game.

♠ K J 8 3
♥ A 5
♦ K Q J
♣ A K J 4

Raise to 3 ♠. You were planning to rebid 2NT after a 2 ♦ response, but partner's positive response in spades has changed the situation. With excellent support for partner's suit, it's best to settle on the trump suit right away. Once that is done, the partnership can search for slam.

If responder bids 2NT, showing a balanced hand with 8 or more points, the partnership is committed to at least game. Opener makes a natural rebid with the exception that 3 ♣ is now the *Stayman* convention, asking responder for a four-card major. Here are examples after the auction starts:

WEST	NORTH	EAST	SOUTH
2♣	Pass	2NT	Pass
?			

♠ K 3
♥ A K Q 9 3
♦ 5
♣ A K Q J 5

Rebid 3 ♥. This is a natural rebid showing a five-card or longer suit. The partnership is still searching for the best contract. Slam aspirations will have to wait until a fit can be found.

♠ A Q J
♥ K Q 3
♦ Q J 3
♣ A K 7 2

Raise to 3NT. This describes a balanced hand of 22 to 24 points. It won't necessarily end the auction, since responder can have more than 8 points. With only 8 or 9 points, however, responder can pass, leaving the partnership at the game level.

♠ A Q J 3
♥ A K J 5
♦ K 9 3
♣ A 7

Rebid 3♣. This is the *Stayman* convention, asking partner for a four-card major. If partner rebids 3 ♥ or 3♠, showing a four-card suit, raise to the game level. If partner rebids 3 ♦, showing no four-card major suit, rebid 3NT. With more than 8 or 9 points, partner can move toward slam.

RESPONDER'S REBID

If responder initially made a waiting response of 2 ♦, responder has to bid again if opener rebids a suit. Responder is in the same position as if opener started with a strong two-bid.

Responder has the following options:

- Raise opener's suit with three-card or longer support and 4 or more points. This sets the trump suit and leaves room for the partnership to explore slam possibilities.

- Jump raise opener's suit with four-card or longer support but no aces, kings, singletons, or voids. This bid sends the message that responder has no values or distribution useful for a slam contract other than good trump support.

- Bid a reasonable five-card or longer suit, typically J 10 x x x or better. Since responder didn't bid the suit directly over 2♣, responder is showing a suit that wasn't good enough for an immediate positive response.

- Bid notrump at the cheapest available level. This is the catchall bid to keep the auction going, even when responder has a very weak hand. It doesn't promise any strength in the unbid suits.

You are South after the auction has begun:

WEST	NORTH	EAST	**SOUTH**
	2♣	Pass	2 ♦
Pass	2♠	Pass	?

♠ Q 7 5
♥ 9 3
♦ K 9 7 6 2
♣ 8 4 2

Raise to 3 ♠, forcing. Since opener will have a good five-card or longer spade suit for the strong two-bid, agreeing on spades as the trump suit is more important than showing your own suit. There's still room left to explore slam possibilities.

♠ J 8 4 3
♥ J 7 5 2
♦ 9 3
♣ 10 6 4

Raise to 4♠. You have excellent support for partner's suit which should be enough for game opposite the strong two-bid. You don't have anything else that will be of much use, however. The jump to game says you have no interest in reaching a slam contract.

♠ 7 4
♥ Q J 9 7 6
♦ Q 8 5 2
♣ 9 4

Bid 3♥. You don't have much in the way of high cards but you can afford to show your reasonable five-card suit. You denied a positive response with a good five-card suit with the 2♦ response, so opener won't be expecting too much.

♠ 8 5
♥ 10 8 3
♦ 7 6 4 2
♣ J 9 6 3

Bid 2NT. You have to say something to keep the auction going since opener might have 10 or more tricks without any help from you. 2NT shows a weak hand.

If responder originally makes a positive response, the partnership is committed to at least game.

You are South after the auction has begun:

WEST	NORTH	EAST	**SOUTH**
	2♣	Pass	2♥
Pass	3♦	Pass	?

♠ 9 5
♥ A K 8 7 4
♦ J 10 5
♣ 10 8 3

Raise to 4♦. You've already shown a good five-card heart suit and enough for a positive response. Now you can show diamond support. Since opener will have a very good diamond suit, there could be a slam. Show as much encouragement as possible.

♠ 9 6 5
♥ K Q 10 9 7 3
♦ 3
♣ K 8 2

Rebid 3♥. Without support for opener's suit, rebid your excellent six-card heart suit. Hearts could be a reasonable trump suit. Opener's high cards should compensate for any lack of support for your suit.

♠ K 6
♥ K Q 8 7 6
♦ 5 2
♣ J 9 5 3

Rebid 3NT. You've already shown your five-card heart suit. To show your second suit, you would have to go beyond 3NT. Without much of a fit for partner and with some strength in the other suits, 3NT appears to be the best choice. Opener can pass or bid again.

THE SUBSEQUENT AUCTION

Once opener has had a chance to describe the hand, the auction can proceed in many directions.

- If responder started with a positive response, the partnership is committed to at least game.

- If responder makes the waiting response of 2♦, the partnership is forced to game *unless opener rebids 2NT or immediately rebids the same suit.*

Here are examples:

West						East
♠ A K J 9 8	WEST	NORTH	EAST	SOUTH		♠ 4 2
♥ A K Q 6 3	2♣	Pass	2♦	Pass		♥ 10 8 5 2
♦ K Q	2♠	Pass	2NT	Pass		♦ J 9 8 5
♣ 5	3♥	Pass	4♥	Pass		♣ Q 7 6
	Pass	Pass				

Without enough for a positive response, East responds 2♦ to the *strong artificial (conventional) 2♣ opening*. West now shows the higher-ranking of the two five-card suits. West's 2♠ rebid is forcing. Since East doesn't have support for opener's suit, East keeps the auction going with a rebid of 2NT. West shows the other suit. Since this is a new suit by opener, it's a forcing bid. With support for opener's second suit, East raises to the game level. Since East has not expressed any interest in a slam contract, West has nothing further to say.

West	WEST	NORTH	EAST	SOUTH	East
♠ A Q J 9 8 5	2♣	Pass	2♦	Pass	♠ 6 3
♥ A Q 3	2♠	Pass	3♥	Pass	♥ J 8 7 6 5 2
♦ K 3	4♥	Pass	Pass	Pass	♦ 9 7 4
♣ A K					♣ J 6

East doesn't have enough for a positive response and starts by making a waiting response of 2♦. West shows the spade suit and now East has an opportunity to show the hearts. West raises responder's suit, and the partnership has arrived at game.

West	WEST	NORTH	EAST	SOUTH	East
♠ A K J 10 7 3	2♣	Pass	2♥	Pass	♠ Q 9 2
♥ 4	2♠	Pass	3♠	Pass	♥ K Q 10 6 5
♦ A K J 4	4NT	Pass	5♣	Pass	♦ 8 3
♣ A Q	6♠	Pass	Pass	Pass	♣ J 7 4

East has enough to make a positive response and shows the good five-card suit. West now shows the spade suit and East raises to show the support. Having found a fit and knowing that East has enough strength for a positive response, West launches into *Blackwood* to check for aces. East's 5♣ response shows no aces, so West settles for a small slam.

West	WEST	NORTH	EAST	SOUTH	East
♠ K 5	2♣	Pass	2♦	Pass	♠ J 8 4 2
♥ A K Q J 8 6 2	2♥	Pass	2NT	Pass	♥ 5
♦ A Q 5	3♥	Pass	Pass	Pass	♦ 9 7 6 3 2
♣ Q					♣ 10 7 4

West's 2♥ rebid is forcing after the 2♦ response, so East bids 2NT with no support for opener's suit and no reasonable suit to show. West's immediate rebid of the original suit isn't forcing. It shows a hand which can take about nine tricks, and partner can pass with no help — which West is happy to do.

West	WEST	NORTH	EAST	SOUTH	East
♠ A K J 9 7 3	2♣	Pass	2♦	Pass	♠ 10 6 4 2
♥ Q 3	2♠	Pass	4♠	Pass	♥ 10 8 2
♦ A K Q	Pass	Pass			♦ 3 2
♣ K J					♣ Q 7 6 5

After West shows the spade suit, East has nothing much except four-card trump support. An immediate raise to the game level is commonly used to show this type of hand — a hand with no aces, kings, singletons, or voids, but with good trump support. With a better hand, East simply raises to 3 ♠, leaving room for opener to explore for a slam contract. The immediate jump to game is essentially a discouraging bid, telling opener that you are willing to play at the game level but aren't interested in a slam contract. Upon hearing this response, opener has no desire to bid any higher.

West	WEST	NORTH	EAST	SOUTH	East
♠ 6	2♣	Pass	2 ♦	Pass	♠ J 8 7 5 2
♥ A K Q 9 7	2 ♥	Pass	2 ♠	Pass	♥ 2
♦ K Q 10 6 2	3 ♦	Pass	4 ♦	Pass	♦ A J 7 5
♣ A K	4NT	Pass	5 ♦	Pass	♣ Q 10 8
	6 ♦	Pass	Pass	Pass	

Holding enough for a positive response but with no good five-card suit to show, East makes a waiting bid of 2 ♦. West shows the heart suit and East shows the spade suit. Without a fit in spades, West shows a second suit, diamonds. East raises to show the fit. Having found a fit, West can use the *Blackwood* convention to ask for aces. East's 5 ♦ response shows one ace and West bids the slam.

West	WEST	NORTH	EAST	SOUTH	East
♠ A K 5	2♣	Pass	2 ♦	Pass	♠ 10 8 7 4
♥ K Q 7 3	2NT	Pass	Pass	Pass	♥ 8 4
♦ A Q J 5					♦ 10 6 4
♣ K 3					♣ J 9 8 2

West's 2NT rebid shows a balanced hand of 22 to 24 points and is not forcing. With nothing that suggests that the partnership can make a game, East passes.

If opener rebids 2NT, the partnership uses the same methods as when responding to an opening bid of 2NT. For example, responder can use both the *Stayman* convention and the *Jacoby transfer* bid after a 2NT rebid. Here are some examples.

West	WEST	NORTH	EAST	SOUTH	East
♠ K Q 9 4	2♣	Pass	2♦	Pass	♠ J 10 6 3
♥ K Q J	2NT	Pass	3♣	Pass	♥ 8 7 4
♦ A 5	3♠	Pass	4♠	Pass	♦ 9 3
♣ A Q J 3	Pass	Pass			♣ K 10 8 6

After West shows a balanced hand of 22 to 24 points, East has enough to put the partnership in game. East checks for a major suit fit along the way by using the *Stayman* convention. West shows the four-card spade suit and East puts the partnership in game in its eight-card fit.

West	WEST	NORTH	EAST	SOUTH	East
♠ A Q J	2♣	Pass	2♦	Pass	♠ 7 3
♥ K 9	2NT	Pass	3♦	Pass	♥ Q 8 7 5 4
♦ A K 8 7 5	3♥	Pass	3NT	Pass	♦ J 10 4
♣ K Q 3	Pass	Pass			♣ J 6 2

Following West's 2NT rebid, East's 3♦ is a *Jacoby transfer* bid. West dutifully accepts the transfer by bidding 3♥. East's 3NT rebid gives partner the choice of playing game in notrump or hearts, and with only two hearts, West elects to play in 3NT.

HANDLING INTERFERENCE AFTER
A 2♣ OPENING

Responder's Bid when the 2♣ Opening Is Doubled

If the opening 2♣ bid is doubled, responder's bids retain their usual meaning, including 2♦ as a waiting bid.

WEST	NORTH	**EAST**	SOUTH
2♣	Double	?	

♠ K Q 10 7 5
♥ 4
♦ Q J 8 3
♣ 7 4 2

Respond 2♠. This is the same response you would have made without the double.

Responder's Bid when the 2♣ Opening Is Overcalled

If there is an overcall of the 2♣ bid, responder can now pass with a weak hand. With enough for a positive response, responder can bid a five-card or longer suit, bid notrump with some strength in the opponent's suit, double for penalty, or *cuebid* the opponent's suit. Here are some examples after the auction begins:

WEST	NORTH	**EAST**	SOUTH
2♣	2♠	?	

♠ 4 3
♥ J 8 6 2
♦ J 9 7 3
♣ 8 7 4

Pass. You are no longer forced to respond after the overcall. Partner will get another opportunity to describe the hand.

♠ 6 3
♥ 9 5
♦ A J 9 8 5 3
♣ J 8 7

Bid 3♦. With a good six-card suit, you have enough for a positive response — 6 high-card points plus 2 length points. It's best to bid now, even if you have to stretch a little. You may not get another opportunity to show your suit, especially if the opponents compete further.

♠ Q 10 3
♥ 9 5
♦ J 7 5 2
♣ K Q 8 3

Bid 2NT. The 2NT response still shows a balanced hand of about 8 or more points, but you need some strength in the opponent's suit to make this bid.

♠ A J 9 3
♥ J 6
♦ Q 8 6 3
♣ 7 5 3

Double. Your double shows an interest in defending for penalties.

♠ 6 4
♥ A 9 7 3
♦ K Q 4
♣ 10 8 6 2

Cuebid 3♠. After an overcall, a cuebid shows 8 or more points with no good five-card or longer suit and not enough strength in the opponent's suit to bid notrump or to double.

Opener's Rebid when an Opponent Overcalls

If the 2♣ opener can't make a natural rebid because of an opponent's interference, a double is for penalty and a pass or a cuebid of the opponent's suit is for takeout. For example:

WEST	NORTH	EAST	SOUTH
2♣	2♠	Pass	Pass
?			

♠ 3
♥ A K Q J 7 6
♦ A K J 2
♣ K J

Rebid 3♥. The opponent's interference hasn't prevented you from making a natural rebid, showing your suit.

♠ A J 10 8
♥ A Q
♦ K Q J
♣ K Q 7 3

Double. This is a penalty double of the opponent's contract. With a hand less suitable for defending for penalty, you could make your natural rebid of 2NT.

♠ —
♥ A K Q 3
♦ K Q 9 8 5
♣ A K J 2

Cuebid 3♠. A double would be for penalty, not for takeout. A cuebid of the opponent's suit is used to ask partner to pick a trump suit.

Consider this auction:

WEST	NORTH	EAST	SOUTH
2♣	Pass	2♦	3♦
?			

♠ A Q
♥ A 7 3
♦ K 4
♣ A K Q 10 8 6

Rebid 3NT. The opponent's interference hasn't left enough room to show your suit without getting past 3NT. Best to treat this as a balanced hand and bid what you think you can make.

♠ A K Q 5
♥ A Q J 5
♦ 9 4
♣ A Q J

Pass. Your pass forces partner to take action — a forcing pass. A double by you would be for penalty, so pass suggests that partner bid something. Partner can bid a four-card or longer suit or double for penalty.

Note: See the Appendix (pages 333–335) for a discussion of these supplemental conventions and/or treatments.

Second Negative

Double Negative

Step Responses

SUMMARY

When the partnership uses weak two-bids, strong hands of 22 or more points are opened with an artificial (conventional) 2♣ bid.

Strong 2♣ Opening

An opening bid of 2♣ is artificial (conventional) and shows:

- A balanced hand with 22 or more high-card points, or

- An unbalanced hand with 22 or more points (nine or more playing tricks).

Responding to 2♣

- With a good five-card or longer suit and 8 or more points, responder bids 2♥, 2♠, 3♣, or 3♦ (not 2♦). This is a *positive* response and commits the partnership to game.

- With a balanced hand of 8 or more points, responder bids 2NT. This is also a *positive* response, committing the partnership to game.

- With all other hands, responder makes the artificial (conventional) response of 2♦. The 2♦ bid is a *waiting* bid and includes all those hands with fewer than 8 points as well as those unsuitable for a positive response.

Opener's Rebid after a 2♦ Response

With a balanced hand:

- Rebid 2NT with 22 to 24 points.

- Rebid 3NT with 25 to 27 points.

- Rebid 4NT with 28 to 30 points . . . and so on.

With an unbalanced hand:

- Bid your longest suit.

- Bid the higher-ranking of two five-card or six-card suits.

NOTE: *If opener rebids a suit after the 2♦ response, the partnership is forced to the game level unless opener immediately bids the suit again after responder's next bid.*

Handling Interference after a 2♣ Opening

If an opponent doubles, both responder and opener can ignore the double.

If an opponent overcalls, responder can pass with less than the values for a positive response. With enough for a positive response, responder can:

- Bid a five-card or longer suit.

- Bid notrump with some strength in the opponent's suit.

- Double for penalty.

- Cuebid the opponent's suit.

If an opponent overcalls and the 2♣ opener no longer has room to make a natural rebid, opener can:

- Double for penalty.

- Cuebid the opponent's suit for takeout.

- Make a forcing pass.

These exercises assume you are using the methods outlined in the summary.

Exercise One — Strong Opening Bids

What is your opening call with each of the following hands?

1) ♠ K Q 9 4
♥ A K Q 10 8 4
♦ A K
♣ J _____

2) ♠ A K J 4
♥ K 3
♦ A J 10 8
♣ A K 9 _____

3) ♠ K J 9 5 3
♥ A K J 6
♦ A 4
♣ Q J _____

Exercise Two — Responding to 2♣

What do you respond with each of the following hands when partner opens the bidding 2♣ and the next player passes?

1) ♠ 9 8 7 4
♥ J 8 6 5 2
♦ 8 3
♣ 7 4 _____

2) ♠ J 5
♥ A Q J 8 3
♦ 8 7 6 3
♣ 9 4 _____

3) ♠ K 2
♥ 9 5 4
♦ A J 10 8 6 3
♣ 7 2 _____

4) ♠ Q 9 3
♥ K 10 8 4
♦ Q J 4
♣ J 5 4 _____

5) ♠ 6
♥ J 7 6 5 3
♦ K 8 5
♣ A 8 7 4 _____

6) ♠ Q 9 7 5 4 2
♥ 8 3
♦ J 6 2
♣ 5 3 _____

Exercise Three — Rebids after 2♣

As West, what would you rebid with each of the following hands after the auction starts:

WEST	NORTH	EAST	SOUTH
2♣	Pass	2♦	Pass
?			

1) ♠ A Q 10 7 5
♥ A K Q J 3
♦ 7
♣ A Q _____

2) ♠ —
♥ A K Q 3
♦ A K J 10 4 2
♣ K Q 4 _____

3) ♠ A Q
♥ K Q 8
♦ A Q 7
♣ K Q 10 6 2 _____

4) ♠ A
♥ A K Q J 10 7 5
♦ K Q 5
♣ A 3 _____

5) ♠ K J
♥ A K Q
♦ A K J 3
♣ K Q J 5 _____

6) ♠ A Q 9 6
♥ A
♦ A K 8 4
♣ A Q 10 3 _____

Exercise One — Strong Opening Bids

1) 2♣. You plan to show the heart suit on your rebid.

2) 2♣. You plan to rebid 2NT.

3) 1♠. This hand is a little short of a strong opening two-bid.

Exercise Two — Responding to 2♣

1) 2♦. Make the *waiting* response of 2♦.

2) 2♥. Make a *positive* response of 2♥.

3) 3♦. A response of 2♦ would be a waiting bid.

4) 2NT. A positive response with 8 or more points and no good five-card suit.

5) 2♦. This hand is good enough for a positive response but your five-card suit is too weak.

6) 2♦. You don't have enough for a positive response.

Exercise Three — Rebids after 2♣

1) 2♠. Bid the higher-ranking suit first. Show the hearts on the next round.

2) 3♦. Bid the longer suit first. When you later bid hearts, partner will know you have longer diamonds.

3) 2NT. This shows a balanced hand with 22 to 24 points.

4) 2♥. There's no need to jump. The 2♥ rebid is forcing.

5) 3NT. This shows a balanced hand with 25 to 27 points.

6) 2NT. Awkward. The hand isn't balanced but there's no five-card suit to bid. Treat the hand as balanced . . . and hope for the best!

Exercise Four — The Subsequent Auction

You hold the following hand as West:

♠ A K Q J 9 6
♥ K Q 4
♦ 3
♣ A Q 3

What is your next bid in each of the following auctions?

1)
	WEST	NORTH	EAST	SOUTH
	2♣	Pass	2♦	Pass
	2♠	Pass	2NT	Pass
	? _____			

2)
	WEST	NORTH	EAST	SOUTH
	2♣	Pass	2♦	Pass
	2♠	Pass	3♥	Pass
	Pass	? _____		

3)
	WEST	NORTH	EAST	SOUTH
	2♣	2♦	Pass	3♦
	? _____			

4)
	WEST	NORTH	EAST	SOUTH
	2♣	Pass	2♦	Pass
	2♠	Pass	3♠	Pass
	? _____			

Exercise Four — The Subsequent Auction

1) 3♠. Partner's 2NT rebid shows a weak hand. With a positive response, partner would bid 2NT right away. The 3♠ rebid isn't forcing, but if partner passes you are unlikely to make game.

2) 4♥. Show the fit with partner. Partner may have a very weak hand since partner didn't respond 2♥ initially, but partner still has an opportunity to move toward slam with a little something.

3) 3♠. Time to show your suit. If you had a balanced hand, you could pass and leave any decision to partner.

4) 4♣ or 4NT. Having found a fit, you can make a move toward slam — either cuebidding the ♣A or using the *Blackwood* convention. Partner should have some high cards. With a weak hand and a fit, partner could have jumped directly to 4♠.

Exercise Five — Handling Interference

As East, what would you rebid with each of the following hands?

WEST	NORTH	**EAST**	SOUTH
2♣	2♥	?	

1) ♠ 8 6 3
♥ J 7 3
♦ J 9 8 6 4
♣ 10 3 _____

2) ♠ K Q 10 8 5
♥ 9 7
♦ K 10 6 3
♣ 8 4 _____

3) ♠ 8 2
♥ K J 8
♦ Q 10 7 2
♣ Q J 7 4 _____

4) ♠ 8 3
♥ Q 10 9 7 5
♦ K 7 6
♣ 9 4 2 _____

5) ♠ K 10 6 5
♥ 5
♦ A 7 6 3
♣ K 6 4 2 _____

6) ♠ 10 8 7 4
♥ 9 5
♦ Q 9 8 4 3
♣ K 6 _____

Exercise Five — Handling Interference

1) Pass. You don't have to bid with a weak hand when there is an over-call. Partner will get another chance to bid.

2) 2♠. The opponent's overcall doesn't prevent you from showing your good suit with enough for a positive response.

3) 2NT. This shows a positive response with 8 or more points and some strength in the opponent's suit.

4) Double. With partner holding a strong hand, your best spot may be defending. Let partner know.

5) 3 ♥. A *cuebid* of the opponent's suit shows a positive response but no good suit of your own and no stopper in the opponent's suit.

6) Pass. You have a little something but it's best to wait and see what partner has to say. Your pass is forcing — partner will have to do something.

Bid and Play — Deal 1

(E-Z Deal Cards: #8, Deal 1 — Dealer, North)

Suggested Bidding

WEST	NORTH	EAST	SOUTH
	Pass	Pass	2♣
Pass	2NT	Pass	3♠
Pass	4♠	Pass	4NT (6♠)
Pass	5♣	Pass	6♠
Pass	Pass	Pass	

After two passes, South, with an unbalanced hand with 23 high-card points and 2 points for the six-card suit, opens 2♣. North has enough for a positive response. With no good five-card suit, North bids 2NT. South now shows the spade suit, and with three-card support, North raises to game. Since partner has shown 8 or more points with the 2NT response, South knows the partnership has a chance for slam. South might simply jump to 6♠ or

```
Dlr: North    ♠ Q 10 6
Vul: None     ♥ 9 6 3 2
              ♦ K J
              ♣ K 8 7 2
♠ 8                      ♠ 5 4 3
♥ J 10 8 7      N        ♥ A 5 4
♦ 9 7 6 5     W   E      ♦ 10 8 4 3 2
♣ J 6 5 3       S        ♣ Q 10
              ♠ A K J 9 7 2
              ♥ K Q
              ♦ A Q
              ♣ A 9 4
```

take the more scientific route of asking for aces using the *Blackwood* convention. When North shows no aces with the 5♣ response, South settles for a small slam.

Suggested Opening Lead

West is on lead and would start with the ♥J, top of a sequence.

Suggested Play

The duplication of values in the diamond suit is unfortunate for declarer. If one of North's low hearts or clubs were a low diamond, South would have 12 easy tricks. As it is, there is some work to do. There's a sure loser in hearts and another in clubs. The contract might look hopeless since there's no place for the club loser to be discarded, but declarer shouldn't give up hope. There's always the possibility that the defenders will discard incorrectly or that something unforeseen will happen. Declarer should take a careful look at the ♥ 9 in dummy. It's surprising how valuable it may prove to be.

When West leads the ♥ J, suppose East wins the first trick with the ♥ A and returns a heart. After winning the second trick, declarer has nothing better to do than to draw the defenders' trumps. With this done, declarer should continue leading spades, hoping the defenders may carelessly discard too many clubs. Declarer can take the two diamond winners, but should play all of the spade winners before touching the club suit. Good things may happen, especially if declarer keeps that ♥ 9 in the dummy.

Why is the ♥ 9 so important? If West originally led from a holding such as ♥ J 10 x x — as looks likely — West will have to hold on to the ♥ 10 to prevent dummy's ♥ 9 from becoming a trick. That means that West can't hold on to clubs. If East started with only two clubs, or throws some away, declarer can take three club tricks. On the actual layout of the cards, this is the position when South leads the last spade winner after taking the diamond tricks:

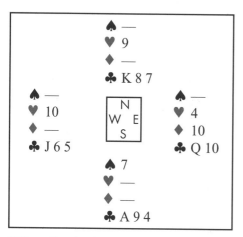

When South leads the last spade winner, West must find a discard. If West discards the ♥ 10, dummy's ♥ 9 is a winner. Declarer can cross to dummy's ♣ K and discard the club loser on the ♥ 9. If West discards a club, declarer takes the last three club tricks, since East started with only two clubs.

It's a bit like magic — manufacturing an extra trick out of thin air. The technical term is a squeeze.

When South plays the last spade, West's hand is squeezed out of one of the winners. There's nothing West can do, provided South was carefully watching the heart suit and that precious ♥ 9 in the dummy.

Will declarer find this line of play? Perhaps not, but in such situations — where you are one trick short of your contract — it is generally a good idea to run all of your winners and make the defenders discard. Anything may happen. On this deal, something does.

Suggested Defense

Can the defenders defeat the contract? Although the ♥ J is the standout lead from West's hand, an original club lead could defeat the contract if East returns a club after winning the ♥ A. It's difficult to see why this works even when you play out all of the cards, but it does. Squeeze plays and defense can be quite complicated, but it's a fascinating area of the game. On this deal, East–West will probably have to hope that declarer doesn't put dummy's ♥ 9 to good use.

Bid and Play — Deal 2

(E-Z Deal Cards: #8, Deal 2 — Dealer, East)

Suggested Bidding

WEST	NORTH	EAST	SOUTH
		2♣	Pass
2♦	Pass	2♠	Pass
2NT	Pass	3♥	Pass
4♥	Pass	Pass	Pass

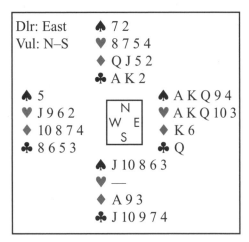

Dlr: East
Vul: N–S

♠ 7 2
♥ 8 7 5 4
♦ Q J 5 2
♣ A K 2

♠ 5
♥ J 9 6 2
♦ 10 8 7 4
♣ 8 6 5 3

♠ A K Q 9 4
♥ A K Q 10 3
♦ K 6
♣ Q

♠ J 10 8 6 3
♥ —
♦ A 9 3
♣ J 10 9 7 4

With 23 high-card points plus 1 point for each of the two five-card suits, East has a hand strong enough to open at the two level. Playing weak two-bids, East starts to show this hand by opening with a strong artificial 2♣ bid.

After South passes, West must respond to partner's forcing bid and uses the artificial (conventional) waiting bid of 2♦. East rebids 2♠, the higher-ranking of the two five-card suits. This is still a forcing bid, so West must say something. West can't support spades and doesn't have a good suit to bid, so West bids 2NT. East now shows a second suit by bidding 3♥. This is another forcing bid, so West shows support for hearts by raising to the game level. West probably didn't expect to make three bids with this hand! Having forced the partnership to game and hearing no encouragement from West, East has nothing further to add and settles for a contract of 4♥.

Suggested Opening Lead

South is on lead. Since East has bid spades, South should avoid leading that suit and start with the ♣J, top of a sequence.

Suggested Play

Declarer has two potential losers in spades, two in diamonds, and one in clubs. If the defenders' spades divide 4–3, East can establish an extra winner in that suit through length. There is also the possibility of trumping one or two spades in the dummy. In diamonds, East could try leading toward the ♦ K, hoping that North holds the ♦ A.

The safest play for the contract is to plan to trump both spade losers in the dummy. That way, East doesn't need to rely on a favorable division of the spade suit or a favorable location for the ♦ A. To follow this plan, declarer must be careful of three things. Since the defenders have led clubs, and may continue leading them, declarer must be careful not to run out of trumps while ruffing the spade losers. Declarer must be careful to make the best use of entries. Finally, declarer wants to avoid having North overruff when ruffing losers in the dummy.

Suppose North wins the first club trick and leads another club which East trumps. East should immediately play a high spade and then trump a low spade with dummy's ♥9. Declarer crosses back to the East hand with a trump — discovering the 4–0 break in that suit — and leads another low spade which declarer trumps with dummy's ♥J. Declarer leads dummy's last trump to cross back in order to draw the remaining trumps in North's hand. After drawing all of the trumps, declarer takes the last two spade winners.

The ♦ A is unfavorably located. The spades divide 5–2 and the trumps divide 4–0. The contract can be defeated if East isn't careful. If East tries to play three spade winners early, North will ruff one of them. If East ruffs the third round of spades with a low trump, North will overruff. Because of the bad trump break, East can't afford to play even one round of trumps before ruffing a spade loser. For example, if the defenders lead two rounds of clubs, declarer must ruff and has only four hearts left. If declarer has to ruff again to get back to the East hand, North will have more trumps than declarer and will eventually get a trump trick. When the hearts break badly, declarer can't afford to try the diamond finesse by leading toward the ♦ K. When it loses, the defenders can force declarer to ruff and North will again have more trumps than declarer.

Suggested Defense

After winning the first trick with the ♣K, North's best defense is to lead another club, forcing East to use a trump to win the trick. Holding four trumps, North would like to run declarer out of trumps. It won't do any harm if North switches to a diamond after winning the first club trick. South can win two diamond tricks and then the defenders can lead either a club or a diamond to force declarer to ruff.

As outlined above, declarer can make the contract with careful play. Declarer may play a round of trumps too soon, and that will give the defenders an opportunity to defeat the contract. For example, suppose the defenders start with two rounds of clubs. Declarer ruffs and plays one round of trumps. On seeing the bad break, declarer plays a high spade and trumps a spade in dummy. Declarer crosses back with a trump and ruffs another spade in dummy. Now declarer has no quick entry back to the East hand to draw trumps. Whether declarer leads a diamond or a club from dummy, the defenders can force declarer to ruff again and North will get a trump trick.

If declarer doesn't ruff two spades in the dummy, South can defeat the contract by holding on to all of the spades. Since East bid spades in the auction, South should be aware that it's important not to discard one.

Bid and Play — Deal 3

(E-Z Deal Cards: #8, Hand 3 — Dealer, South)

Suggested Bidding

WEST	NORTH	EAST	SOUTH
			2♣
Pass	2♦	Pass	2NT
Pass	3♣	Pass	3♠
Pass	3NT	Pass	Pass
Pass			

With 23 high-card points, South is too strong to open 2NT if the partnership uses weak two-bids. A 2NT opening bid would show only 20 or 21 high-card points. Instead, South starts with a strong artificial 2♣ bid. After West passes, North makes the artificial (conventional) waiting response of 2♦. This allows South to describe the nature of the hand by rebidding 2NT, showing a balanced hand of 22 to 24 points. With 5 points, North has enough to take the

```
Dlr: South    ♠ 6 5 2
Vul: E–W      ♥ K J 10 3
              ♦ 9 4
              ♣ J 10 6 2
♠ A J 9 7            ♠ Q 8
♥ 8 5        N      ♥ 9 7 4 2
♦ J 10 7 6 3  W  E   ♦ Q 8
♣ 7 4        S      ♣ Q 9 8 5 3
              ♠ K 10 4 3
              ♥ A Q 6
              ♦ A K 5 2
              ♣ A K
```

partnership to game. Holding a four-card heart suit, North can use the *Stayman* convention to discover if the partnership has an eight-card major-suit fit. When South responds 3♠, showing a four-card spade suit, North signs off in 3NT. North was able to make three bids with only 5 points!

Suggested Opening Lead

West is on lead against 3NT and should start with the ♦ 6, fourth from the longest and strongest suit. West should avoid a spade lead, since South showed a four-card spade suit.

Suggested Play

Declarer starts with eight sure tricks: four hearts, two diamonds, and two clubs. One possibility for a ninth trick is the spade suit. South could try leading a spade from dummy toward the ♠K, hoping East holds the ♠A. If that doesn't work, there's still the possibility that the missing spades divide 3–3. But there's a much safer alternative in the club suit. Declarer can use dummy's ♣J and ♣10 to promote a trick in that suit by driving out the ♣Q.

To develop and take an extra trick in the club suit, declarer must be careful with entries to dummy. After winning a diamond trick, South starts by playing the ♣A and ♣K to unblock that suit. South then plays the ♥A and the ♥Q, overtaking with the ♥K in dummy — or South can play the ♥6 to dummy's ♥J or ♥10. Next, declarer leads a club from dummy to drive out the defenders' ♣Q. On regaining the lead, declarer can cross to dummy with a heart, take the established club winner and the remaining heart winner, and finish with nine tricks.

Having spotted the possibility of developing an extra club trick, declarer must be careful to use the heart suit to provide two entries to the dummy.

Suggested Defense

The defenders should try to develop enough winners from West's diamond suit to defeat the contract. There's no way to defeat the contract if declarer plays carefully. But if declarer fails to take proper advantage of the club suit, the defense will have a chance, provided they don't give South a ninth trick in another suit. West must be careful not to lead a spade, giving South a trick with the ♠K. East can lead a spade to trap declarer's ♠K, but the defender's can't continue leading the suit before establishing their diamond winners or South will take a trick with the ♠10.

Bid and Play — Deal 4

(E-Z Deal Cards: #8, Deal 4 — Dealer, West)

Suggested Bidding

WEST	NORTH	EAST	SOUTH
Pass	2♣	Pass	2♦
Pass	2♠	Pass	2NT
Pass	3♥	Pass	3♠
Pass	4♠	Pass	Pass
Pass			

With 24 high-card points plus 1 for the five-card suit, North is in the range of a strong two-bid. Since an opening bid of 2♠ would be a weak two-bid, North starts with the strong artificial 2♣. After East passes, South has to say something. South responds 2♦, an artificial (conventional) waiting bid, showing a weak hand or a hand unsuitable for a positive response in notrump or a suit.

```
Dlr: West      ♠ A K 9 7 5
Vul: Both      ♥ A K Q 3
               ♦ A
               ♣ A 10 3
♠ Q 10 8 3            ♠ 4
♥ 10 8        N      ♥ 7 6 5 4
♦ 10 9 8 7 2  W   E  ♦ K Q J 5
♣ K J           S    ♣ Q 9 6 4
               ♠ J 6 2
               ♥ J 9 2
               ♦ 6 4 3
               ♣ 8 7 5 2
```

North now gets to bid the spade suit and the bidding comes back to South. North's 2♠ bid is forcing — just as if North had opened a strong 2♠ bid. With nothing much to say, South bids 2NT to keep the bidding going. North can now show a second suit by bidding 3♥. This is another forcing bid, so South gives preference back to 3♠. Needing very little from partner to make game, North continues to 4♠.

(North might suggest 3NT on the fourth round of bidding — having shown five spades and four hearts — but South should correct back to 4♠, knowing there is an eight-card fit.)

Suggested Opening Lead

East is on lead and has an easy choice, the ♦K, top of a sequence.

Suggested Play

There are two sure losers in the club suit, so North's main concern is to avoid losing more than one trick in the trump suit. If the missing trumps divide 3–2 or the ♠Q is singleton, there won't be a problem. Declarer should concentrate on the possibility that the missing trumps might divide 4–1.

After winning the ♦A at trick one, North can afford to play the ♠A to see if the ♠Q is singleton or if the defenders' spades are divided 5–0. When both defenders follow suit with low cards, the missing trumps can be divided no worse than 4–1. Declarer must still be careful. If declarer plays the ♠K at this point, the contract will be defeated if the missing spades divide 4–1. The defenders will get tricks with both the ♠Q and ♠10. To guard against this, North should lead a low spade toward dummy's ♠J. This guarantees only one spade loser and making contract.

If both defenders follow suit, their trumps have divided 3–2 and declarer, after regaining the lead, will pick up the last trump with the ♠K. If East has the ♠Q, declarer, will get a trick with dummy's ♠J, even if East started with four trumps. If West started with all four trumps, as on the actual layout, declarer can still make the contract. When East shows out, declarer plays dummy's ♠J, losing to West's ♠Q. On regaining the lead, declarer plays the ♥3 over to dummy's ♥J and leads dummy's remaining spade. When West follows with a low spade, declarer finesses the ♠9 and draws West's last trump.

Notice how declarer makes good use of both of dummy's jacks. South's 2 points were just enough to let declarer make the contract despite the unfortunate trump division.

Suggested Defense

The defenders can't do much if declarer handles the spade suit correctly in a contract of 4♠. If declarer does give up two trump tricks, the defenders should defeat the contract if East holds on to clubs.

If North–South play in 3NT, the defenders can lead diamonds to defeat the contract. If South is declarer and West leads the ♦10, East must be careful to unblock the ♦K under North's ♦A. Otherwise, East won't have a low diamond left to lead back to West's winners.

APPENDIX

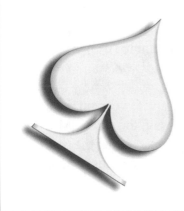

THE CONVENTION CARD

For a club or tournament game, both members of a partnership are expected to have a completed *convention card* describing the general style and the conventional bids they have agreed to use. Both cards must be identical.

Writing down the conventions is useful to make sure that both partners are playing the same methods. If you are playing with an unfamiliar partner, it gives the partnership a chance to discuss the methods that will be used. The real purpose of the convention card, however, is for the benefit of the opponents. When you sit down at a table, the opponents can look at your convention card to familiarize themselves with your methods. Likewise, you can look at the opponents' convention card. You don't have to ask a lot of questions about the methods your opponents are using. You need to look only at the information you feel might be relevant. You can look at the opponent's convention card any time during the auction when it's your turn to call and at any time during the play when it's your turn to play. On the other hand, you're not to look at your own convention card during the bidding to remind yourself of what you are playing. Your convention card is for the benefit of the opponents.

The ACBL has developed a classification system for all conventional bids. The purpose is to allow some events to be restricted to a subset of all possible conventions. In this way, inexperienced players don't have to play against complex systems and conventions which would put them at a distinct disadvantage. For example, some games for beginners are restricted to only those conventions on the ACBL Limited Convention Chart, which includes such favorites as *Stayman*, *Blackwood*, and *Gerber*. As players become more familiar with handling a wider variety of conventions, they could move into games with fewer and fewer restrictions powered by the ACBL General Convention Chart and the ACBL Mid-Chart. Only in the last stages of some NABC championships are the restrictions lifted to permit nearly all of the recognized conventions. These games use the ACBL Superchart.

Convention cards come in different formats and colors, depending on the type of game in which they are being used. Periodically, the design of these cards is changed to reflect new regulations. There are three types of convention cards currently in use:

- **General Convention Card** — The most common format is the white General Convention Card, designed to cover the widest variety of conventions. This can be used at virtually any level of competition — provided you put only allowable conventions on it.

- **Standard American Yellow Card** — There's an ACBL Standard American Yellow Card (SAYC) which is pre-filled with many popular conventions and is designed for games where everyone plays the same methods. It is popular among players on the Internet.

- **"Fat Free" Simplified Card** — There's a simplified convention card (Form SS4) which is affectionately know as the "Fat Free" Card. It is streamlined and perfect for both newer players and those who play less complicated systems.

ACBL GENERAL CONVENTION CARD

LEFT SIDE OF CARD (not actual size)

SPECIAL DOUBLES

Negative □: thru_____thru 4♠ +___
Responsive □: thru _____ Maximal □
Support: Dbl. □ thru _____Redbl □
Card-showing □   Min. Offshape T/O □

SIMPLE OVERCALL

1 level_____to_____HCP (usually)
often 4 cards □   very light style □

Responses

New Suit: Forcing □ NFConst □ NF □
Jump Raise: Forcing □ Inv. □ Weak □

JUMP OVERCALL

Strong □   Intermediate □   Weak □

OPENING PREEMPTS

	Sound	Light	Very Light
3/4-bids	□	□	□
Conv./Resp.			

DIRECT CUEBID

OVER:	Minor	Major	Artif. Bid
Natural	□	□	□
Strong T/O	□	□	□
Michaels	□	□	□

NOTRUMP OVERCALLS

Direct: _____to_____Systems on □
Conv. □ _____
Balancing: _____to_____
Jump to 2NT: Minors □ 2 Lowest □
Conv. □ _____

DEFENSE VS NOTRUMP

vs:		
2♣		
2♦		
2♥		
2♠		
Dbl:		
Other		

OVER OPP'S T/O DOUBLE

New Suit Forcing: 1 level □ 2 level □
Jump Shift: Forcing □ Inv. □ Weak □
Redouble implies no fit □

2NT Over	Limit+	Limit	Weak
Majors	□	□	□
Minors	□	□	□
Other			

VS Opening Preempts Double Is

Takeout □ thru _____   Penalty □
Conv. Takeout: _____
Lebensohl 2NT Response □
Other: _____

SLAM CONVENTIONS   Gerber □: 4NT: Blackwood □ RKC □   1430 □

vs Interference: DOPI □   DEPO □   Level: _____ ROPI □

LEADS (circle card led, if not in bold)

versus Suits		versus Notrump	
X x	x x x **X**	**X** x	**X** x x x
x x **X**	x x x x **X** x	**X** x x	x x x x **X** x
A **K** x	**T** 9 x	A **K** J x	A **Q** J x
K Q x	K **J** T x	A **J** T 9	A **T** 9 x
Q J x	K **T** 9 x	**K** Q J x	K **Q** T 9
J T 9	Q **T** 9 x	**Q** J T x	Q **T** 9 x
K Q T 9		**J** T 9 x	**T** 9 x x

LENGTH LEADS:

4th Best   vs SUITS □ vs NT □
3rd/5th Best   vs SUITS □ vs NT □
                       Attitude vs. NT □

Primary signal to partner's leads

Attitude □   Count □   Suit preference □

DEFENSIVE CARDING

	vs SUITS	vs NT
Standard:	□	□
Except □		

Upside-Down:		
count	□	□
attitude	□	□

FIRST DISCARD

Lavinthal	□	□
Odd/Even	□	□
	□	□

OTHER CARDING

Smith Echo	□	□
Trump Suit Pref.	□	
Foster Echo	□	□

SPECIAL CARDING □   PLEASE ASK

ACBL GENERAL CONVENTION CARD
RIGHT SIDE OF CARD (not actual size)

NAMES _____

GENERAL APPROACH

Two Over One: Game Forcing ☐   Game Forcing Except When Suit Rebid ☐
VERY LIGHT: Openings ☐   3rd Hand ☐   Overcalls ☐   Preempts ☐
FORCING OPENING: 1♣ ☐   2♣ ☐   Natural 2 Bids ☐   Other ☐ _____

NOTRUMP OPENING BIDS

1NT	3♣ _____
____ to ____	3♦ _____
____ to ____	3♥ _____
5-card Major common ☐	3♠ _____
System on over ____	
2♣ Stayman ☐ Puppet ☐	
2♦ Transfer to ♥ ☐	4♦, 4♥ Transfer ☐
Forcing Stayman ☐	Smolen ☐
2♥ Transfer to ♠ ☐	Lebensohl ☐ (____denies)
2♠ _____	Neg. Double ☐: _____
2NT _____	Other: _____

2NT ____ to ____
Puppet Stayman ☐
Transfer Responses:
Jacoby ☐   Texas ☐
3♠ _____
3NT ____ to ____

Conventional NT Openings
_____

MAJOR OPENING			MINOR OPENING			
Expected Min. Length	4	5	Expected Min. Length	4	3	2 Other
1st/2nd	☐	☐	1♣	☐	☐	☐ ☐
3rd/4th	☐	☐	1♦	☐	☐	☐ ☐

RESPONSES

MAJOR	MINOR
Double Raise: Force ☐ Inv. ☐ Weak ☐	Double Raise: Force ☐ Inv. ☐ Weak ☐
After Overcall: Force ☐ Inv. ☐ Weak ☐	After Overcall: Force ☐ Inv. ☐ Weak ☐
Conv. Raise: 2NT ☐ 3NT ☐ Splinter ☐	Forcing Raise: J/S in other minor ☐
Other: _____	Single raise ☐ Other: _____
1NT: Forcing ☐ Semi-forcing ☐	Frequently bypass 4+♦ ☐
2NT: Forcing ☐ Inv. ☐ ___to___	1NT/1♣ ____to____
3NT: ____to____	2NT Forcing ☐ Inv. ☐ ___to___
Drury ☐: Reverse ☐ 2-Way ☐ Fit ☐	3NT: ____to____
Other: _____	Other _____

		DESCRIBE	RESPONSES/REBIDS
2♣	____to____ HCP		
	Strong ☐ Other ☐		
	2♦ Resp: Neg ☐ Waiting ☐		
2♦	____to____ HCP		
	Natural ☐ Conv. ☐		2NT Force ☐ New Suit NF ☐
2♥	____to____ HCP		
	Natural ☐ Conv. ☐		2NT Force ☐ New Suit NF ☐
2♠	____to____ HCP		
	Natural ☐ Conv. ☐		2NT Force ☐ New Suit NF ☐

OTHER CONV. CALLS: New Minor Forcing: ☐ ____ 2-Way NMF ☐ ____
Weak Jump Shifts ☐ _____ 4th Suit Forcing: 1 Round ☐ Game ☐
_____
_____
_____

Items appearing in grey are blue on the actual convention card.

ACBL STANDARD AMERICAN YELLOW CARD (SAYC)
LEFT SIDE OF CARD (not actual size)

SPECIAL DOUBLES (Describe)
Negative ———➔ **2♠**

SIMPLE OVERCALL
8 to **16** HCP

Cuebid is: One-Round Force

JUMP OVERCALL
Preemptive

OVER OPP'S TAKEOUT DOUBLE
New Suit Force 1-level

Other **2NT = Limit Raise or Better over Majors & Minors**

OPENING PREEMPTS

	Sound	Light
3-bids	☐	☐

Psychics: Very Rare

DIRECT NT OVERCALLS
1NT **15** to **18** HCP

2♣ = Stayman

Other **Other Systems Off**

Unusual 2 NT = 2 Lower Unbid

OVER OPPONENT'S NT
| 2♣ shows ♣ | 2♦ shows ♦ |
| 2♥ shows ♥ | 2♠ shows ♠ |

VS. OPP'S OPENING PREEMPTS
Dbl. Is Takeout — Takeout

Wk. 2s ☐ — Wk. 3s ☐

2 NT / Weak 2 = 16–19 HCP Bal.

DIRECT CUEBID
Two Suits ☒ **Michaels (5-5) or Longer**

Natural ☒ **In either suit if opponents have bid 2 suits**

SLAM CONVENTIONS

Gerber ☒ **Over 1 NT & 2NT openings, responses, rebids**

Blackwood ☒ — Grand Slam Force ☒

After Interference over 4♣ or 4 NT ☒ **Double = 0, Pass = 1, Next Suit = 2, Etc.**

Defenses vs. Opp's Conventions **SOS Redoubles**

DEFENSIVE CARD PLAY

Opening lead vs. SUITS: 4th best ☐ 3rd and 5th best ☐

K Q x — Q J x — J 10 x — 10 9 x — K J 10 x — K 10 9 x — Q 10 9 x

Must mark card led: x x x — x x x x — x x x x x — A K x

Opening lead vs. NT: 4th best ☐ 3rd and 5th best ☐

A K J x — A Q J x — A J 10 9 — A 10 9 8 — K Q J x — K Q 10 9

K J 10 9 — K 10 9 8 — Q J 10 x — Q 10 9 8 — J 10 9 x — 10 9 8 x

Must mark card led: x x x — x x x x — x x x x x

ACBL STANDARD AMERICAN YELLOW CARD (SAYC)
RIGHT SIDE OF CARD (not actual size)

Names _____   Pair # _____

ACBL STANDARD YELLOW CARD

Strong Forcing Opening: 2♣

NOTRUMP OPENING BIDS

1 NT __15__ to __17__ HCP   2 NT __20__ to __21__ HCP

2♣ Non-Forcing Stayman   3 NT __25__ to __27__ HCP

Transfers: Jacoby for majors over 1, 2 and 3 NT (on over dbls.)

2♠ forces 3♣ (for signoff in either minor)

1 NT - 3♣/3♦ Is Game Invitational; 1 NT - 3♥/3♠ Is Slam Invitational

---

MAJOR OPENINGS
Normally Five-Card Majors

RESPONSES:

2 NT = Forcing Raise (Jacoby)

Double Raise = Limit (10-12 pts.)

Double Raise = Preemptive
        Over Double

Be Courteous –
Opponents May Just
Be Friends We
Haven't Met Yet!

MINOR OPENING
Length Promised

	4+	3+
1♣		☐
1♦	☐	☐

RESPONSES:

Double Raise = Limit (10-12 pts.)
Double Raise = Preemptive
        Over Double

1 NT/1♣ or 1♦ __6__ to __10__ HCP

2 NT/1♣ or 1♦ __13__ to __15__ HCP

3 NT/1♣ or 1♦ __16__ to __17__ HCP

Describe __22+ Balanced Points or 9+ Tricks__

2♣ STRONG Conventional Response __2♦ Artificial,__

__May be waiting lacking a good suit__

__5__ to __11__ HCP   __Normally a good 6 card suit__

2♦ WEAK   __RONF__

2♥ WEAK Conventional Response: 2 NT ☒ __if maximum__

2♠ WEAK   __requests feature__

THE ALERT PROCEDURE

The opponents fill out a convention card so you can familiarize yourself with their bidding style and any conventions they use. When two or three boards are played against a set of opponents, you don't want to spend time reading their entire convention card and asking questions about special bids which are unlikely to be used. To make things as easy as possible, the ACBL has developed a procedure to inform the opponents whenever a player makes a conventional bid or play and to give the opponents a chance to ask about it.

The Alert

When someone at the table makes a call that has a special meaning for the partnership, that player's partner says, "Alert." If bidding boxes are being used, the Alert card or strip should be tapped as well. This lets the opponents know that the call has been assigned some conventional message, rather than the natural meaning. The player whose turn it is to bid can now ask the person who Alerted for further information by saying, "Please explain."

It is the *partner* of the person making the conventional call who does the Alerting, not the player who makes the call. Otherwise, you could remind partner any time you made a conventional call by saying "Alert." It's up to partner to remember your agreements. Notice also that you ask for an explanation from the partner of the player who made the Alertable call, not the player who made the call. Otherwise, the player who made the call could describe exactly what was meant! It's up to the partner to explain the partnership understanding. It may not be given correctly, but the Alert procedure isn't there to offer a chance to correct any misunderstanding. If the wrong explanation is given, the partner should say nothing and proceed as though the Alert never occurred.

When the auction is over, however, a member of the declaring side who is aware that an incorrect explanation has been given should inform the defenders before the opening lead is made. Likewise, the defenders must reveal any errors, but only at the conclusion of play — so the explanations won't influence the defense. The director should be summoned in both instances to make sure the opponents have not been put at a disadvantage by the mistaken explanation.

The Alert Procedure in Action

If the opponents have agreed to play *splinter bids* in response to major suit opening bids, they've marked this on their convention card. When you sit down against them, you may have no idea what this convention is, even if you happen to notice it on the card. You don't need to ask for an explanation before you start to bid since the convention is unlikely to come up during the couple of boards you play against this pair.

Suppose the opponent on your right opens the bidding 1♥. That doesn't require an Alert since it is a natural bid. You can look at an oppontent's convention card to see whether it promises at least five cards in the suit or only four — if you are interested. After you pass, opener's partner responds 3♠. The natural interpretation of a 3♠ response is that it shows a long spade suit. Since this isn't the case when the opponents are playing *splinter bids*, opener says "Alert."

Your partner now has the option of saying, "Please explain." Opener — the player who made the Alert (not the bid) — might say that 3♠ is a *splinter bid*. If partner is familiar with this convention, the auction will continue. If partner has never heard of *splinter bids*, it's fine to ask for a further explanation. Opener would explain that the 3♠ response shows a hand with four-card or longer support for hearts, enough strength to commit the partnership to game, and a singleton or void in spades. Your partner then decides what to do based on this information.

When it's your turn to call, you can also ask about the conventional 3♠. Ask opener for the explanation of the 3♠ response, not the player who made the bid.

If opener forgets about the convention, or forgets to Alert the 3♠ bid, responder should say nothing during the auction. Responder continues to bid as though the 3 ♠ bid had been Alerted. When the auction is over, responder must inform you before the opening lead is made about what has happened. If your side happens to win the auction, your opponent informs you at the end of play.

Which Bids Are Alertable?

In general, natural bids aren't Alertable. For example, if you open the bidding 1 ♣, showing a club suit, there's no need to Alert, although it may occasionally be a three-card suit. Your opponent can glance at your card, or ask, to find out exactly how many clubs you are promising.

Some conventional bids don't have to be Alerted, since they are used by so many players that they have become the standard use of the bid. For example, a response of 2 ♣ to a 1NT opening bid is assumed to be *Stayman* — you would alert only if your partnership played it as a natural bid! A bid of 4NT after a suit has been agreed is assumed to be the *Blackwood* convention, asking for the number of aces held by partner. On the other hand, conventions such as *splinter bids* are Alertable. To make it easier to determine which calls require Alerts and which do not, Alertable calls are marked in *red* on the general convention card. Non Alertable calls are indicated in black. (Partnerships with very unusual understandings of calls marked in black may have to Alert them.)

Announcements

A few calls require an *Announcement* rather than an Alert. An Announcement is a word or phrase that directly describes the meaning of partner's call. This is done to speed up the Alert process in common situations. There are currently three instances in which an Announcement is used.

The first is when the partnership uses an opening bid of 1NT to describe a balanced hand that falls outside the range of 15 to18 high-card points. If the partnership opens 1NT with 12 to 14 points, responder would Announce "weak" after hearing partner open the bidding 1NT. If there's no Announcement after the 1NT opening bid, assume the opponents are using a range that falls within 15 to 18 points.

The second case occurs when the partnership is using *Jacoby transfer bids* for the major suits (see Chapter 2). When responder bids 2 ♦ or 2 ♥ after a 1NT opening bid, opener Announces "transfer" instead of "Alert."

The third is using a response of 1NT to a major suit as a forcing or semi-forcing bid (see *two-over-one* in *More Commonly Used Conventions*). Opener Announces "forcing" after opening 1 ♥ or 1 ♠ and hearing a 1NT response from partner.

To make it easy to decide which calls require Announcements, they are marked in *blue* on the general convention card.

Skip-Bid Warning

A player planning to skip one or more levels of bidding during the auction gives a *skip-bid warning* by Announcing, "I am about to make a skip bid, please wait." After the bid is made, the opponent on the left is expected to wait for approximately ten seconds before making a call.

The purpose of making this Announcement — letting your opponent know about the impending bid and asking the opponent to deliberately wait before making a bid — is to avoid the difficult problems associated with hesitations. The ten-second wait should give the left-hand opponent enough time to decide on a call even with a difficult hand, and the right-hand opponent will not be given any unauthorized information through the tempo in which the call is made.

Skip-bid warnings should be made consistently, whether the jump bid is weak or strong. For example, before opening a *strong artificial 2 ♣ bid*, you should issue a skip-bid warning.

OTHER CONVENTIONS

This appendix covers conventions and treatments that are outside the scope of this book but may be popular in certain areas. They are included for reference purposes but are not intended for use in casual partnerships. Once you are familiar with the mainstream conventions, you may want to explore some of these variations in more detail. There are many books and articles available that cover specific conventions in more detail.

The following conventions are arranged by topic and supplement the eight chapters in the text.

OTHER NOTRUMP CONVENTIONS
(Supplement to Chapter 1)

Gambling/Acol 3NT Opening

This convention is used only when the partnership has some other method for showing a strong balanced hand of 25 to 27 points — for example, when the partnership uses 2♣ as a strong artificial opening bid (see Chapter 8). This allows an opening 3NT bid to be used for other purposes.

Some partnerships like to use an opening bid of 3NT to show a hand with a "solid" seven-card or eight-card minor suit, with little strength outside the minor suit. The following hand would be opened 3NT.

♠ 6
♥ 7 3
♦ A K Q J 9 7 6
♣ 10 9 3

The idea is that, if you can get the lead, you can probably take seven or eight tricks in your minor suit. That's why this bid is referred to as a *gambling 3NT opening* bid — the opponents may be the ones who take the first nine tricks. Partner isn't expected to leave in you in 3NT without some strength in the other suits. With a weak hand, partner can bid 4♣, expecting you to pass or bid 4♦, depending on which minor suit you hold.

A popular variation of the *gambling 3NT* is the *Acol 3NT* . You also need a long, strong minor suit, but with stoppers — high cards — in at least two of the other three suits.

For example:

♠ A 3	You're gambling that whatever suit the opponents
♥ K 4	lead, you can win a trick and take enough tricks with
♦ K 6	your minor suit and other high cards to make the
♣ A K J 10 8 7 3	contract — even if your partner has no strength.

There are many other treatments besides *gambling 3NT* and *Acol 3NT* openings — usually dependent on the solidity of the suit and the number of outside stoppers that are held. There are some, such as *Kantar 3NT*, which provide for opening 3NT with a long solid major suit.

Forcing Stayman

A common variation of *Stayman* is technically referred to as *non-forcing Stayman*. This is a little confusing since the 2♣ response itself is a forcing bid — opener cannot pass. If responder subsequently bids 2♥ or 2♠, however, opener doesn't have to bid again. This is where the term *non-forcing Stayman* comes from. *Forcing Stayman* is a variation in which the 2♣ response forces the partnership to keep bidding to at least 2NT.

For example:

WEST	EAST
1NT	2♣
2♦	2♥
?	

Playing *non-forcing Stayman*, East's 2♥ bid is invitational — opener can pass at this point. Playing *forcing Stayman*, opener must bid again, since the partnership has not yet reached 2NT. *Forcing Stayman* is rarely used by partnerships these days.

Double-barreled Stayman (Two-Way Stayman)

In this variation of the *Stayman* convention, a response of 2♣ is similar to *non-forcing Stayman*. It doesn't commit the partnership to the game level. A response of 2♦ is also *Stayman* — initially asking opener to bid a four-card or longer major suit — but commits the partnership to the game level. Any subsequent bids below the game level are forcing. Consider the following hands for responder after an opening bid of 1NT:

1) ♠ J 3
    ♥ K J 8 2
    ♦ 9 7 5
    ♣ K 10 5 2

2) ♠ A 3
    ♥ K J 8 2
    ♦ 9 7 5
    ♣ A K J 2

With the first hand, responder bids 2♣ as *non-forcing Stayman*. If opener bids 2♦ or 2♠, responder rebids 2NT as a non-forcing bid, inviting opener to game. If opener bids 2♥, responder raises to 3♥ as an invitation. With the second hand, responder bids 2♦ as *forcing Stayman*. If opener bids 2♠, responder can rebid 2NT as a forcing bid. Opener has to bid again and can mention a four-card club suit, perhaps leading to a slam in clubs. If opener bids 2♥, responder raises to 3♥ as a forcing bid, initiating a slam investigation. *Double-barreled Stayman* is incompatible with *Jacoby transfer bids* (see Chapter 2), since the 2♦ response can no longer be used as a transfer to 2♥.

Puppet Stayman

This is a variation of *Stayman* that allows responder to ask if opener holds a five-card major, in addition to enquiring about four-card majors. With no five-card major, opener responds 2♦. Responder then rebids:

- 2♥ to show a four-card *spade* suit.

- 2♠ to show a four-card *heart* suit

- 2NT to show four hearts and four spades with invitational strength.

- 3NT to show four hearts and four spades with game-going strength.

Opener now determines whether the partnership has an eight-card major suit fit and places the contract. An advantage of *puppet Stayman* is that opener's distribution tends to remain concealed, making it more difficult for the defenders. *Puppet Stayman* is useful for those partnerships concerned about 'losing' the five-card major when they open 1NT with a balanced 5–3–3–2 hand. The responses are somewhat complex, and many partnerships use this variation only in response to 2NT because there is more room to explore using standard methods after 1NT.

Negative Doubles after 1NT

When an opponent overcalls directly over an opening 1NT bid, some partnerships prefer to use a double for takeout — *negative* — rather than penalty. It shows enough strength to compete and tends to show four cards in any unbid major suit. For example:

West			East
♠ Q J 9 3			♠ K 10 8 2
♥ A 10 5			♥ 7 2
♦ A J 6 2			♦ Q 8 3
♣ K 8			♣ Q 9 6 2

WEST	NORTH	EAST	SOUTH
1NT	2♥	Double	Pass
2♠	Pass	Pass	Pass

This is similar to the use of the *negative double* after an opening bid of one in a suit which is discussed in *More Commonly Used Conventions*. Some partnerships, especially those that use the *lebensohl* convention, use *negative doubles* only after an overcall at the three level, leaving the double of a two-level overcall for penalties.

Lebensohl

Although the standard approach for handling interference after a 1NT opening bid is quite workable, there are more complex methods that can be used. An opponent's overcall often makes things difficult for responder. 2♣ is no longer available as *Stayman* and there is less bidding room left for responder to handle all of the combinations of weak, invitational, and strong hands. The *lebensohl* convention is a method for meeting some of these challenges. Playing this convention, the partnership has the following agreements when there is a direct overcall at the two level following an opening bid of 1NT:

- A double of the overcall is for penalties.

- A response in a suit at the two level shows a five-card or longer suit and is non-forcing.

- A response in a suit at the three level shows a five-card or longer suit and is forcing.

- A cuebid of the opponent's suit is *"Stayman"* but denies a stopper — a high card — in the opponent's suit. Opener will bid a four-card or longer major. With no four-card major, opener rebids 3NT with a stopper in the opponent's suit, otherwise bids a minor suit looking for a better spot than 3NT.

- 2NT is a transfer to 3♣ (see below).

- 3NT is a raise to game but denies a stopper in the opponent's suit. If opener also doesn't have a stopper in the opponent's suit, opener can bid a minor suit looking for a better contract than 3NT.

This 2NT response is the heart of *lebensohl*. It gives up the natural raise to 2NT, but as compensation responder has several possible continuations after opener rebids 3♣ in response to the transfer:

- Pass to play in partscore when responder has a weak hand with long clubs.

- Bid a new suit at the three level that is lower-ranking than the overcalled suit as a signoff in that suit — since an immediate bid of a new suit at the three level was available as a forcing bid.

- Bid a new suit at the three level that is higher-ranking than the overcalled suit as an invitational bid in that suit — since responder could have bid the suit immediately at the two level with a weak hand or jumped to the three level with a strong hand.

- Cuebid the opponent's suit as *Stayman*. This also shows a stopper in the opponent's suit, since an immediate cuebid would be *Stayman* without a stopper.

- Bid 3NT. This shows a raise to 3NT with a stopper in the opponent's suit. Without a stopper, responder would have jumped to 3NT immediately.

Here are some examples of *lebensohl* in action:

West	WEST	NORTH	EAST	SOUTH	East
♠ A K 9 3	1NT	2♥	2NT	Pass	♠ Q 2
♥ 9 8 5	3♣	Pass	3♦	Pass	♥ J 3
♦ K 8	Pass	Pass			♦ Q J 10 9 4 3
♣ A J 10 4					♣ 9 7 3

After North's overcall, East bids 2NT as the *lebensohl* convention to ask West to bid 3♣. After West bids 3♣, East corrects to 3♦, showing the diamond suit. This is non-forcing, allowing the partnership to play in partscore. If East had bid 3♦ directly over 2♥, it would be a forcing bid. If the partnership were not playing *lebensohl*, East would have no satisfactory method of competing on this hand after the overcall.

West	WEST	NORTH	EAST	SOUTH	East
♠ A K 9 3	1NT	2♥	3♥	Pass	♠ Q J 5 2
♥ 9 8 5	3♠	Pass	4♠	Pass	♥ J 3
♦ K 8	Pass	Pass			♦ Q J 10 3
♣ A J 10 4					♣ K 7 3

After the overcall, East cuebids the opponent's suit to find out if opener has four spades. West shows the four-card suit and East puts the partnership in game. In this sequence, East denied a stopper in hearts. With some strength in hearts, East would first bid 2NT to ask West to bid 3♣ and then cuebid 3♥.

West	WEST	NORTH	EAST	SOUTH	East
♠ A K 9 3	1NT	2♥	3NT	Pass	♠ 6 5 2
♥ 9 8 5	4♣	Pass	5♣	Pass	♥ J 3
♦ K 8	Pass	Pass			♦ A Q J 3
♣ A J 10 4					♣ K Q 7 3

East's jump to 3NT shows the values to go to game but denies a stopper in the opponent's suit. West also doesn't have a stopper and looks for a better spot by showing the club suit. East puts the partnership in game in the minor suit. The partnership avoids playing in 3NT, where the opponents are likely to take enough heart tricks to defeat the contract.

There are other variations of this convention and some modifications are often used when an opponent makes a two-suited overcall — such as *Landy* or *Astro* (see *More Commonly Used Conventions*). *Lebensohl* is popular among those partnerships that can remember the various sequences, but it isn't recommended for casual partnerships.

OTHER NOTRUMP CONVENTIONS
(Supplement to Chapter 2)

Four-Suit Transfer Bids

A popular method for handling minor suits following an opening bid of 1NT is *four-suit transfer bids*. This is more complex than using 2♠ to sign off in either minor, but it has some advantages. The partnership will have to decide whether the advantages outweigh the additional complexity. *Four-suit transfer bids* work like this:

> • A response of 2 ♦ is a transfer to 2 ♥.
>
> • A response of 2 ♥ is a transfer to 2 ♠.
>
> • A response of 2 ♠ is a transfer to 3 ♣.
>
> • A response of 2NT is a transfer to 3 ♦.

The first two responses are the standard *Jacoby transfers* for the major suits. The 2♠ and 2NT responses are used to show the minor suits, either when responder wants to sign off in the minor suit or when responder is interested in bigger things. These transfer bids give opener some latitude. With a minimum-strength hand and poor support for responder's minor, opener simply accepts the transfer. With extra strength and a good fit with the minor suit, opener makes the bid below the minor suit — 2NT in reply to the 2♠ transfer bid, 3♣ in reply to the 2NT transfer bid. This allows responder to still stop at the three level in the minor suit with no interest in anything else, but encourages responder to bid more with a hand of at least invitational strength.

For example:

West	WEST	EAST	East
♠ Q 9 5 4	1NT	2NT	♠ 8 3
♥ A K 5 4	3♦	Pass	♥ 6 3
♦ 9 3			♦ K Q 10 6 5 2
♣ A Q 10			♣ J 5 2

East bids 2NT as a transfer to diamonds. With a minimum-strength hand and no fit for diamonds, opener simply accepts the transfer. Responder has no reason to go any further, and the partnership rests in partscore.

West	WEST	EAST	East
♠ Q 9 5 4	1NT	2NT	♠ 8 3
♥ A K 5 4	3♣	3NT	♥ 6 3
♦ A 9 3	Pass		♦ K Q 10 6 5 2
♣ A 10			♣ J 5 2

In this example, opener has a maximum-strength hand for the 1NT bid and a fit with responder's diamonds. Opener shows this by bidding 3♣, rather than 3♦. Responder could still sign off by bidding 3♦, but encouraged by opener's bid decides to push on to a game contract.

If 2NT is used as a transfer bid, it's no longer available as a natural invitation to game, which is a disadvantage. This can be overcome by starting all invitational hands with 2♣, *Stayman*, even when responder has no interest in playing in a major suit. For example:

West	WEST	EAST	East
♠ Q 10 4	1NT	2♣	♠ J 8 3
♥ K J 5 4	2♥	2NT	♥ A Q 3
♦ A K 3	Pass		♦ Q 8 6
♣ Q 9 5			♣ 10 7 4 2

After West's 1NT opening, East would like to invite game by raising to 2NT. Playing *four-suit transfers*, East can't bid 2NT directly since that would be a transfer to diamonds. Instead, East starts by bidding 2♣, the *Stayman* convention. West dutifully shows the four-card heart suit. East now rebids 2NT, showing an invitational-strength hand. With a minimum hand for the 1NT opening, West passes and the partnership rests in partscore. The sequence is ambiguous. West can't be sure whether or not East holds a four-card spade suit in addition to a hand of invitational strength. That's a small disadvantage to this method.

The partnership will need to discuss several such possible bidding sequences to ensure that there are no misunderstandings when *four-suit transfers* are used.

Minor-Suit Stayman

Instead of using the 2♠ response to 1NT as a transfer to 3♣ — allowing responder to sign off in either minor suit — partnerships using *Jacoby transfer bids* sometimes prefer to use the 2♠ response as an inquiry about opener's minor suits. Opener rebids 2NT with no four-card or longer minor suit, rebids 3♣ or 3♦ with one four-card minor suit, and rebids the longer major — 3♥ or 3♠ — with four cards in both minor suits. The 2♠ response can also be used when responder holds a five-card or longer minor suit and is interested in slam.

For example:

West		WEST	EAST		East
♠ K Q 7 2		1NT	2♠		♠ A 8
♥ A 8 6		3♦	4♦		♥ 9 5
♦ A J 7 3		4♥	4NT		♦ K Q 10 4
♣ J 4		5♥	6♦		♣ A Q 9 6 3

Partnerships that use *Jacoby transfers* in response to 2NT sometimes use a response of 3♠ in a similar fashion.

Texas Transfers

Texas transfers are similar to *Jacoby transfers* for the major suits but are used at a higher level. They are commonly used in response to both a 1NT opening bid or a 2NT opening bid as follows:

> • A response of 4♦ is a transfer to 4♥.
> • A response of 4♥ is a transfer to 4♠.

For example:

West		East
♠ K 9		♠ A J 10 8 7 4
♥ A 9 7 5		♥ 3
♦ K 6 3		♦ 7 4 2
♣ A J 8 5		♣ K Q 4

WEST	EAST
1NT	4♥
4♠	Pass

Since responder can essentially accomplish the same thing by using a *Jacoby transfer bid* and then raising to the game level, this convention may appear unnecessary. Nonetheless, *Texas transfers* can be used in conjunction with *Jacoby transfers* by experienced partnerships to distinguish between signoff bids and slam invitations. Typically, responder would use a *Texas transfer* to stop at the game level in the major suit. With some interest in going beyond game, responder would start with a *Jacoby transfer* and then jump to game. Such distinctions are not for the casual partnership.

Smolen Transfers

Holding a game-going hand with both a four-card major and a five-card or longer major, responder usually starts with the *Stayman* convention. If opener rebids 2♦, responder then jumps to the three level in the longer major, asking opener to choose between the major and 3NT. This has the disadvantage that responder will become declarer if opener holds three cards in the major suit and raises to game. The *Smolen* convention ensures that opener is always the declarer. After the 2♣ response and 2♦ rebid, responder jumps to the three level in the four-card major suit, showing five or more cards in the other major. For example:

West		East
♠ A 8 6		♠ Q J 9 7 2
♥ Q 7		♥ A K 9 4
♦ A Q 7 4 2		♦ 5
♣ K 9 4		♣ 8 6 5

WEST	EAST
1NT	2♣
2♦	3♥
4♠	Pass

Singleton-Showing Responses (Splinter)

There are various methods that can be used to show shortness — a singleton or a void — in response to an opening 1NT bid. For example, a jump to the three level in a suit can be used to show shortness, allowing the partnership to avoid 3NT when the opponents can run a long suit. Such bids must be integrated carefully into the partnership methods, since they may conflict with other conventions. They are not recommended for casual partnerships.

MAJOR SUIT OPENINGS AND RESPONSES
(Supplement to Chapter 3)

Splinter Bids

Splinter bids, or *splinter raises*, are similar to *Jacoby 2NT* in that they are used by responder to show a forcing raise after an opening bid of 1 ♥ or 1 ♠. Instead of asking about opener's shortness, however, a splinter bid shows responder's shortness as follows:

> • In response to an opening bid of 1 ♥ or 1 ♠, a double jump in a new suit shows a singleton or void in that suit, four-card or longer support for opener's major, and 13 to 16 dummy points.

It's then up to opener to decide whether to stop at the game level in the agreed major suit, or try for a slam contract. Some partnerships allow responder to make a splinter bid with more than 16 points, in which case responder will bid again even if opener shows no interest in slam. Here is an example of an auction involving a *splinter bid*:

West					East
♠ A Q 9 8 3 2					♠ K 10 7 4
♥ Q 8					♥ K J 7 3
♦ K J 2					♦ 3
♣ 8 4					♣ A 9 5 2

WEST	NORTH	EAST	SOUTH
1 ♠	Pass	4 ♦	Pass
4 ♠	Pass	Pass	Pass

East's hand is worth a forcing raise in response to West's opening bid — 11 high-card points plus 3 dummy points for the singleton. East's double jump to 4 ♦ is a *splinter bid* — a non-jump response of 2 ♦ would be natural, showing diamonds, and a single jump response of 3 ♦ would be a jump shift, showing a strong hand. 4 ♦ shows diamond shortness and a fit for opener's suit. West has wasted high cards in diamonds opposite East's announced shortness, so there's no reason to move beyond the game level. West signs off in the agreed trump suit, and East has nothing further to say. If opener's hand is changed slightly, a slam contract becomes more probable:

West	WEST	NORTH	EAST	SOUTH	East
♠ A Q 9 8 3 2	1 ♠	Pass	4 ♦	Pass	♠ K 10 7 4
♥ A Q	4 ♥	Pass	5 ♣	Pass	♥ K J 7 3
♦ 8 7 2	6 ♠	Pass	Pass	Pass	♦ 3
♣ 8 4					♣ A 9 5 2

West has no more strength than in the previous example, but the hand appreciates considerably in value when East shows a forcing raise with shortness in the diamond suit. West cuebids the ♥A to show some slam interest and bids to the excellent slam contract when East cooperates by cuebidding the ♣A.

Most partnerships continue to use splinter bids after a takeout double. After an overcall, *splinter bids* — like *Jacoby 2NT* — are usually considered to be "off," but some partnerships prefer to continue to use them.

Extended Splinter Bids

Splinter bids can be used by the partnership in situations other than as a response to the opening bid. Many partnerships treat any unnecessary jump in a new suit — where a lower-level bid of the new suit would be forcing — as a *splinter bid*. For example:

WEST	NORTH	EAST	SOUTH
1 ♥	Pass	1 ♠	Pass
4 ♣			

A rebid of 2♣ by West would be natural and non-forcing. A jump to 3♣ would be a jump shift and would be forcing. West's double jump to 4♣, therefore, isn't needed to show clubs. It's an unnecessary jump and can be used as a *splinter bid* showing four-card support for East's spades, a game-going hand, and club shortness.

WEST	NORTH	EAST	SOUTH
1♠	Pass	2♥	Pass
4♦			

After East's 2♥ response, a rebid of 3♦ by West would be forcing. 4♦, therefore, is an unnecessary jump and would show diamond shortness and a fit with East's hearts.

Swiss

Swiss is another form of forcing major-suit raise that makes use of the jumps to 4♣ and 4♦ in response to an opening bid of one-of-a-major. Instead of using these responses as splinter bids — showing shortness — they can be used to distinguish between different types of raises to the game level. There are a number of variations. *Trump Swiss* uses the jumps to 4♣ and 4♦ to distinguish between hands with excellent trump support for opener's major suit — A–Q–x–x, A–x–x–x–x — and those with mediocre support — Q–x–x–x, 10–x–x–x–x. *Control Swiss* uses the responses of 4♣ and 4♦ to distinguish hands with lots of aces and kings — controls — and those with fewer controls. *Value Swiss* uses 4♣ and 4♦ to more narrowly define the strength of responder's hand.

None of these variations are recommended for the casual partnership. They involve considerable partnership discussion and a fair degree of judgment.

Bergen Major-Suit Raises

This is a scheme of major suit raises designed to get the partnership quickly to the three level or higher whenever there are nine or more combined trumps. It was developed by Marty Bergen, a well-known expert, based on Marty's experiences in partnership with Larry Cohen — which also resulted in Larry's books on *The Law of Total Tricks*. The most common variation of *Bergen raises* in response to an opening bid of 1 ♥ or 1 ♠ is the following:

Bergen Raises

- A raise of opener's suit to the two level shows 6 to 9 points and *precisely* three-card support.

- A raise of opener's suit to the three level is weak — preemptive — showing 0 to 6 points and four-card support.

- A jump to 3 ♣ is artificial (conventional) and shows four-card support with 7 to 10 points.

- A jump to 3 ♦ is artificial (conventional) and shows four-card support with 11 or 12 points — a limit raise.

- A jump to the three level in the other major is artificial (conventional) and shows a game-forcing raise with shortness — a singleton or a void — in one of the side suits. Opener can ask where the shortness is by making the next cheapest bid.

- A jump to 3NT shows a balanced hand with *precisely* three-card support, game-going strength, and stoppers in all of the unbid suits. Opener can pass, bid the major-suit to game, or look for slam.

For example, consider the following hands for South after the auction has started:

WEST	NORTH	EAST	**SOUTH**
	1 ♠	Pass	?

♠ K J 7 3
♥ 7 6
♦ J 10 6 5
♣ 9 7 3

Jump to 3 ♠. A jump to 3 ♠ is a preemptive raise showing 0 to 6 points and four-card support. The idea is to make it difficult for the opponents to get into the auction. If North–South can't make 3 ♠, presumably the opponents can make at least a partscore, and perhaps a game contract.

♠ Q J 8 4 ♥ A 8 ♦ 9 6 3 ♣ J 8 7 4	Jump to 3♣. With 8 high-card points and four-card support for opener, South would make the artificial response of 3♣. With a minimum hand, opener can rebid 3♠. With a medium-strength hand, opener can jump to 4♠.
♠ K 9 7 4 ♥ A J 10 8 ♦ 9 3 ♣ Q J 5	Jump to 3♦. This shows four-card support and the strength for a limit raise. North can return to 3♠ to reject the invitation or jump to 4♠ to accept the invitation. This is similar to 1♠–3♠ when the partnership plays limit raises — opener passes or bids 4♠.
♠ Q 9 7 3 ♥ A Q 8 ♦ 3 ♣ K 8 6 4 2	Jump to 3♥. A jump to 3♥, the other major suit, shows a forcing raise with shortness — a singleton or a void — in a side suit. Opener can simply rebid 4♠ with no interest in slam. With slam interest, opener makes the next cheapest bid, 3♠, to ask about

the shortness. South would now bid 4♦ to show the singleton, and North could evaluate the hand accordingly.

Weak Jump Raises

Some partnerships prefer to treat the immediate jump raise to the three level in opener's major suit as a weak, preemptive raise, rather than as a limit or forcing raise. This style is referred to as *weak jump raises*. It's a feature of *Bergen major-suit raises* as outlined above.

Most partnerships prefer to use limit raises — or forcing raises — in response to 1♥ or 1♠ when there is no interference. If there is a takeout double or an overcall over the 1♥ or 1♠ bid, some partnerships now shift to weak jump raises. After a takeout double, 2NT is commonly used to show a limit raise as discussed earlier in the chapter. After an overcall, a cuebid of the opponent's suit can be used to show a limit raise or better in support of opener's suit.

3NT as a Balanced Forcing Raise

Rather than using the *Jacoby 2NT* response to show a forcing raise of opener's major suit, some partnerships that play limit raises prefer to use 3NT to show a forcing raise with no shortness. With shortness, responder can make a splinter bid. For example:

♠ K 10 3
♥ A Q 7 5
♦ J 3
♣ A 8 7 3

To bid 3NT in response to an opening bid of 1♥, responder could hold a hand like this. With no interest in slam, opener would sign off in 4♥. Any other rebid by opener would show interest in slam.

MAJOR SUIT OPENINGS AND RESPONSES
(Supplement to Chapter 4)

Weak Jump Shifts

Instead of using strong jump shifts, some partnerships prefer to use a jump shift by responder as a weak non-forcing bid, showing a long suit but no desire to bid any higher. For example, consider the following hand in response to an opening bid of 1♥.

♠ K J 10 8 7 6 3
♥ 7
♦ 9 8 3
♣ J 3

Playing *weak jump shifts*, responder would bid 2♠ with this hand, rather than 1♠. This serves as both a descriptive bid — telling opener that you have a long spade suit and a weak hand — and as a preemptive bid — making it more difficult for the opponents to enter the auction at a convenient level. Holding a strong hand with spades, responder would bid 1♠, intending to show the extra strength on the next round.

Soloway Jump Shifts

Paul Soloway, a well-known bridge expert and former member of the Dallas Aces, puts a tight limit on the types of hands with which responder can jump shift. A jump shift into a new suit shows a hand worth 17 or 18 points and one of three types of hand:

- A strong one-suiter, which is shown by rebidding the suit at responder's next opportunity.

- A balanced hand, which is shown by rebidding in notrump at responder's next opportunity.

- A hand with support for opener's suit, which is shown by raising opener's suit at responder's next opportunity or by bidding a new suit to imply shortness in the unbid suit.

Apart from the narrow range for responder's strength, this is close to the style of jump shift recommended in Chapter 4. Responder can hold a hand stronger than 17 or 18 points but would then have to bid again if opener signs off.

Preemptive Re-raises

Consider the meaning of North's 3 ♥ bid in the following auction:

WEST	NORTH	EAST	SOUTH
	1 ♥	Pass	2 ♥
Pass	3 ♥	Pass	?

Using standard methods, North's 3 ♥ bid would be considered an invitational bid. South can pass with minimal values, or continue to game with a good hand for the raise. Some partnerships prefer to treat the re-raise of the trump suit as a preemptive bid, designed to keep the opponents from easily coming into the auction. With a hand of invitational strength, North could invite game by bidding something other than 3 ♥.

MINOR-SUIT OPENING BIDS AND RESPONSES
(Supplement to Chapter 5)

Inverted Minor-Suit Raises

Some partnerships prefer to reverse the meaning of a raise of opener's minor to the two level and a jump raise to the three level. This is referred to as *inverted minor-suit raises* and works as follows:

- A raise of opener's minor to the two level shows 10 or more points and is forcing for one round.

- A jump raise of opener's minor to the three level is weak, showing fewer than 10 points.

The advantages to this approach are:

- Responder can raise preemptively to the three level with a weak hand and a good fit for opener's suit. This is more effective in keeping the opponents out of the auction than a raise to the two level. This is similar to the concept of *weak jump raises* over a major suit.

- When responder has a limit raise of opener's minor — 10 or more points — the partnership has more opportunity to explore for the best contract. An immediate limit raise to the three level leaves less room to explore for a contract of 3NT — a more likely contract than 5♣ or 5♦ when opener has enough to accept responder's invitation.

- With a forcing raise of opener's minor suit, responder can start with a single raise, since it's forcing for one round. Having shown support for the minor suit, responder can then keep the bidding going until game is reached. Playing limit raises with no immediate forcing raise, responder has a more difficult time showing support — often having to go through *fourth suit forcing* (see Chapter 6) before raising opener's minor.

Here are some examples of responding to an opening bid of 1♣ when the partnership uses *inverted minor-suit raises*:

♠ 9 5	Raise to 3♣. This is a weak — preemptive — raise.
♥ 7 6 4	Hopefully, the partnership can take eight or nine
♦ Q 3	tricks with clubs as the trump suit, even if opener
♣ K J 9 6 3 2	has a minimum-strength hand. At the same time, it
	will be more difficult for the opponents to enter the

auction following a 3♣ bid than if you raised to only 2♣.

♠ 4 2
♥ K J 8
♦ Q 8 3
♣ A J 8 7 5

Raise to 2♣. This is forcing for one round and shows at least the values for a limit raise. If opener has some strength in spades, the partnership is likely to belong in a notrump contract. If not, the partnership can settle for partscore in clubs — or game if opener has extra strength. After the 2♣ response, opener can bid 2NT with a minimum-strength balanced hand suitable for notrump, or rebid 3♣ with a minimum-strength hand unsuitable for notrump. With extra strength, opener can bid a new suit to probe for the best contract.

♠ A 9 3
♥ 8 6
♦ A 4 2
♣ K Q J 8 6

Raise to 2♣. This would be an awkward hand playing standard methods, since there is no way to immediately show a forcing raise with club support. Responder would have to temporize with a response of 1♦, and continue to make forcing bids until game is reached. Playing inverted raises, responder starts by raising to 2♣ — showing the fit — and can then continue to game over opener's rebid.

The partnership must agree on whether this convention still applies if responder is a passed hand and whether it applies if the opponents interfere with an overcall or takeout double. The standard agreement is that it still applies when responder is a passed hand — although opener can pass since responder can no longer have a forcing raise — but raises revert to their natural meaning after an overcall or double. Some partnerships prefer to continue using the convention after a takeout double or a simple overcall.

Jump Shift in Other Minor as a Forcing Raise

If responder's jump raise of opener's minor suit is used as a limit raise, responder doesn't have a way of immediately showing a forcing raise. Some partnerships use a jump shift in the other minor as an artificial (conventional) bid, showing a forcing raise in opener's minor. For example, consider the following hand for responder after an opening bid of 1♣.

♠ A Q 7
♥ 8 6
♦ 10 8 3
♣ A K J 8 7

Using this convention, responder would jump shift to 2♦. This is an artificial response, showing a game-forcing raise in clubs. Playing standard methods, responder would have difficulty showing this hand — perhaps starting with a *temporizing* response of 1♦.

The partnership has to give up the standard use of the jump shift response in the other minor — as a natural bid showing a strong hand with interest in a slam contract.

Splinter Bids

Splinter bids can be used in response to a minor suit in a similar fashion as in responding a major suit (see page 308):

> • In response to an opening bid of 1♣ or 1♦, a double jump in a new suit shows a singleton or void in that suit, support for opener's minor, and at least game-going values.

In reply to the splinter bid, opener can decide whether to play game in notrump, to play game in the minor suit, or to try for a slam contract.

For example:

West					East
♠ K Q 10 8	WEST	NORTH	EAST	SOUTH	♠ 5
♥ Q 8 4	1♦	Pass	3♠	Pass	♥ A 7 6
♦ K 9 6 4	3NT	Pass	Pass	Pass	♦ A Q 10 8 7 3
♣ K 6					♣ Q 7 5

In response to West's opening bid, East's hand is worth a forcing raise — 12 high-card points plus 3 dummy points for the singleton spade. Playing standard methods, with no immediate forcing raise, East would have to manufacture a forcing response of 2♣, intending to show diamond support later. Playing *splinter bids*, East can make a double jump to 3♠, showing diamond support and shortness in spades. With a lot of strength in spades, opener elects to play in 3NT. Having described the hand, responder has nothing further to say.

West		East
♠ J 7 4		♠ 5
♥ K Q 9 4		♥ A 7 6
♦ K J 6 4		♦ A Q 10 8 7 3
♣ K 6		♣ Q 7 5

WEST	NORTH	EAST	SOUTH
1♦	Pass	3♠	Pass
5♦	Pass	Pass	Pass

After East shows a singleton spade, West knows that 3NT won't be a good spot. With a minimum-strength hand for the opening bid, West settles for a game contract in the minor suit.

West		East
♠ A 9 7 2		♠ 5
♥ 8 3		♥ A 7 6
♦ K 9 6 4		♦ A Q 10 8 7 3
♣ A K 4		♣ Q 7 5

WEST	NORTH	EAST	SOUTH
1♦	Pass	3♠	Pass
4♣	Pass	4♥	Pass
4NT	Pass	5♥	Pass
6♦	Pass	Pass	Pass

Opposite East's diamond fit and singleton spade, West's hand holds excellent slam potential, since there will be no losers in the spade suit. West *cuebids* to show strength in clubs and East cooperates by *cuebidding* the ♥ A (see *More Commonly Used Conventions*). West checks for aces using the *Blackwood* convention (see *More Commonly Used Conventions*). When East shows two aces, West bids to the excellent slam contract.

Most partnerships continue to use splinter bids after a takeout double but not after an overcall — although some partnerships continue to use them in all competitive situations. The partnership can also use splinter bids in other bidding sequences to show support for partner's suit and shortness in the bid suit.

Bypassing Diamonds

While the standard style is to bid four-card suits up the line when responding to an opening bid of 1♣, some partnerships prefer to bypass a four-card diamond suit when holding a four-card major suit. The idea is that it's unlikely that opener has a four-card diamond suit — with both four-card minors, opener usually starts with 1♦ — and it's more important to find a major-suit fit. It is especially important to show the major suit when responder has a weak hand. If responder starts with 1♦ and the next opponent overcalls, the partnership may not find it's major suit fit — neither opener nor responder may have the strength to introduce the major suit on their rebid. Some partnerships take this concept further, bypassing a five-card or longer diamond suit in favor of bidding a four-card major suit. Here are some examples of responding to 1♣:

♠ 9 4
♥ A J 7 3
♦ Q 10 8 4
♣ J 6 5

The standard method is to respond 1♦, bidding four-card suits up the line. Partnerships using the above approach would respond 1♥ and ignore the possibility of a diamond fit. The advantage is that if opener holds four hearts and the next opponent overcalls 1♠ or 2♠, the partnership will have found its eight-card fit and be able to compete.

♠ K J 6 2
♥ 7 4
♦ J 9 8 7 4 3
♣ 5

Taking this approach one step further, some partnerships would respond 1♠, rather than mention the diamonds. With a minimum-strength hand, responder wants to be sure of getting the major suit introduced.

♠ A J 10 5
♥ 8 3
♦ A Q 8 6 3
♣ Q 5

With enough strength to take the partnership to the game level, responder should bid naturally, showing the diamond suit first by bidding 1♦. Responder has enough strength to show the spade suit later, even if the opponents interfere.

Playing this style, a response of 1♦ implies that responder doesn't have a four-card or longer major suit — unless responder has a game-forcing hand and can afford to bid the major suit later, even if the opponents interfere. If responder bids 1♦, opener can rebid 1NT with a balanced hand, rather than continuing to bid four-card suits up the line.

The partnership doesn't need to warn the opponents when using this approach — it's considered standard practice to occasionally bypass a four-card or longer diamond suit to bid a major suit. If opener's 1NT rebid may bypass a major suit that could have been shown at the one level, however, the opponents must be informed about the 1NT rebid. Opener is expected to bid four-card suits up the line at the one level.

1NT Response to 1 ♣

A response of 1NT to an opening bid of 1 ♣ commonly shows a hand of 6 to 10 points — the same range used for a 1NT response to other opening bids at the one level. Some partnerships prefer to use a higher range for the response, such as 8 to 10 points or 9 to 11 points. The reasoning behind this variation is that responder can usually find some other response with a weaker hand. If responder doesn't have another four-card suit to bid at the one level, responder will have at least four clubs. Responder can raise to 2 ♣ with a weak hand of 6 to 8 points, reserving 1NT for a slightly stronger hand. To avoid raising clubs with only four-card support, some players respond 1 ♦ on a three-card suit with a hand too weak for the 1NT response.

Consider the following hands for responder after an opening bid of 1 ♣.

♠ K 9 4 ♥ Q J 7 ♦ K 9 6 ♣ J 10 6 3	With 10 high-card points, responder has the perfect hand for a response of 1NT.
♠ 9 6 2 ♥ K 3 ♦ J 8 5 ♣ Q 7 6 3 2	With a weak hand containing only 6 high-card points, responder can raise to 2 ♣, rather than respond 1NT.
♠ J 8 3 ♥ 7 6 2 ♦ A 10 4 ♣ Q 9 5 2	If the partnership uses a response of 1NT to show 8 or more points, responder will have to raise to 2 ♣ — or respond 1 ♦ to avoid raising clubs with only four-card support.

2NT as an Invitational Response to a Minor

The standard approach is to play a response of 2NT to a minor suit as a forcing bid, showing 13 to 15 points and a balanced hand. A jump to 3NT shows a balanced hand of 16 or 17 points. With an invitational-strength balanced hand of 11 or 12 points — too strong for a response of 1NT — responder must start by bidding a new suit, planning to make an invitational rebid of 2NT at the next opportunity.

Some players prefer a style of notrump responses similar to that for limit raises of opener's suit. A response of 1NT shows 6 to 10 points. A response of 2NT shows a balanced hand of 11 or 12 points and is only invitational, not forcing. A response of 3NT shows a balanced hand of 13 to 15 points. With 16 or more points, responder starts by bidding a new suit, followed by forcing bids until game, at least, is reached. For example, consider the following hands as responder when partner opens the bidding 1♦.

♠ K Q 7
♥ Q 10 6
♦ J 6 5 3
♣ K 10 5

With a balanced hand and 11 high-card points, this is an ideal hand for an invitational response of 2NT. Using standard methods, a response of 2NT would be forcing, showing 13 to 15 points, so responder would have to find another bid (2♣).

♠ A J 9
♥ K 10 8
♦ J 9 7
♣ A Q 6 2

Playing standard methods, responder would bid 2NT as a forcing response showing a balanced hand of 13 to 15 points. If the partnership plays 2NT as a limited, invitational response, then responder would bid 3NT.

Weak Jump Shifts

As when responding to a major suit, some partnerships prefer to use a jump shift by responder as a weak non-forcing bid in response to a minor suit, showing a long suit but no desire to bid any higher. For example, consider the following hand in response to an opening bid of 1♦:

♠ 6
♥ Q J 10 9 7 5
♦ J 6 5
♣ 10 3 2

Playing *weak jump shifts*, responder would bid 2 ♥ rather than pass or respond 1 ♥. This tells opener about the heart suit while showing a weak hand at the same time. The 2 ♥ response will also make it more difficult for the opponents to enter the auction.

Flip-Flop

One disadvantage of using 2NT to show a limit raise of opener's minor suit after a takeout double is that opener may want to play in a contract of 3NT with enough strength to accept responder's invitation. The 3NT contract will now be played by the weaker hand, with the opening lead through the high-card strength in opener's hand. To avoid this, some partnerships reverse the meaning of the 2NT response and the jump raise in opener's minor after a takeout double. This is sometimes referred to as *flip-flop*:

> • After partner's minor suit opening is doubled for takeout, a jump to 2NT shows a preemptive raise to the three level and a jump to the three level in opener's minor is invitational, showing a limit raise.

The same consideration doesn't apply after a major-suit opening bid has been doubled, since opener will put the partnership in game in the major suit, rather than 3NT, with enough to accept an invitation. Here is an example of *flip-flop* after the auction starts:

WEST	NORTH	EAST	**SOUTH**
	1 ♦	Double	?

♠ 7 5
♥ 4 2
♦ A J 8 6 4
♣ 10 9 6 3

With a preemptive raise to the three level, responder would bid 2NT when playing *flip-flop*. It's unlikely that opener will want to play in notrump when responder has a weak hand. Opener will rebid 3 ♦ with no interest in going any higher.

♠ J 4 3
♥ 9 4
♦ K Q J 7 3
♣ A 8 5

With a limit raise of opener's minor suit, responder jumps to 3 ♦ over the takeout double. This allows opener to pass with a minimum-strength hand, but to bid 3NT with enough to accept responder's invitation. 3NT should be a better contract from opener's side of the table, with the opening lead coming up to opener's high cards in the other suits.

THE SUBSEQUENT AUCTION
(Supplement to Chapter 6)

New Minor Forcing

After a 1NT rebid by opener, a new suit by responder isn't forcing unless it's a jump shift or a reverse, both of which commit the partnership to the game level. This can prove awkward when responder needs to get further information from opener without committing the partnership to a game contract. To get around this difficulty, some partnerships treat the bid of a new minor suit by responder as forcing, while the bid of an old minor suit — one previously bid by the partnership — remains non forcing. For example, consider the following hands for responder after the auction starts:

WEST	NORTH	**EAST**	SOUTH
1♣	Pass	1♠	Pass
1NT	Pass	?	

♠ A K 9 7 3
♥ A 4 3
♦ 7 3
♣ Q 10 6

Responder could raise to 3NT, but the partnership might miss a 5–3 major-suit fit in spades if opener has three-card support. A rebid of 2♠, however, would be a signoff, and a rebid of 3 ♠ would only be invitational and would tend to show at least a six-card suit. Playing *new minor forcing*, responder can bid 2 ♦ — the unbid minor suit — to get more information from opener. If opener bids 2♠, showing three-card support, responder can take the partnership to 4♠.

Otherwise, responder can put the partnership in 3NT.

♠ A J 9 7 4	Responder has an invitational-strength hand, and the
♥ K J 6 5	partnership could have an eight-card fit in either
♦ Q 3	hearts or spades. Using *new minor forcing*, responder
♣ 8 4	bids 2♦. If opener bids 2♥, showing a four-card
	heart suit, responder can raise invitationally to 3♥.

If opener rebids 2♠, showing three-card spade support, responder can
raise to 3♠. If opener rebids 2NT, showing a minimum-strength hand
without four hearts or three spades, responder can pass. With a maximum-strength hand for the 1NT rebid, opener can jump to 3NT without
a four-card heart suit or three-card spade support.

♠ K 9 7 5 3	Responder can return to 2♣. Since that's a minor
♥ J 3	suit previously bid by the partnership, it's not a forc-
♦ 5	ing bid.
♣ Q 10 8 7 5	

♠ A Q 8 6	A bid of 2♣ at this point would be a signoff, and a
♥ 6	jump to 3♣ would be invitational. Responder can
♦ K 7 3	bid 2♦, *new minor forcing*, intending to bid 3♣ at
♣ K J 10 6 2	the next opportunity. That would create a forcing
	sequence — with an invitational hand, responder
	would have jumped to 3♣ on the previous round.

This convention can be used after a 2NT rebid by opener (see also
checkback Stayman and *Wolff signoff*).

Checkback (Delayed) Stayman

After a 1NT rebid by opener, some partnerships use a 2♣ bid by
responder in a manner that is similar to the *Stayman* convention. The 2♣
bid by responder is artificial and asks opener to show a four-card major
suit or three-card support for responder's first bid suit. This is referred to
as *checkback Stayman* or *delayed Stayman*. For example, consider the
following hands after the auction has started:

WEST	NORTH	**EAST**	SOUTH
1♦	Pass	1♠	Pass
1NT	Pass	?	

♠ A Q 7 4 2
♥ K J 7 3
♦ A 4
♣ 8 5

A rebid of 2♥ by responder wouldn't be forcing, since it's not a reverse by responder. A jump to 3♥ would be forcing, but most partnerships prefer to reserve this bid for a hand with at least five cards in each major. Using *delayed Stayman*, responder can rebid 2♣ with this hand. Opener can now show a four-card heart suit or three-card support for spades. With neither, opener can rebid 2♦ with a minimum-strength hand or 2NT with the top of the range for the 1NT rebid.

♠ K Q 10 7 3
♥ 7 4
♦ A J 3
♣ 7 6 2

Responder has an invitational-strength hand with a five-card major suit. By using 2♣ as *checkback Stayman*, responder can find out if opener has three-card support for spades. Using standard methods, responder would have to invite by raising to 2NT — perhaps missing a 5–3 major suit fit — or jumping to 3♠ — which tends to promise a six-card suit.

♠ K 9 7 5 3
♥ J 3
♦ 5
♣ Q 10 8 7 5

The disadvantage of *checkback Stayman* is that responder can no longer sign off in 2♣ with this hand. Instead, responder will either have to pass or bid 2♠, hoping to land in a reasonable spot. This hand would also be a problem if the partnership uses *new minor forcing* rather than *checkback Stayman*.

This convention can also be used over a 2NT rebid by opener — a 3♣ bid by responder would check for a four-card major suit in opener's hand, or for three-card support for responder's first bid suit. Some partnerships only use this convention after a 2NT rebid, preferring *new minor forcing* or other methods after a 1NT rebid.

Wolff Sign-off

After a jump rebid to 2NT by opener, any bid by responder is forcing using standard methods. To allow responder to stop in the best partscore, some partnerships use the *Wolff sign-off* convention:

> • After a jump rebid of 2NT by opener, a response of 3♣ asks opener to bid responder's first suit at the three level with three-card support, otherwise to bid 3♦.

This convention was developed by Bobby Wolff, a many-time world champion from Dallas, Texas. Here is an example after the auction has started:

WEST	NORTH	**EAST**	SOUTH
1♦	Pass	1♥	Pass
2NT	Pass	?	

♠ J 3
♥ Q J 8 4 3
♦ Q 10 6 2
♣ 6 2

Rather than pass 2NT to stop in partscore, responder can bid 3♣ if the partnership uses *Wolff sign-off*. Opener will bid 3♥ with three-card support for responder's suit, or 3♦ without three-card support. In either case, responder can now pass, leaving the partnership in its best fit.

WEAK TWO-BIDS
(Supplement to Chapter 7)

Ogust Responses to Weak Two-bids

Instead of showing a feature with a maximum hand after a forcing 2NT response to a *weak two-bid*, some partnerships prefer a rebid that describes both the strength of the hand and the quality of the suit. The following rebid structure was developed by Harold Ogust, an expert international player:

- 3♣ shows a minimum-strength hand (5 to 8) and a poor suit.
- 3♦ shows a minimum-strength hand but a good suit.
- 3♥ shows a maximum-strength hand (9 to 11) but a poor suit.
- 3♠ shows a maximum-strength hand and a good suit.

Here are some examples of opener's rebid when playing *Ogust responses* after the auction starts:

WEST	NORTH	EAST	SOUTH
2♥	Pass	2NT	Pass
?			

♠ 8 2
♥ Q J 9 7 6 4
♦ K 7 3
♣ 6 4

Rebid 3♣. This shows a hand with minimum strength for a *weak two-bid* and a suit of relatively poor quality.

♠ 2
♥ K Q J 10 8 4
♦ 10 8 3
♣ 9 6 5

Rebid 3♦. The hand is of minimum strength but the heart suit is very good.

♠ 9 4
♥ K 10 9 6 5 3
♦ J 3
♣ A J 5

Rebid 3♥. This rebid shows a hand in the upper range of the strength for a *weak two-bid* but with a relatively poor suit.

♠ 8 3 2
♥ A Q J 8 7 4
♦ 8 4
♣ K 3

Rebid 3♠. This shows both a good hand and a good suit.

Ogust responses are quite useful if the partnership plays undisciplined *weak two-bids*, where the suit quality could vary considerably. They are less useful if opener always promises a good suit — two of the top three honors, or three of the top five.

Flannery 2♦

Consider the following hand:

♠ A Q 7 4   Playing standard methods, this hand would be opened
♥ K 9 5 4 3   1♥. That could leave opener with a difficult choice
♦ K 8 5   of rebid if, for example, responder bids 1NT. With
♣ 6   an unbalanced hand, opener doesn't want to pass and
                  leave responder playing in 1NT, but any other op-
tion could get the partnership into more trouble. Opener's hearts are too
weak to rebid. A rebid of 2♠ would be a *reverse*, forcing for one round
(see Chapter 6), and since responder didn't bid 1♠, it's unlikely the partnership has an eight-card fit in that suit. A rebid of 2♦ on a three-card suit
is also unappetizing, although partner could have length in that suit. Opener
would have a similar rebid problem if responder bid 2♣, rather than 1NT.

To avoid this predicament, William Flannery, suggested using an
opening bid of 2♦ to show an opening bid of 11 to 15 points with exactly four spades and five hearts. Responder then bids as follows:

- 2♥ or 2♠ is a sign-off in a major suit.

- 2NT is artificial (conventional) and forcing. It asks opener to
  further describe the hand as follows:

  - 3♣ or 3♦ shows three cards in the suit.

  - 3♥ shows a minimum (11 to 13) with two cards in
    each minor.

  - 3♠ shows a maximum (14 or 15) with two cards in
    each minor.

  - 3NT shows a maximum with a doubleton honor in both
    minors.

  - 4♣ or 4♦ shows four cards in the suit (and a void in
    the other minor).

- 3♣ or 3♦ asks opener to bid 3NT with one of the top three honors in that suit.
- 3♥ or 3♠ is invitational in the major suit.
- 3NT, 4♥, and 4♠ are sign-offs.
- 4♣ asks opener to bid 4♥ (transfer) and 4♦ asks opener to bid 4♠ (transfer).

For example, consider the following hands for responder after partner opens with a *Flannery 2♦*:

♠ J 8 3   Respond 2♥. This is a signoff bid in one of opener's
♥ J 10 2   suits. The partnership will be playing in an eight-
♦ Q J 7 4   card fit.
♣ Q 8 7

♠ K 10 8 3 2 Respond 4♠ (or 4♦, or 2NT). The partnership
♥ Q 8   should have a chance for a game contract playing in
♦ Q 9 3   the nine-card fit. A response of 4♦ would be a trans-
♣ A J 5   fer to 4♠, allowing the contract to be played from
partner's side. Responder could also start with 2NT
to find out more about opener's hand — although a slam is unlikely.

Flannery 2♦ is the most popular opening bid that shows a two-suited hand. It can be used if the partnership has another method of showing a strong opening bid in diamonds. It's commonly used in conjunction with *weak two-bid* openings in the majors — 2♥ and 2♠ — and an artificial strong 2♣ opening. It replaces the weak 2♦ opening bid.

Namyats

To distinguish between a weak four-level preempt in a major suit and a stronger preempt, some players use a convention commonly known as *Namyats*. Playing this convention, an opening bid of 4♣ shows a strong preempt in hearts — typically about eight or nine playing tricks — and an opening bid of 4♦ shows a strong preempt in spades. As a corollary, opening bids of 4♥ and 4♠ show weaker hands. After the 4♣ or 4♦ opening, responder usually signs off in the appropriate major suit, but with interest in a slam contract, responder can bid the next higher suit. For example, consider the following hands for opener:

♠ 3
♥ A Q J 8 7 6 4 3
♦ 9 3
♣ 7 4

This hand is a standard preemptive opening bid of 4♥. Opener has an eight-card suit and the bid is primarily defensive in nature. It is unlikely that there is a slam unless responder has a very strong hand.

♠ 3
♥ A K Q 10 8 7 5 3
♦ K 8 3
♣ 5

Playing *Namyats*, this hand would be opened 4♣. Opener has a hand likely to take eight or nine tricks with little help from partner. Responder wouldn't need too much for the partnership to make a slam.

With no interest in going beyond game, responder will bid 4♥ as a signoff. With interest in slam, responder can start by bidding 4♦. How the auction continues from that point depends on the partnership methods.

Namyats was devised by the English partnership of Terence Reese and Jeremy Flint, but it was introduced to North America by Sam Stayman. Since *Stayman* already had one convention named after him, this convention bears his name spelt backwards.

To use this convention, the partnership gives up the natural opening preempts of 4♣ and 4♦ showing a weak hand with a long minor suit. To compensate for this, some partnerships use an opening bid of 3NT as a weak preempt in either minor suit. Balanced hands of 25 to 27 points are opened with an artificial 2♣.

STRONG 2♣ OPENING
(Supplement to Chapter 8)

Second Negative

When responder has used the artificial 2♦ waiting bid in response to a strong 2♣ bid and opener rebids a suit, responder must bid again. Some partnerships prefer to have a *second negative* bid available to show a very bad hand of 0 to 4 points. There are two common methods. One method is to use the next cheapest suit as the second negative. This is referred to as the *Herbert negative*. The other method is to use the cheapest minor suit, if available at the three level, as the second negative. This is referred to as *cheaper minor second negative*. For example, suppose you are South and the auction starts like this:

WEST	NORTH	EAST	SOUTH
	2♣	Pass	2♦
Pass	2♥	Pass	?

♠ J 8 6 2
♥ 6 4
♦ 10 7 3
♣ J 9 6 4

Playing *Herbert negative*, South would rebid 2♠, artificial and showing a very weak hand. If the partnership is using *cheaper minor second negative*, South would rebid 3♣ to show a poor hand. If North had rebid 3♦ to show a strong hand with diamonds, partnerships playing *Herbert* would be able to bid 3♥ as a second negative, while those using *cheaper minor* wouldn't have that bid available at the three level and would probably bid 3NT, rather than bypass that contract.

Double Negative

Some partnerships prefer to have the responder to the strong artificial 2♣ opening bid show a weak hand immediately, rather than use 2♦ as an ambiguous waiting bid. One way to do this is to use the 2♦ response as a *double negative*, showing 0 to 3 points. Using this method, most partnerships then use a 2♥ response as the waiting bid, showing 4 or more points. For example, consider the following hands in response to partner's opening bid of 2♣:

♠ 9 5   Playing *double negative*, responder would bid 2 ♦
♥ J 3   with this hand to immediately show opener a hand
♦ 8 7 6 4   of 0 to 3 points.
♣ 10 8 7 5 3

♠ Q 8 7 4   Playing *double negative*, responder would bid 2 ♥
♥ K 8   with this hand. This is an artificial waiting bid, show-
♦ 9 7 5 3   ing a hand with 4 or more points that is unsuitable
♣ 10 8 2   for a positive response in a suit.

Some partnerships prefer to reverse the meanings of the artificial
2 ♦ and 2 ♥ responses — using 2 ♦ as the waiting bid and 2 ♥ as the
double negative. This approach is sometimes referred to as *Jacoby responses to 2♣* — another method named for Oswald Jacoby, a great
player and theorist — and includes the use of 2NT as the bid to show a
positive response with a good heart suit.

Step Responses

Another approach that can be used in response to the strong artificial
2♣ opening is *step responses*. These show the number of *controls* held
by responder — where an ace counts as two controls and a king counts as
one control — using a scheme such as the following:

- 2 ♦ shows 0 or 1 control.

- 2 ♥ shows 2 controls (an ace or two kings).

- 2♠ shows 3 controls, specifically an ace and a king.

- 2NT shows 3 controls, specifically three kings.

- 3♣ shows 4 controls.

- 3 ♦ shows 5 controls . . . . and so on.

For example, consider the following hand for responder after an opening bid of 2♣:

♠ 9 7 4
♥ J 6 3
♦ A 6
♣ K 9 7 6 3

Playing *step responses*, responder would bid 2♠ to show an ace and a king. Once responder has shown the number of controls, the rest of the auction continues naturally.

1NT forcing —The conventional agreement that a response of 1NT to an opening bid of 1♥ or 1♠ is forcing for one round; often used in conjunction with *two-over-one*.

1NT response to 1♣—A conventional agreement to use a higher range (8 to 10 or 9 to 11, rather than 6 to 10 points) for a 1NT response to an opening 1♣ bid.

2NT as a limit raise—See *Truscott 2NT*.

2NT as a non-forcing response to a minor —An agreement that a response of 2NT to 1♣ or 1♦ is invitational, showing 10 to 12 points.

2NT as an invitational response to a minor— An agreement that a response of 2NT shows a balanced hand of 11 or 12 points and is only invitational, not forcing. This is used when a response of 1NT shows 6 to 10 points and 3NT shows a balanced hand of 13 to 15 points.

3NT as a balanced forcing raise—The conventional use of a 3NT response to an opening bid of 1♥ or 1♠ to show a forcing raise with no short suit.

3NT as a weak preempt in either minor suit —The conventional use of an opening bid of 3NT to show a weak hand with a long minor suit; often used in conjunction with *namyats*.

ACBL Standard Yellow Card—The list of conventions that must be used by a partnership in "Yellow Card" events and that can serve as a starting point for partnerships in other events. Frequently used by new partnerships playing on the Internet.

Acol—A bidding system popular in the United Kingdom featuring a weak notrump, four-card majors, and limit raises.

Acol 3NT opening—An opening bid of 3NT based on a long, solid suit with stoppers in at least two of the other suits; this falls somewhere between the gambling 3NT opening and the more traditional strong balanced hand of 25 to 27 points.

Alert—A warning to the opponents that the last call by your partner has been assigned a conventional message, rather than the natural or literal meaning they might expect.

Announcement—A word or phrase that directly describes the meaning of partner's call. This is part of the Alert process and is used in three cases: when the partnership's range for an opening bid of 1NT falls outside the range of 15 to 18 high-card points; when the partnership uses a *Jacoby transfer bid*; when the partnership uses a *forcing 1NT response*.

Astro—A conventional overcall of a minor suit after a strong or weak notrump, in the direct or reopening position, to show a two-suited hand. 2♣ shows hearts and a minor suit; 2♦ shows spades and another suit.

Attitude signal—An attitude signal tells partner whether or not you like a particular suit. It can be used when you have a choice of cards to play in a suit that partner has led or when discarding in a suit. The conventional agreement is: a high card is encouraging; a low card is discouraging.

Becker—A conventional agreement to use an overcall of 2♣ over 1NT to show both minor suits and an overcall of 2♦ to show both major suits.

Bergen major-suit raises—See *Bergen raises*.

Bergen raises—A structure of major suit raises that puts the emphasis on quickly getting to the three level with four-card support.

Better minor—A bidding style in which the better (stronger) minor suit is opened when the hand doesn't contain a five-card major suit and the minor suits are of equal length.

Bidding box—A mechanical device that allows bids to be made silently, rather than verbally; often used in bridge clubs and at tournaments.

Blackwood—A conventional bid of 4NT after a trump suit has been agreed to ask partner to show the number of aces held: 5♣—0 or 4; 5♦—1; 5♥—2; 5♠—3. A subsequent bid of 5NT asks for the number of kings held.

Brozel—A conventional agreement that assigns the following meanings to overcalls of an opponent's 1NT opening bid: Double shows a one-suited hand (partner bids 2♣ to find out which suit); 2♣ shows hearts and clubs; 2♦ shows hearts and diamonds; 2♥ shows hearts and spades; 2♠ shows spades and a minor suit (partner bids 2NT to find out which minor); 2NT shows clubs and diamonds.

Bypassing diamonds—The conventional agreement following an opening 1♣ bid to bypass a four-card diamond suit when holding a four-card major suit.

Call—Any bid, double, redouble, or pass.

Cappelletti (also called Hamilton, Pottage)—A conventional agreement that assigns the following meanings to overcalls of an opponent's 1NT opening bid: Double is for penalty; 2♣ shows a one-suited hand; 2♦ shows hearts and spades; 2♥ shows hearts and a minor suit; 2♠ shows spades and a minor suit.

Cheaper minor second negative—A rebid of 3♣ to deny strength following a strong artificial 2♣ opening, a 2♦ waiting response, and opener's rebid of 2♥ or 2♠; if opener rebids 3♣, responder's 3♦ rebid denies strength.

Checkback Stayman—The use of 2♣ after opener's rebid of 1NT— or 3♣ after opener's rebid of 2NT—to ask about opener's major suit holdings.

Constructive raises—The use of an immediate raise of a major suit to the two level to show 8 to 10 points, rather than 6 to 10 points.

Control—A holding that prevents the opponents from taking a trick in a suit: aces and voids are *first-round controls*; kings and singletons are *second-round controls*.

Control Swiss—A variation of the *swiss* convention which focuses on the number of controls (aces and kings) held.

Convenient club—Another name for the bidding style in which the longer minor suit is opened with no five-card major suit; this term is used because opener bids 1♣ with three cards in both minors.

Convention—A call or play which may be artificial and which has a defined meaning for the partnership; it may not suggest playing in the denomination named.

Count signals (length signals)—A count signal tells partner how many cards you have in a suit. The standard conventional agreement to show length in a suit is: high-low shows an even number of cards; low-high shows an odd number of cards.

Cuebid—An artificial forcing bid in a suit in which the bidder cannot wish to play: a bid in the opponents' suit or a bid to show a control in a slam-going auction.

Cuebid as a limit raise—Responder's use of a cuebid of the opponent's suit following an overcall to show the values for a limit raise or better in opener's suit.

Deal—1. The distribution of the pack to form the hands of the four players. 2. The cards so distributed considered as a unit, including the auction and play.

Delayed Stayman—See *checkback Stayman*.

Distribution points—Hand valuation points that take into account the shape of the hand (see length points and short suit points).

DONT—A conventional agreement that assigns the following meanings to overcalls of an opponent's 1NT opening bid: Double shows a one-suited hand (usually not spades); 2♣ shows clubs and another suit; 2♦ shows diamonds and a major suit; 2♥ shows hearts and spades; 2♠ shows spades.

DOPI—When an opponent overcalls after a 4♣ Gerber bid or a 4NT Blackwood bid, the partnership can use D-O-P-I: Double is no aces; Pass is one; cheapest bid is two; next cheapest bid is three, etc.

Dormer 2NT—See *Truscott 2NT*.

Double-barreled Stayman—See *two-way Stayman*.

Double negative—A response that immediately denies strength in response to a strong forcing bid when responder also had the option of making a waiting bid.

Double raise—See *jump raise*.

Drury—A conventional response of 2♣ to an opening bid of 1♥ or 1♠ in third or fourth position, asking if opener has a full opening bid.

Dummy points—Valuation points for short suits when planning to raise partner's suit: void— 5; singleton—3; doubleton—1.

Extended Jacoby transfers—Use of 2♠ in response to 1NT as a transfer to 3♣ when holding a weak hand with either clubs or diamonds; with diamonds, responder then bids 3♦.

Extended splinter bids—Use of splinter bids in situations other than a direct response to an opening bid.

First-round control—An ace, or a void in a suit contract.

Fit-showing jump—An agreement to use a jump shift in competitive situations to show a strong hand of at least nine cards in the two suits (partner's suit and the suit in which you jump) and invitational strength. Usually shows five cards in the suit you bid and four cards in support of partner's suit.

Five-card majors—A bidding style where opening bids of 1♥ or 1♠ usually promise a five-card or longer suit.

Flannery 2♦—A conventional use of a 2♦ opening bid to show four spades, five hearts, and 11 to 15 points.

Flip-flop—The conventional use of 2NT by responder to show a pre-emptive raise after opener's minor suit opening has been doubled for takeout; responder's jump raise of opener's minor is then a limit raise. This is a reversal of the usual agreement when playing *Truscott 2NT*.

Forcing bid—A bid which requires partner to bid again if there is no intervening bid.

Forcing club system—A bidding system in which an opening bid of 1♣ is artificial and shows a strong hand.

Forcing for one round—A bid that requires partner to make a call other than pass if there is no intervening call.

Forcing raise—A style of responding to an opening bid of one-of-a-suit where a jump raise to the three level is forcing to at least the game level.

Forcing Stayman—A variation of the *Stayman* convention in which a rebid of 2♥ or 2♠ by responder is forcing to at least 2NT.

Four-card majors—A bidding style where opening bids of 1♥ or 1♠ can be made on a four-card suit.

Four-suit transfer bids—Transfer bids into all four suits over an opening bid of 1NT: 2♦ for hearts, 2♥ for spades, 2♠ for clubs, and 2NT for diamonds.

Fourth suit forcing and artificial —An agreement that the bid of the fourth suit by responder is artificial and forcing; usually played as forcing to game.

Gambling 3NT—An opening bid of 3NT based on a long, solid minor suit, rather than the more traditional 25 to 27 HCPs.

Game-forcing—A bid that, by agreement, commits the partnership to at least the game level.

Gerber—A conventional agreement that following a bid of 1NT or 2NT, a jump to 4♣ asks partner how many aces are held. Partner responds: 4♦ — 0 or 4; 4♥ — 1; 4♠ — 2; 4NT — 3. If the partnership holds all of the aces, a bid of 5♣ asks partner how many kings are held.

Grand slam force—An agreement that a bid of 5NT asks partner to bid a grand slam with two of the top three trump honors, otherwise to bid a small slam in the agreed trump suit.

Grand slam force after Blackwood—An agreement that when 4NT is used as *Blackwood* to ask for aces, 6♣ (rather than 5NT) is used as the *grand slam force* unless the agreed trump suit is clubs.

Hamilton—See Cappelletti.

Hand—The cards originally dealt to a player.

HCPs —The abbreviation for high-card points.

Herbert negative—The use of the cheapest available suit response to deny strength when opener has made a strong forcing bid. Often applied after responder has initially made a waiting bid.

High-card points—The value of the high cards in a hand: ace—4; king—3; queen—2; jack—1.

Informatory double—See *takeout double*.

Ingberman—See *lebensohl over reverses*.

Inverted minor-suit raises—A bidding style in which a single raise of opener's minor suit is forcing for one round while a jump raise shows a weak hand. Essentially, the meaning of raises to the two level and the three level are reversed from standard practice.

Invitational bid—A bid which encourages partner to bid again but gives partner the option of passing with minimal values for what has been promised to date.

Jacoby transfer bid—A conventional response to an opening bid of 1NT where 2♦ shows hearts and 2♥ shows spades. Similar responses can be used over other notrump opening bids.

Jacoby 2NT—A conventional response to an opening bid of 1♥ or 1♠ which shows a forcing raise of the major suit.

Jordan 2NT—See *Truscott 2NT*.

Jump cuebid—An agreement to use a jump cuebid in the opponent's suit to show a hand with four-card or longer support for partner's suit and at least invitational strength.

Jump preference—Returning to partner's original suit at a level one higher than necessary.

Jump raise—A raise of partner's suit skipping a level of bidding (e.g., 1♥ — 3♥).

Jump shift—A jump one level higher than necessary in a new suit.

Jump shift by responder—A jump in a new suit in response to an opening bid of one-of-a-suit.

Jump shift in other minor as a forcing raise—The conventional use of a jump raise in the other minor to show a forcing raise in opener's minor when a jump raise of opener's minor suit is used as a limit raise.

Kantar 3NT—A conventional opening bid to show a solid major suit with no side aces and at most one side king.

Keycard Blackwood—This version of Blackwood assumes that there are five key cards: the four aces and the king of the trump suit. The responses are: 5♣ — 0 or 4; 5♦ — 1 or 5; 5♥ — 2; 5♠ — 3. *See also Roman Keycard Blackwood.*

Kock-Werner redouble—See SOS redouble.

Landy—A conventional overcall of 2♣ after an opposing 1NT opening as a request for a takeout to a major suit. Overcaller promises at least four cards in each major and usually has five.

Lavinthal discards—A complicated partnership agreement with many possible variations that calls for the first discard on defense to give a suit preference signal rather than an attitude signal.

Law of total tricks—An observation that the total number of tricks available to both sides in their best trump suit on any hand is usually equal to the total number of the trumps in each side's best trump suit. It is usually applied in competitive bidding situations.

Lead-directing double—Without specific agreements to the contrary, a double of an opponent's conventional bid shows strength in that suit.

Lead-directing double of 3NT—When the opponents have voluntarily bid to 3NT and the player not on lead doubles, this double conventionally asks partner to lead one of the following suits, in order of priority: a suit bid by the opening leader; a suit bid by the doubler; dummy's first bid suit if it wasn't rebid. When no suit has been bid, the double shows a solid suit which can take five tricks if the opening leader can find it. Without a clue, the opening leader will tend to lead a short major suit.

Lebensohl—A convention to handle interference after partner opens with 1NT (variations of this convention can be used in other situations).

Lebensohl over reverses—A conventional agreement for handling the auction after opener makes a reverse bid.

Leaping Michaels—An extension of the *Michaels cuebid* convention used following a weak 2♥ or 2♠ bid by the opponents. A jump to 4♣ shows at least five clubs and five cards in the unbid major. A jump to 4♦ shows at least five diamonds and five cards in the unbid major.

Length points—The value assigned to long suits in a hand: five-card suit — 1; six-card suit — 2; seven-card suit — 3; eight-card suit — 4.

Light opening bid—An opening bid on a hand that doesn't meet the standard requirements; for example, an opening bid at the one level on fewer than 13 points.

Lightner double—A conventional agreement that a double of a slam by the player not on lead requests partner to make an unusual lead, which hopefully would result in the defeat of the contract.

Limit raise—A style of responding to an opening bid of one-in-a-suit where a jump raise to the three level is invitational rather than forcing.

Longer minor—A bidding style in which the longer minor suit is opened when the hand doesn't contain a five-card major suit; 1 ♦ is usually opened with four cards in both minors; 1 ♣ is usually opened with three cards in both minors.

Mathe—A competitive conventional agreement following a strong, artificial 1 ♣ opening that a double shows both major suits and 1NT shows both minor suits.

Maximal double—A competitive double used by a player as a game try when the opponents' bids have left no bidding room to make any other form of game try.

Minor-suit slam try—A forcing bid in a minor suit asking if partner has interest in a slam contract in the minor suit.

Minor-suit Stayman—A conventional use of the 2 ♠ response to 1NT as an inquiry about opener's minor suits. Opener rebids 2NT with no four-card or longer minor, rebids 3 ♣ or 3 ♦ with one four-card minor suit, and rebids the longer major — 3 ♥ or 3 ♠ — with four cards in both minor suits.

MUD—An agreement on how to lead from a suit containing three low cards — lead the middle (M) card; follow with the highest (Up) card, and finally play the lowest (Down) card — MUD.

Namyats—The conventional use of 4 ♣ to show a strong 4 ♥ opening bid and 4 ♦ to show a strong 4 ♠ opening bid; as a consequence, opening bids of 4 ♥ and 4 ♠ are weak preemptive bids.

Natural bid—A bid which suggests playing in the denomination named.

Negative double—A variation of the takeout double, used when an opponent overcalls at a low level.

Negative doubles after 1NT—The use of a double for takeout, rather than penalty, after a direct overcall by an opponent of an opening 1NT bid. It shows enough strength to compete and tends to show four cards in any unbid major suit.

Negative response—A response that denies strength when partner opens with a strong forcing bid such as 2♣.

New minor forcing—A conventional agreement that the bid of a new minor by responder is forcing after a 1NT (or 2NT) rebid by opener.

Non-forcing Stayman—The standard form of the *Stayman* convention where a rebid of 2♥ or 2♠ by responder is non forcing.

Ogust responses—A method of responding to weak two-bids that asks opener about both the strength of the weak two-bid and the quality of the suit.

Passed hand—A hand which passed when it had an opportunity to open the bidding.

Penalty double—Double of an opponent's bid that suggests defending that contract for penalty.

Positive response—A response that shows some values when partner opens with a strong forcing bid such as 2♣.

Pottage—See Cappelletti.

Precision Club—A complete bidding system centered around a conventional opening bid of 1♣ for strong hands of 16 or more points.

Preemptive bid—A bid made to interfere with the opponents' auction. It is usually made with a long suit and a weak hand.

Preemptive opening bid—Opening bid at the two level or higher based on a long suit and a weak hand; designed to interfere with the opponents' auction.

Preemptive re-raise—The conventional agreement where, after responder has raised opener's suit to the two level, a further raise to the three level shows a minimum-strength hand rather than an invitational, medium-strength hand.

Preempts—Bids that skip one or more levels of the bidding and are based on a long suit and a weak hand; designed to interfere with the opponents' auction.

Principle of fast arrival—A bidding concept that the faster a contract is reached, the weaker the hand that places the contract; conversely, the slower the approach, the stronger the suggestion that a higher contract might be appropriate.

Psychic call—A deliberate and gross misstatement of honor strength and/or suit length.

Puppet Stayman—A variation of the *Stayman* convention which can be used to discover whether opener holds a four-card or a five-card major suit.

Quantitative—A natural, limited, non-forcing bid. For example, a raise of an opening 1NT bid to 4NT—inviting opener to bid slam but not forcing.

Redouble—A redouble shows 10 or more points with interest in doubling the opponents for penalty. Responder usually won't have a good fit with opener's suit.

Responsive double—When partner makes a takeout double and the next opponent raises opener's suit, some partnerships agree to treat a double as responsive rather than as a penalty double. The responsive double acts like a takeout double, asking partner to pick a suit.

Reverse—A rebid of a new suit that prevents responder from returning to opener's original suit at the two level.

Reverse by responder—A bid of a second suit by responder that prevents opener from returning to responder's first suit at the two level.

Reverse Drury—A variation of the *Drury* convention in which opener rebids the major suit to show a sub-standard hand.

Ripstra—A conventional agreement to overcall 1NT with your better minor as a takeout for the major suits. Partner has the advantage of passing your overcall leaving you to play in your better minor suit when holding no fit for either major suit.

Roman Keycard Blackwood—A version of Blackwood that assumes five key cards: four aces and the king of the proposed trump suit. It also takes into consideration the queen of the proposed trump suit. The responses are: 5♣ — 0 or 3; 5♦ — 1 or 4; 5♥ — 2 (or 5) key cards without the queen of trumps; 5♠ — 2 (or 5) key cards and the queen of trumps.

RONF—An acronym for 'Raise is the Only Non Force' when responding to a weak two-bid.

Rule of two and three—See *rule of 500*.

Rule of 5 and 10—A guideline for responding 2♥ over partner's 1♠ opening bid: responder needs at least five hearts and at least 10 points.

Rule of 15—A guideline for opening the bidding in fourth position on marginal hands: if the high-card points plus the number of spades adds to 15 or more, open the bidding; otherwise, pass.

Rule of 20—A guideline for opening marginal hands: if the high-card points plus the number of cards in the two longest suits adds to 20 or more, open the bidding.

Rule of 500—A guideline for opening preemptive bids based on the penalties for being doubled and defeated: a non vulnerable preempt should not risk being defeated more than three tricks; a vulnerable preempt should not risk being defeated more than two tricks.

Second negative—A rebid by the responder to a strong forcing bid that denies strength when responder initially made a waiting bid.

Second-round control —A king, or a singleton in a suit contract.

Short club—A bidding style in which an opening bid of 1♥ or 1♠ shows a five-card or longer suit and an opening bid of 1♦ shows a four-card or longer suit. This style sometimes result in an opening bid of 1♣ being made on a two-card suit (4–4–3–2 distribution).

Short suit points—The value assigned to short suits in a hand (usually applied when showing support for partner's suit — see dummy points): void—5; singleton—3; doubleton—1.

Sign-off bid—A bid which partner is expected to pass.

Simple preference—Returning to partner's first suit at the cheapest available level when partner has shown two suits.

Smolen transfers—A convention for ensuring that the 1NT opener declares the contract when responder is 5–4 in the major suits.

Soloway jump shift—A conventional agreement that responder's jump shift falls into one of three types of hand: a strong single-suiter; a strong hand with a fit for opener's suit; a strong balanced hand.

SOS redouble—A redouble when your side has been doubled for penalties in a low-level contract. It requests partner to pick another contract. (Partnerships must be clear when the redouble is for rescue and when it's strength-showing.)

Splinter bid—A conventional double jump in a new suit to show a fit with partner and a singleton or void in the suit bid.

Splinter raise—See *splinter bid.*

Stayman—An conventional response of 2♣ to an opening 1NT bid that asks whether opener has a four-card major suit and a 3♣ response to an opening 2NT.

Step responses—A conventional set of responses to an a strong forcing bid that shows the number of *controls* (aces and kings) held.

Stopper—A holding in a suit that is likely to prevent the opponents from taking all of the tricks in a suit (Q–J–3, for example).

Strong artificial (conventional) 2♣—The use of an opening bid of 2♣ to show a strong hand of about 22 or more points; commonly used in conjunction with weak two-bids.

Strong club—An artificial (conventional) opening bid of 1♣ to show a strong hand.

Strong notrump—An opening bid of 1NT that falls in the range of 15 to 18 points.

Strong two-bid—An opening bid in a suit at the two level to show a strong hand (21 or more points); it is forcing to game unless opener rebids 2NT or rebids the original suit at the three level.

Suit preference signals—A suit preference signal indicates a preference for one of the two remaining suits (it doesn't apply to the suit led or to the trump suit). A high card shows preference for the higher-ranking suit; a low card shows preference for the lower-ranking suit.

Super acceptance— A jump of a level when accepting partner's transfer bid to show a maximum-strength hand and good fit.

Support double—Used by opener to show exactly three-card support for responder's suit following an overcall on opener's right after partner has responded in a suit. By agreement, opener can redouble to show three-card support when the intervening call is a double.

Swiss—A conventional response of 4♣ or 4♦ to an opening bid of 1♥ or 1♠ to show a forcing raise of the major suit. (Not to be confused with Swiss teams, which is a method of pairing up teams with similar records in a bridge event.)

Takeout double—A double that asks partner to bid rather than defend for penalty.

Temporizing bid—See *waiting bid*.

Texas transfer bids—A conventional set of responses to an opening bid of 1NT or 2NT where 4♦ shows six or more hearts and 4♥ shows six or more spades.

Treatment—A natural bid that indicates a desire to play in the denomination named (or promises or requests values in that denomination), but that also, by agreement, gives or requests additional information on which further action could be based.

Trump echo—A high-low in the trump suit is commonly used to show three or more trumps.

Trump Swiss—A variation of the *Swiss* convention which focuses on trump quality.

Truscott 2NT—A conventional jump to 2NT after an opponent's takeout double to show a limit raise or better in partner's suit.

Two-over-one—A bidding style in which a new suit response at the two level is forcing to at least game after partner opens one-of-a-suit.

Two-way Stayman—A variation of the *Stayman* convention in which a response of 2♣ is non-forcing *Stayman* and a response of 2♦ is game-forcing *Stayman*.

Unusual notrump—A conventional agreement that a jump overcall of 2NT over a major suit shows a two-suited hand with two five-card or longer suits that promise to be weak. The majority of players use this bid to show both minor suits. Modern partnerships use the bid to show the two lowest-ranking unbid suits.

Unusual over unusual—An agreement that responder will take the following action when an opponent makes a two-suited overcall, such as *Michaels* or *unusual notrump*, that takes away some of your bidding room: double is penalty-oriented; raising partner at the cheapest available level is invitational; a bid of the suit not shown by partner or the opponent's bid is invitational; a cuebid of the lower-ranking of the suits shown by the opponent's bid shows the lower-ranking of the other two suits and is forcing for one round; a cuebid of the higher-ranking of the suits shown by the opponent's bid shows the higher-ranking of the other two suits and is forcing for one round.

Upside-down attitude signals—An agreement that a low card is encouraging and a high card is discouraging. The exact opposite to standard attitude signals.

Upside-down count signals—An agreement that a low card followed by a higher card would show an even number of cards in the suit; a high card followed by a low card would show an odd number of cards in the suit. The exact opposite to standard count signals.

Up-the-line—The practice of making the cheapest bid when responding or rebidding with two or three four-card suits (responding 1♥ to an opening bid of 1♣ or 1♦, for example, when holding four hearts and four spades).

Value Swiss—A variation of the *Swiss* convention which accommodates forcing major-suit raises with balanced hands.

Waiting bid—A bid asking for a further description of partner's hand while saying nothing specific about the bidder's hand.

Weak jump raises—Conventional use of a jump raise of partner's suit to show a weak hand with good support.

Weak jump shifts—The conventional use of a jump shift response to show a weak hand with a long suit.

Weak notrump—An opening bid of 1NT with a minimum-strength opening hand, usually 12 to 14 or 13 to 15 points.

Weak two-bid—The use of an opening bid of 2♦, 2♥, or 2♠ as a preemptive bid, usually showing a six-card suit with 5 to 10 points.

Wolff signoff—A conventional method for allowing responder to sign off in a suit at the three level after opener's 2NT rebid.

**ACBL has what you need to brush up or polish your skills and techniques, or even learn new ones!
We can help you with great gift ideas for any occasion!**

Your "Source" for information

✔ Playing cards	✔ Bridge software,
✔ Duplicate boards	including
✔ Bidding boxes	CD ROM
✔ Convention cards	✔ Tablecloths
and holders	✔ Windbreakers,
✔ Movement cards	shirts, aprons
✔ Bridge games	✔ Dangle earrings
✔ Tote bags	and LM jewelry
✔ Bridge books with	✔ Over 100 bridge
coded cards	books by great
for practice	authors
✔ Videos	✔ Bridge Bucks and
	other prizes

Call, write, e-mail, or fax your request for a free catalog today!

Your friendly Sales Representative will be happy
to help your with your order.

Orders are shipped the next day.

Same day service is available if you call early.

Browse our web page, **www.acbl.org**
and shop our new, secure catalog at your convenience.

NOTES

NOTES

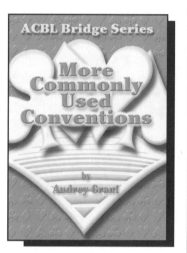